IMAGES
of America

RUSH

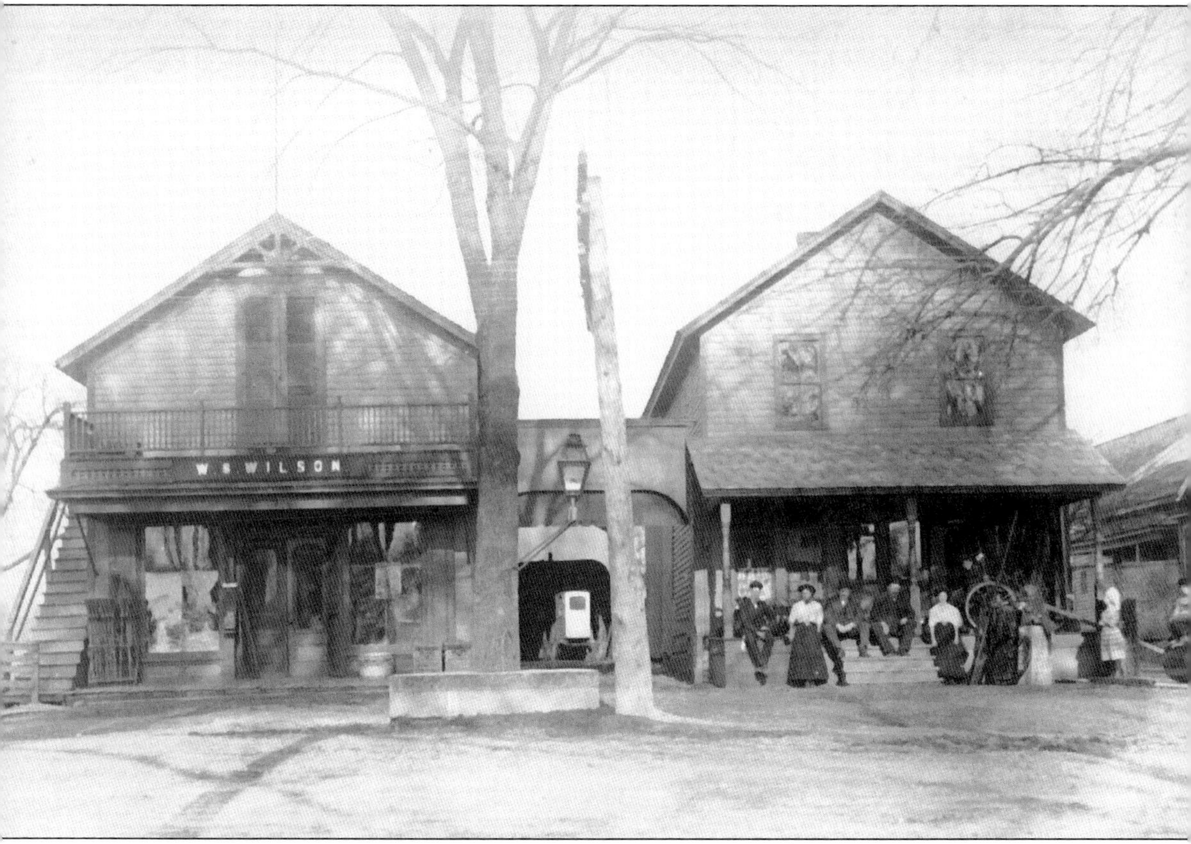

On the Cover: The cover image is a photograph printed as a postcard and mailed from Rush to Mrs. William Prudom in Middleport, New York, in 1908. The picture is of the W.S. Wilson General Store and the message on the back of the card reads, "Dear Cousins, This is a picture of one of our stores in Rush. See the mail wagon in the shed. This is the first picture I have taken in about a week. Your cousin, Franklin." The Prudom and Wilson families were related, and their descendants still reside in the Middleport area today. (Courtesy of George Murray Stahl.)

IMAGES
of America

RUSH

Susan Bittner Mee

ARCADIA
PUBLISHING

ISBN 978-1-4671-3195-7

Published by Arcadia Publishing
Charleston, South Carolina

Printed in the United States of America

Library of Congress Control Number: 2013957656

For all general information, please contact Arcadia Publishing:
Telephone 843-853-2070
Fax 843-853-0044
E-mail sales@arcadiapublishing.com
For customer service and orders:
Toll-Free 1-888-313-2665

Visit us on the Internet at www.arcadiapublishing.com

This book is dedicated to the memories of the early families of Rush. They were a group of hardworking and stalwart individuals who forged a town from the wilderness lands of the Genesee region.

Contents

ACKNOWLEDGMENTS

This book, and the wonderful photographs within, is a result of the generous spirit and open hearts of the families and friends of Rush. The Rush Historian's Office provided a tremendous foundation for our Rush book, but many photographs came from personal collections as well. I thank you for searching through boxes, scrapbooks, and photo albums tucked away in attics and for also reaching out to other family members for their photographs. Thank you to those who let me borrow framed photographs from the walls of their homes, mantels, and end tables. It is these unique and individual contributions that help to more fully represent Rush and all those who came before us.

In some cases, I found I had received multiple copies of the same photograph from different sources. Ultimately, I chose to use the copy that was in the best condition for reproduction purposes. Again, I thank everyone for his or her contributions.

In particular, I would like to acknowledge Marjorie Kirch, Rush historian, for providing welcome access to the Rush historical files; to Selden Price Chase for his personal historical knowledge; and to my dad, Walter Bittner, for his knowledge in identifying automobiles and dating photographs based on vehicles in the pictures. Former historian Jeanne Yawman was also a beneficial resource. I would especially like to acknowledge Eleanor Mason DeFreze for sharing her extensive personal history collection. Ms. DeFreze's great-uncle, Dean Norris, was the official photographer for Rush in the early 1900s, and she graciously shared many photographs and documents. I would also like to acknowledge Karen Hopkins for her assistance and attention to detail in editing and proofreading this book prior to publication. Lastly, I would like to thank my husband, Tim, for supporting and sharing in this great adventure.

One photographic book cannot fully represent multiple generations, or all the life, work, and dedication that created Rush, but hopefully, this will help serve to both represent and preserve in pictures the life and culture that built our town.

Photographs are courtesy of Rush Historian's Office unless otherwise indicated.

INTRODUCTION

Carving a town from the wilderness takes not only courage, but also foresight and a good dose of fortitude. Those who came before us and entered the vast Genesee region possessed those traits and more. They were a strong and proud people who endured hardship and celebrated success, supporting one another and working together.

The first settlers to arrive in the region were James and John Ganson, arriving in 1788. Their father, Capt. John Ganson, recommended the area to his sons as he had become familiar with the land as a Revolutionary soldier during General Sullivan's campaign. Gen. John Sullivan was charged with targeting the Iroquois nation and breaking their alliance. Sullivan's campaign traveled through the Genesee Country region in 1779. Several of his soldiers were impressed with the beauty and natural richness of the area and returned later as settlers.

The Gansons cleared their newly claimed land, built a cabin, and constructed a mill. After this work had been done, they learned the title to their land was not legitimate, and they had to abandon the property. The Gansons left the area and resettled in LeRoy. They had purchased their land prior to the Treaty of Hartford. The treaty resolved a lengthy dispute over the Genesee Country lands by awarding jurisdiction to New York and preemption rights to Massachusetts.

In 1790, Col. Jeremiah Wadsworth sent his two younger cousins James and William Wadsworth to act as his agents in selling his portion of the Phelps and Gorham Purchase. Oliver Phelps and Nathaniel Gorham, Massachusetts businessmen, had purchased preemption rights to six and a quarter million acres in 1788. The Wadsworth land extended from Geneseo to Lake Ontario. Joseph Morgan and the Wadsworths owned, and then sold, parcels of this tract. Some of this acreage would later become Rush.

Col. William Markham ended up purchasing a portion of the former Ganson land. Colonel Markham was a member of the Ontario County Assembly and the first supervisor of the town of Rush. Colonel Markham became a large landowner in Rush and a prominent member of the community. The brick house on East River Road, close to the southern border of Rush, was his home.

The town of Hartford was created in 1789 and was part of Ontario County. Hartford became Avon in 1808 and included Rush. Around 1815, people in the northern parts of Avon began talking about separating from Avon and forming their own town. On March 13, 1818, the town of Rush was formed, but at that time, it was still a part of Ontario County. That changed in 1821 when Monroe County was formed in February and Rush was reassigned to Monroe County.

As has been discussed in other documents regarding the history of Rush, the details of how the town came to be named Rush are not known for certain. Three possible theories prevail: one, the town was named after the quantities of rushes growing on the flats, which were used to feed the cattle of the early settlers; two, the town was named for Dr. Benjamin Rush, Surgeon General to the Continental Army during the American Revolution, a member of the first Continental Congress, and a signer of the Declaration of Independence; or three, named for Richard Rush, son of Dr. Benjamin Rush. Richard was an American statesman and diplomat, and served as attorney general in Pres. James Madison's administration, from 1814 to 1817. Since no documentation has been discovered to determine the reason for the name Rush, one could potentially build a case for any of the above theories. Regardless of how the name came to be, the first town meeting was held at the home of Benejah Billings, located at the corner of West Rush and Stonybrook Roads.

Serving along with Colonel Markham in 1818, Peter Price was chosen as the first town clerk. Nathan Jeffords, Jacob Stull, and John Markham were selected as assessors. In 1820, the town had a population of 1,001. By 1835, the number had more than doubled to 2,026. The number of improved acres was 12,800. Farm animals consisted of 2,171 cattle, 679 horses, 5,580 sheep, and 2,335 hogs. In 1858, improved land had increased to 14,837 acres and the population had decreased slightly to 1,750. Farmers were primarily growing wheat, potatoes, and apples. That same year, 78,910 pounds of butter were produced along with 4,400 pounds of cheese.

Rush has continued at a steady pace, never becoming a big town, but always holding its own with its farms producing solid quantities of crops and often exceeding in quality. Descendants of some of the early settlers have remained here—happy with the choice of place their ancestors selected to settle those many years ago.

Life moves forward at a much faster pace today than in the early years of the town. The horizons have expanded in countless ways. In looking back at how life was, like the often referenced "simpler times," it is easy to wish we were "back then." With that, we must also recognize that life "back then" was not easy. Today, we have many conveniences and tools, which make our lives easier and more comfortable. We cannot go back, but we can make every effort to remember, to preserve, and to protect the legacy that our ancestors have left us.

Though written more than 130 years ago, the meaning of the words of Prof. W.H. McIntosh in the *History of Monroe County 1788–1877* can be still be applied to the residents of the town today, where the value and importance placed on home, family, and education hold a prominent role: "Limited in area, old in settlement, Rush is rich in farms, and occupied by an intelligent, sober, and religious people, worthy descendants of a superior class of pioneers."

One

Early Rush

The late 1790s and beginning of the 1800s saw the arrival of the first settlers to Rush. Among the earliest is William Markham, considered to be the first permanent settler. Another early name in Rush's history is Christle Thomas. The Thomas family was Amish and arrived about 1801, settling in the area of Fishell and West Rush Roads. It was Christle Thomas who built the first sawmill in Rush. That same time period also brought John Bell, who settled north of the creek. Also arriving in 1801 were Capt. Philip Price and his family, settling near what came to be called Mann's Corners. Jacob Stull, a family friend from Maryland, arrived about the same time. Elder Goff brought 16 families from Connecticut in 1804 and settled in the area of West Rush and Stonybrook Roads. Elnathan Perry brought his family from Vermont in 1806 and settled on Fishell Road. That year was also the time Nathan Jeffords Sr. arrived, as did Thomas Daily, who left Ireland in 1793. Jacob Martin left Maryland in 1809 and came to Rush. All of these families, along with others, were already here when John Webster arrived in 1810 and began building the foundation for a town center.

Many of the earliest settlers had also served in the American Revolution. Some had passed through this area during Sullivan's Campaign and were able to appreciate the beauty and wealth of the land.

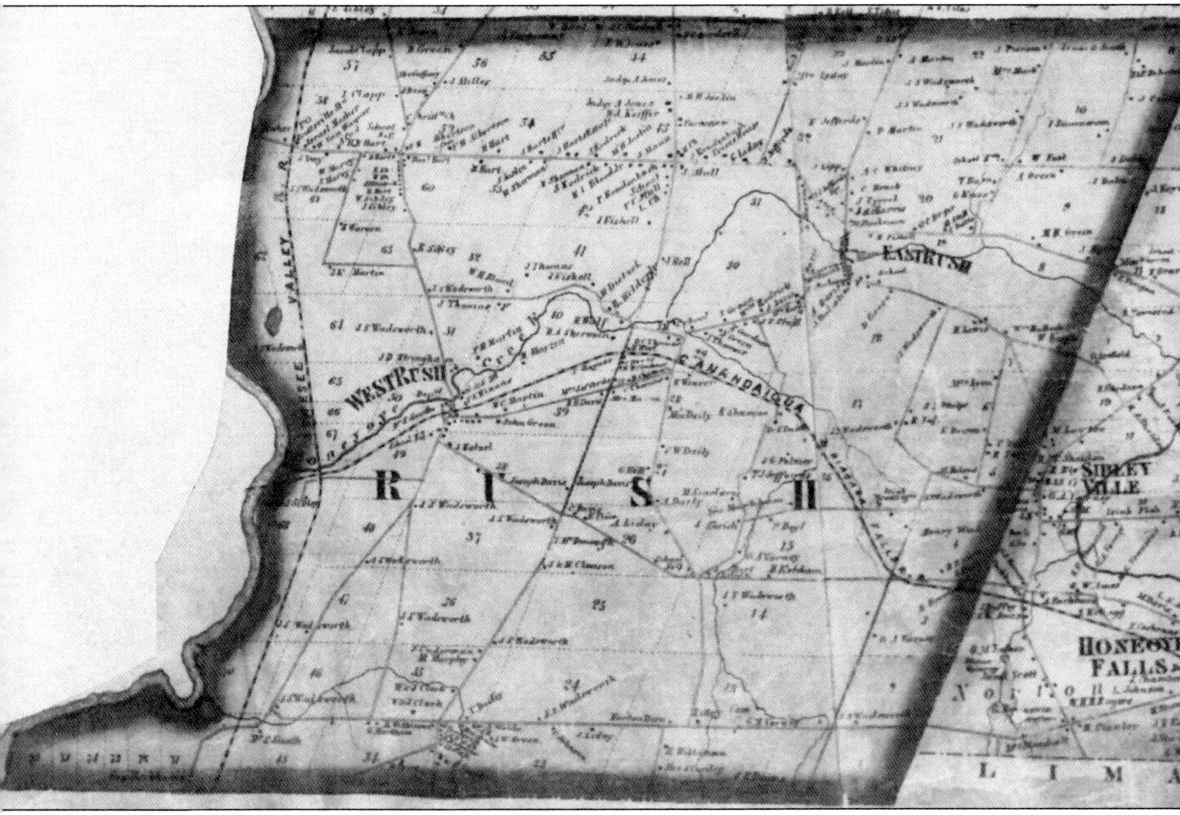

This map of the town of Rush in 1858 was sold by Whitlocks in New Haven, Connecticut. In 1804, only the families of John Bell, Peter Price, and Jacob Stull were living north of the creek. By 1858, there were 318 families living in Rush with a total population of 1,750 and 301 houses. Of the town's nearly 18,400 acres, 14,837 were reported as improved and agriculture was flourishing.

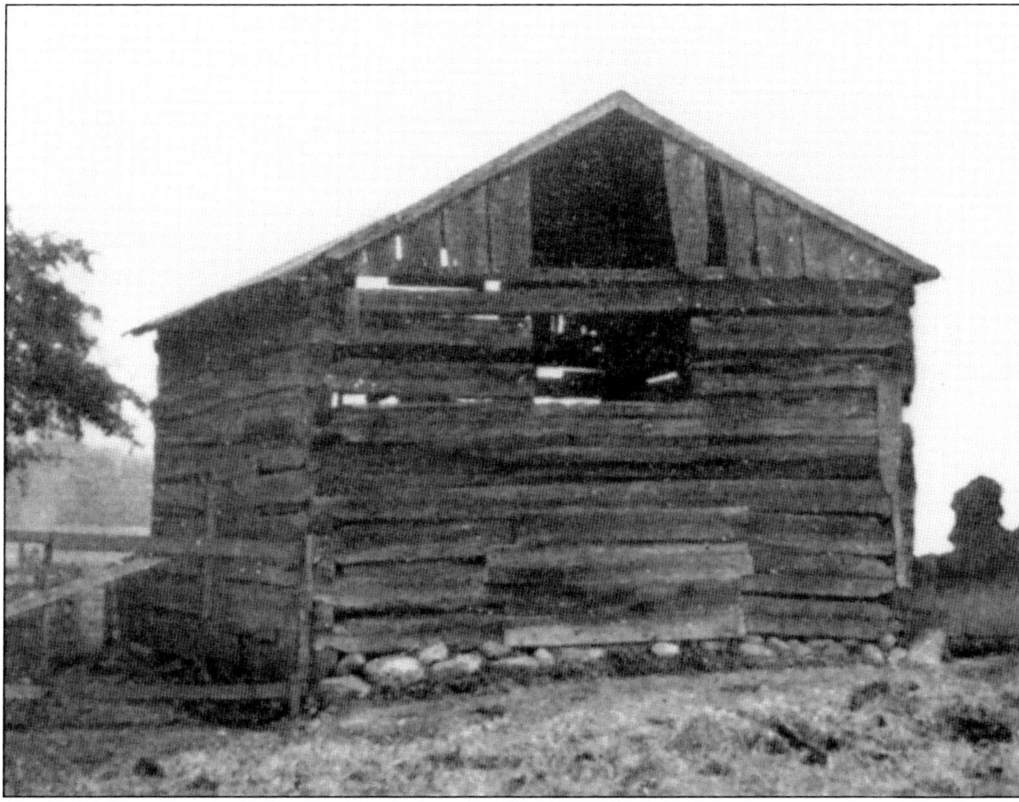

Jacob Stull was one of the first settlers in Rush. He built this cabin in 1802, and his family lived here until the larger Stull homestead was erected in 1814. The cabin was located approximately where the present-day Colby's Ice Cream, Bakery and BBQ is, near the intersection of West Henrietta and Rush-Scottsville Roads. Jacob married Susannah Price, the only daughter of Capt. Philip Price and Susannah Layman Price. (Courtesy of Eleanor Mason DeFreze.)

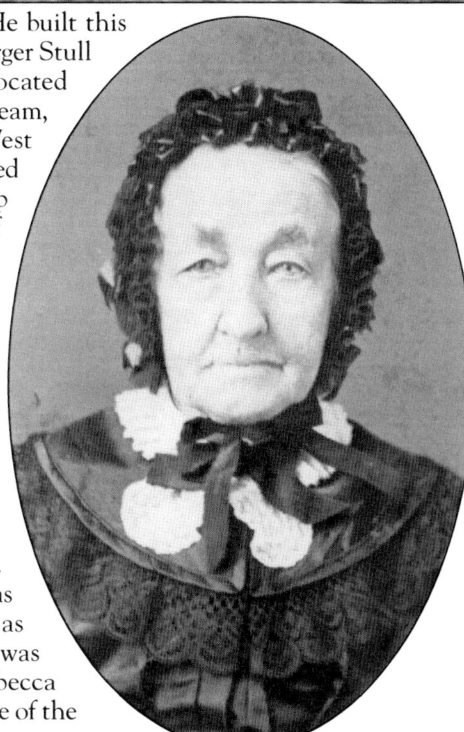

Rebecca Jeffords Price was born September 2, 1791, to Nathan Jeffords and Rebecca Sherwood. Rebecca married the Honorable Peter Price in January 1809. He was the first lawyer in Rush, served four years as justice of the peace, 18 years as town supervisor, as president of the county board of supervisors, and was also a member of the Constitutional Assembly. Rebecca died November 25, 1888, at the age of 97 and was one of the oldest residents of Monroe County at that time.

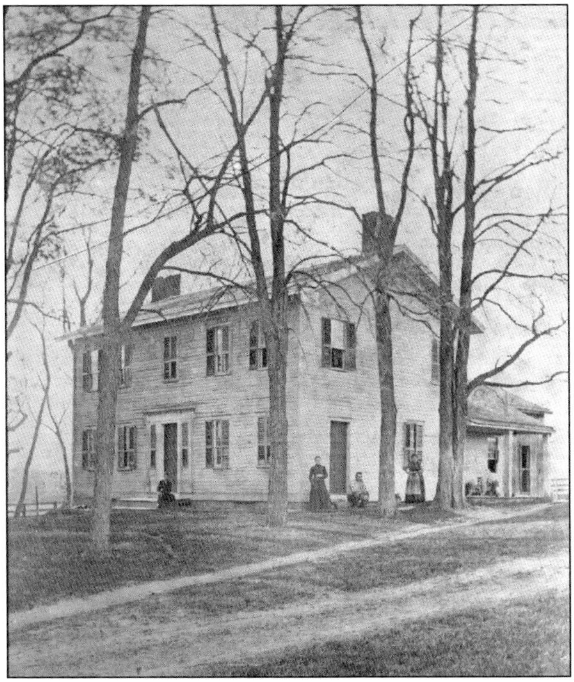

Capt. Philip Price and his family arrived from Maryland in 1801. The original Price home was a log cabin located near Chase's Farm Market on Rush-Scottsville Road. In 1827, Peter Price erected a frame house on the north side of the road. Family history holds that James Wadsworth helped build the family home. Years later, Frank Price installed greenhouses on the farm and formed the beginning of what eventually became Chase's Greenhouses and Florists. The house remained in the family for many years, but is no longer standing. Ruth Laraby's home at 1484 Rush-Scottsville Road now sits in that location. (Courtesy of Selden Price Chase.)

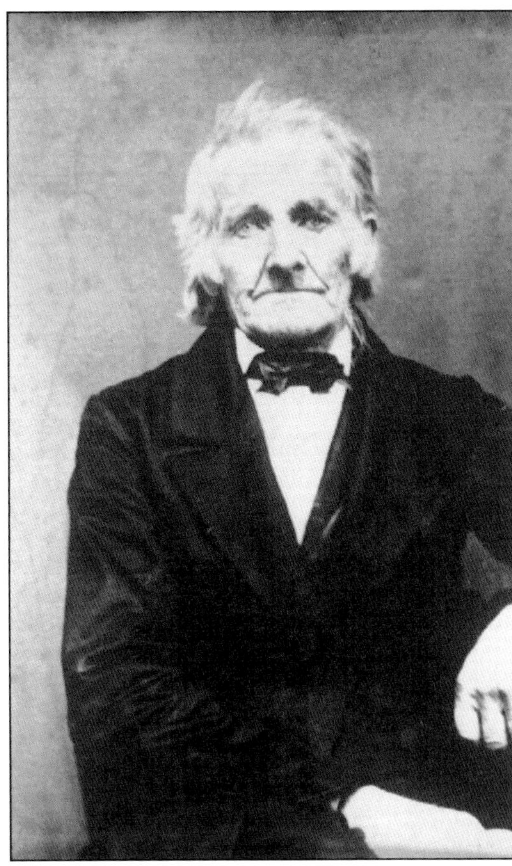

Capt. Nathan Jeffords Sr. (1755–1819) was the father of Rebecca Jeffords Price. Captain Jeffords, veteran of the American Revolution, arrived in the spring of 1806 from Richfield Springs. Along with his family, he brought five hired men, four horses, and three cows. Nathan was married to Rebecca Sherwood Jeffords (1762–1801).

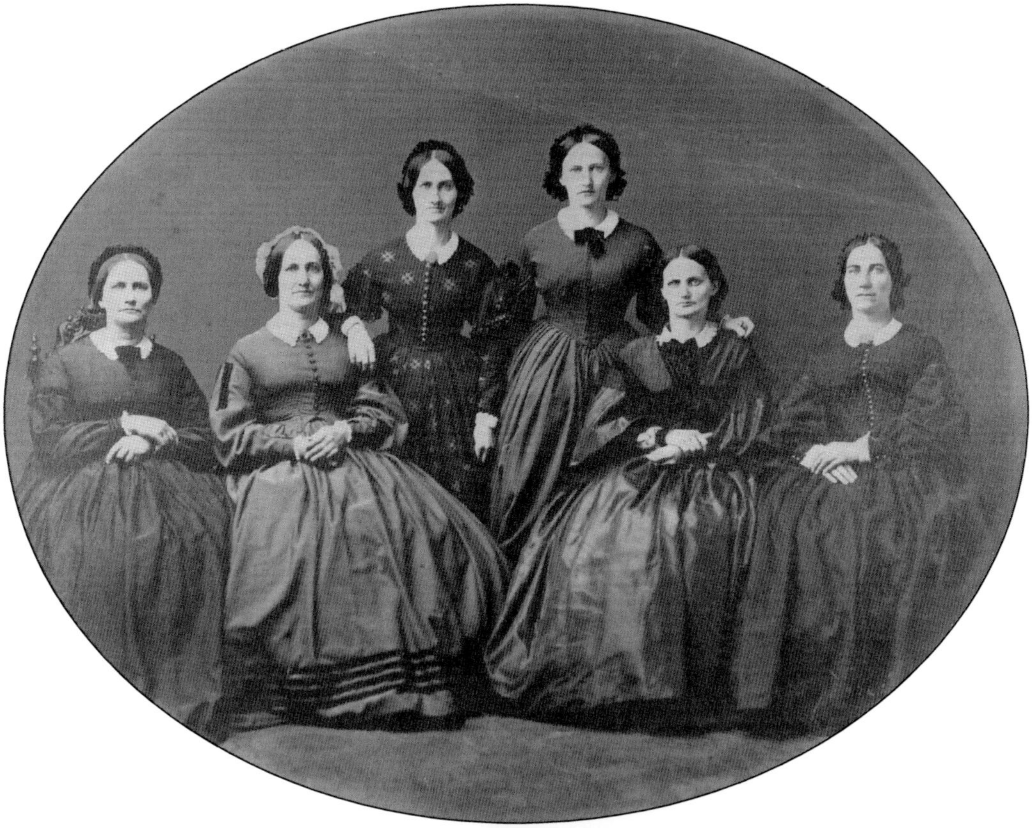

Pictured here are the six Jefferds sisters, daughters of Capt. Nathan Jefferds Jr. (1786–1867) and Polly Green Jefferds (1793–1877). The daughters are Orphelia Sybil, Sarah Malora, Cornelia, Elizabeth, Rebecca, and Julia. This photograph was taken around 1865–1870. Nathan and Polly had a family of 12 children.

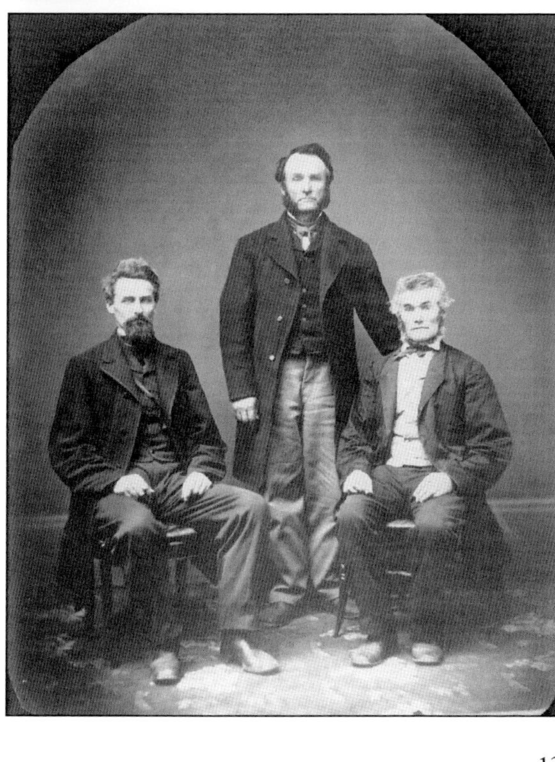

From left to right are William Jefferds, Bruce Jefferds, and Capt. Nathan Jefferds Jr. William and Bruce were the sons of Captain Jefferds, a veteran of the War of 1812, and Polly Green Jefferds. The photograph was taken around 1860 to 1865.

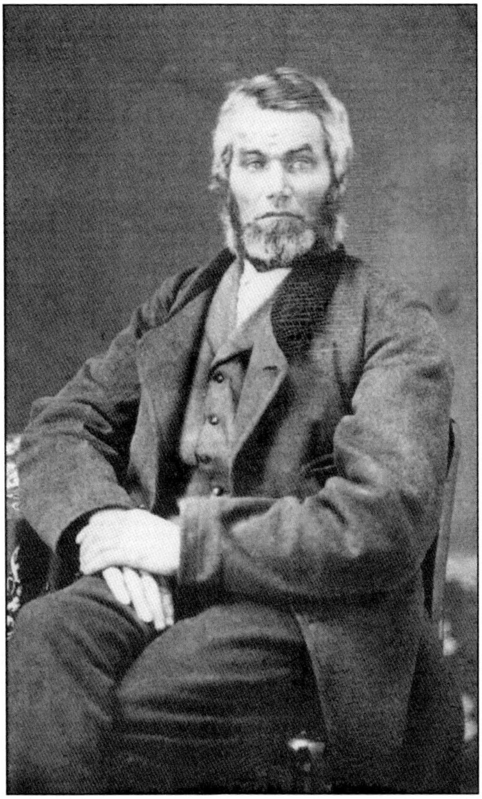

Pictured here around 1880 is Nathan Haden Jefferds, the son of Nathan Jefferds Jr. and Polly Green Jefferds.

Julia Jefferds Stull is shown around 1895 with her grandchildren. She is seated and holding her granddaughter Susie Provost. Her grandson Harold Stull is seated in front of her. Standing, from left to right, are Elvie, Wayne, Elsie, and Harry Jefferds, Frank Provost, Sadie Provost, Clyde Jefferds, and Ora Provost. Julia, the daughter of Capt. Nathan Jefferds Jr. and Polly Green Jefferds, was married to Peter Price Stull and lived to age 90.

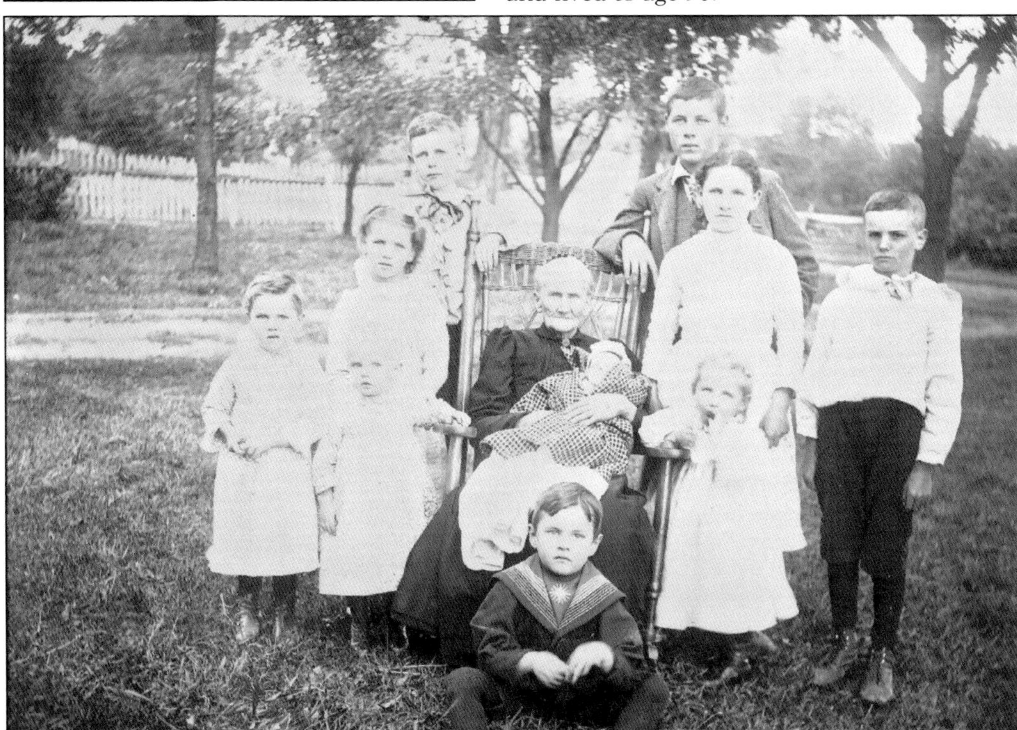

Two

EAST RUSH

East Rush was the largest of the town's hamlets and eventually became known as simply Rush. It was originally named Webster's Mills, after John Webster. He had arrived from Connecticut in 1810 and purchased land along the creek from James Wadsworth. Webster laid the foundation for a town by building a sawmill, a gristmill, a carding machine, a fulling mill, a store, and then a hotel and a schoolhouse. Other settlers were also arriving and building, some in East Rush, others nearby. Additional stores opened, more houses were built, and more businesses came along.

Along with these developments came a number of different churches. The East Rush hamlet has been home to Baptist, Methodist, Evangelical Lutheran (also called the "German Church" or the "Old Dutch" church), and Catholic churches.

The 1860 *Gazetteer and Business Directory of Monroe County* lists the number of residents of East Rush as 250, and by 1895, the count had increased to 500.

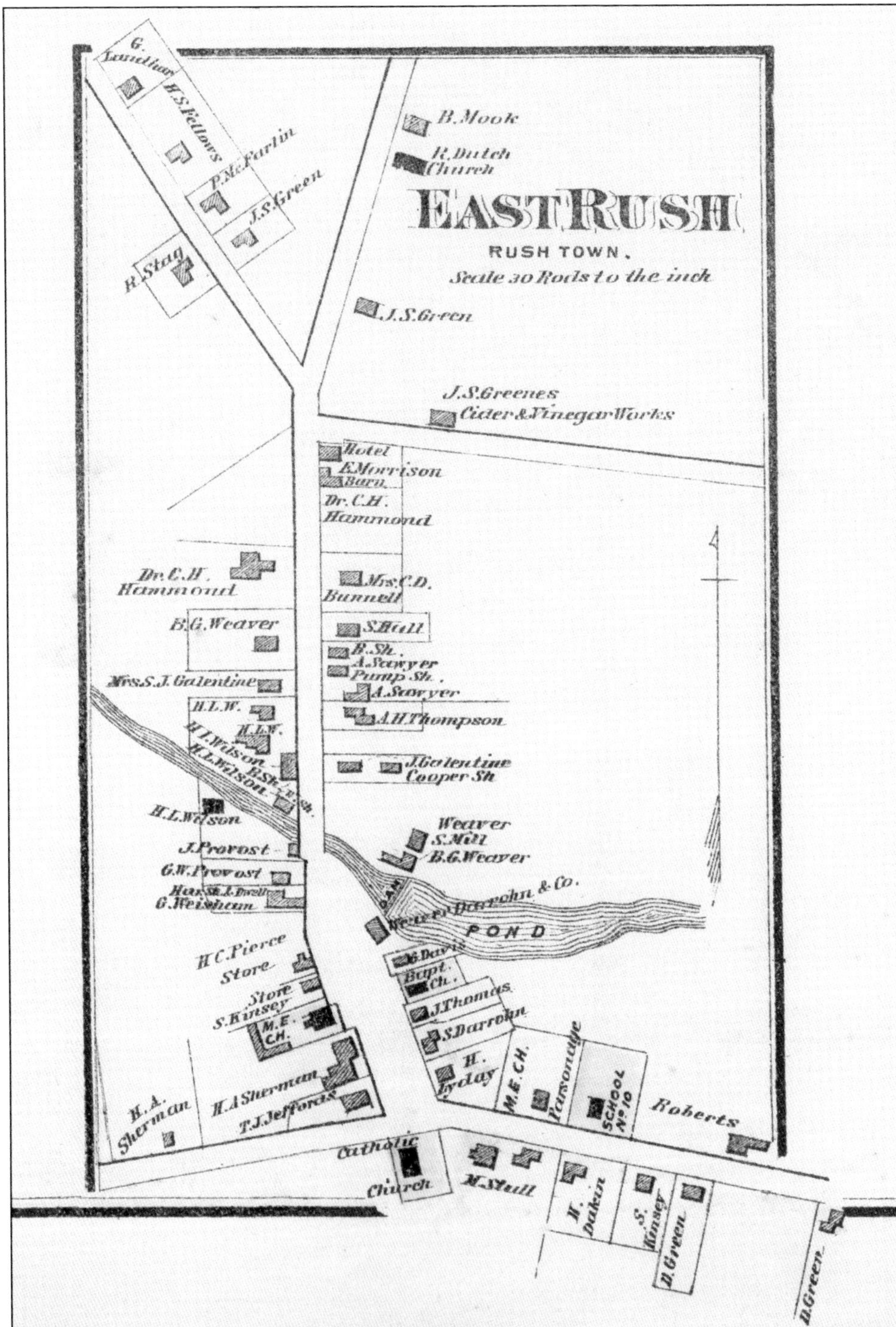

This 1872 map of the hamlet of East Rush from the *Beers' Atlas* shows a thriving, small town center. Businesses included J.S. Greene's Cider and Vinegar Works; Morrison's Hotel; Jacob Galentine's Cooper Shop; Benjamin Weaver's Mill; Morris R. Darrohn, Miller; the H.C. Pierce and the S. Kinsey Stores; and H.L. Wilson, Wagon and Carriage Maker.

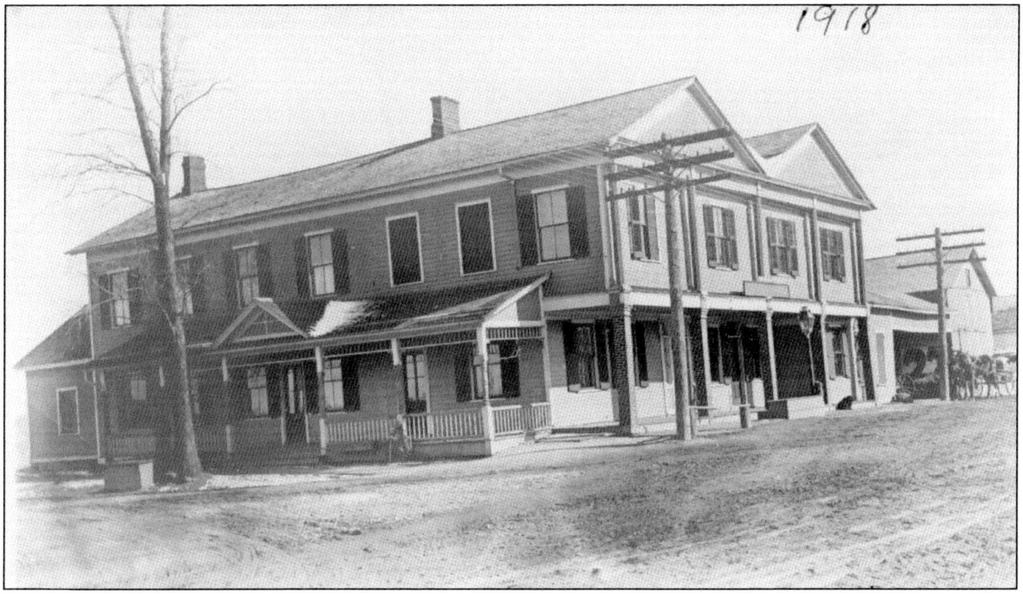

This is a 1918 photograph of the hotel that once stood at the southeast corner of East Henrietta and Rush-Mendon Roads. John Webster came to Rush in 1810 and is said to have built the hotel in 1826. In addition to overnight rooms, the hotel had a lobby, horse barn, wagon shed, and a water trough for drivers to stop and water their horses. Throughout the years, the hotel was owned and managed by a number of different people.

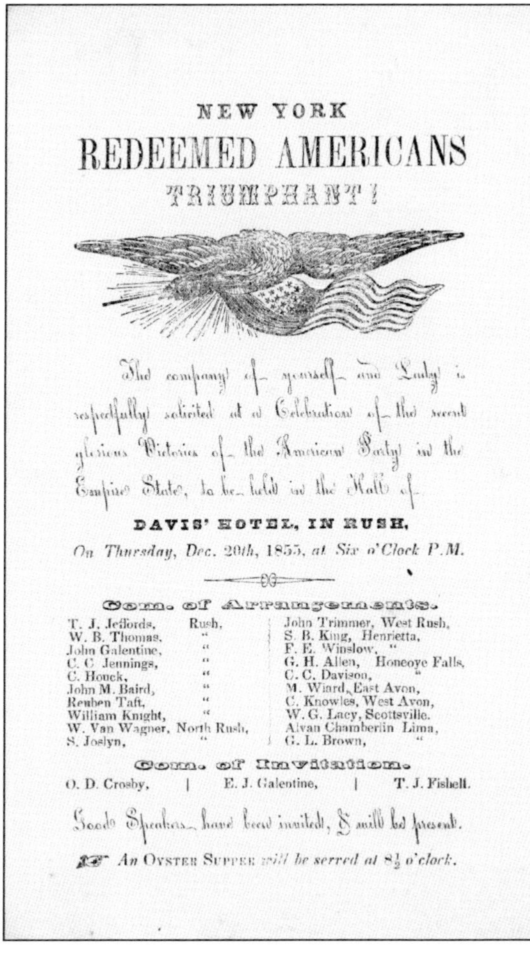

NEW YORK

REDEEMED AMERICANS

TRIUMPHANT!

The company of yourself and Lady is respectfully solicited at a Celebration of the recent glorious Victories of the American Party in the Empire State, to be held in the Hall of

DAVIS' HOTEL, IN RUSH,

On Thursday, Dec. 20th, 1855, at Six o'Clock P.M.

Com. of Arrangements.

T. J. Jeffords,	Rush,	John Trimmer,	West Rush,
W. B. Thomas,	"	S. B. King,	Henrietta,
John Galentine,	"	F. E. Winslow,	"
C. C Jennings,	"	G. H. Allen,	Honeoye Falls,
C. Houck,	"	C. C. Davison,	"
John M. Baird,	"	M. Wiard,	East Avon,
Reuben Taft,	"	C. Knowles,	West Avon,
William Knight,	"	W. G. Lacy,	Scottsville.
W. Van Wagner,	North Rush,	Alvan Chamberlin	Lima,
S. Joslyn,	"	G. L. Brown,	"

Com. of Invitation.

O. D. Crosby, | E. J. Galentine, | T. J. Fishell.

Good Speakers have been invited, & will be present.

☞ *An* OYSTER SUPPER *will be served at 8½ o'clock.*

John Webster's hotel was known as the Davis Hotel in the 1850s. This invitation is in celebration of the 1855 New York State election results. The American Party rose to popularity in the early 1850s, replacing the Whigs as the opposition party to the Democrats by 1854. By the end of 1856, the American Party had all but disappeared. Though the party was short-lived, it played a key role in the transformation of the American political system.

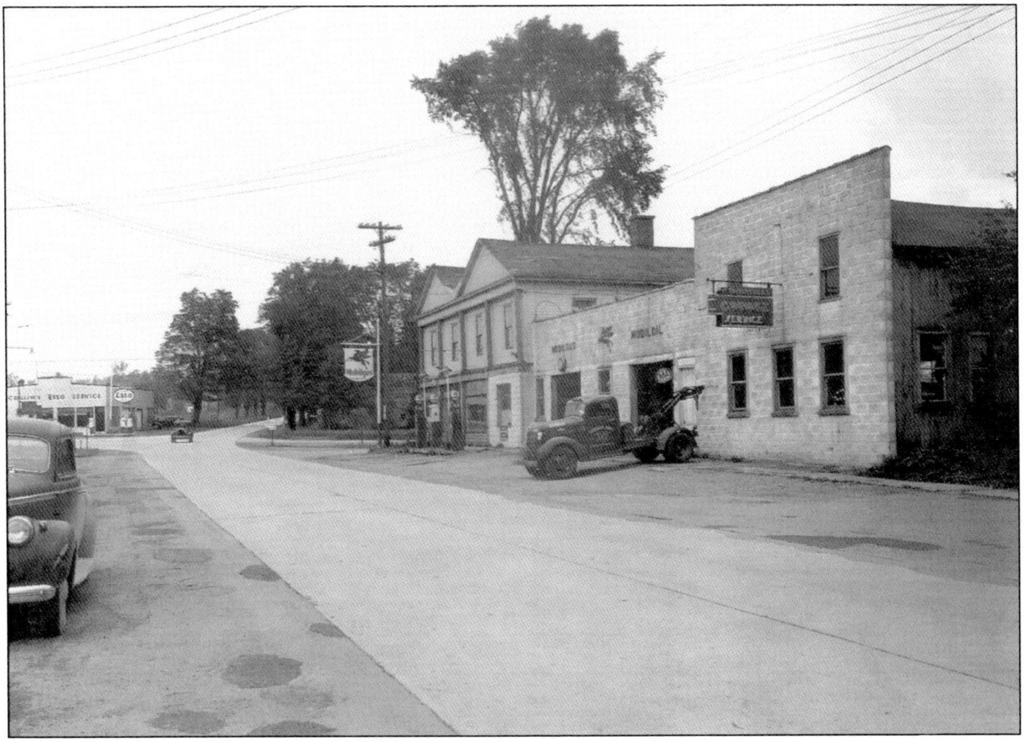

After its years as a hotel, the building became a repair garage, first as a Ford dealership owned by Roscoe Tompkinson and then by George Thitchener. The above photograph depicts a view from 1945 showing Thitchener's as a Mobilgas station and garage. The sign at the far left end of the building also advertises Frigidaire Appliances. On the corner diagonally across, where the 7-Eleven is located today, is Collin's Service Station selling Esso gasoline. The below photograph, taken around the 1950s, shows that Thitchener's was also a DeSoto and Plymouth dealership. Mr. and Mrs. Thitchener sold the old hotel in March 1967 to the Atlantic Refining Company. The Thitcheners became the 28th owners of the building when they purchased it in 1940 and continued to operate their business for the next 27 years. More recently, it was known as the Townline Garage. (Above, courtesy of Gail Mack.)

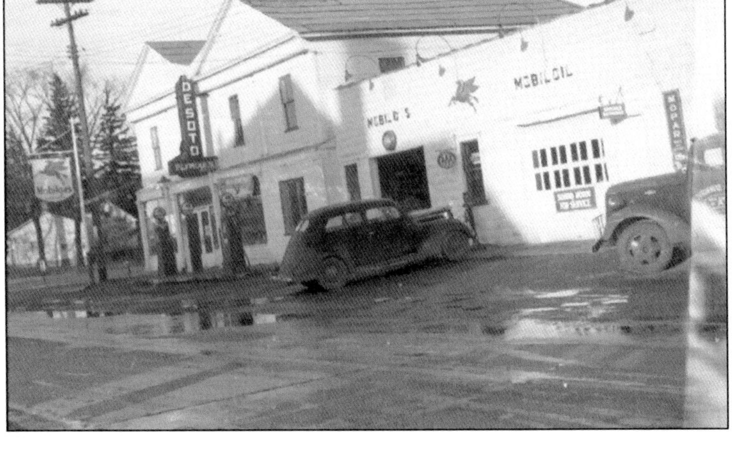

In the 1930s, the "Owen-Wiles Garage" was located at the site of the Webster Hotel and was a Ford dealership.

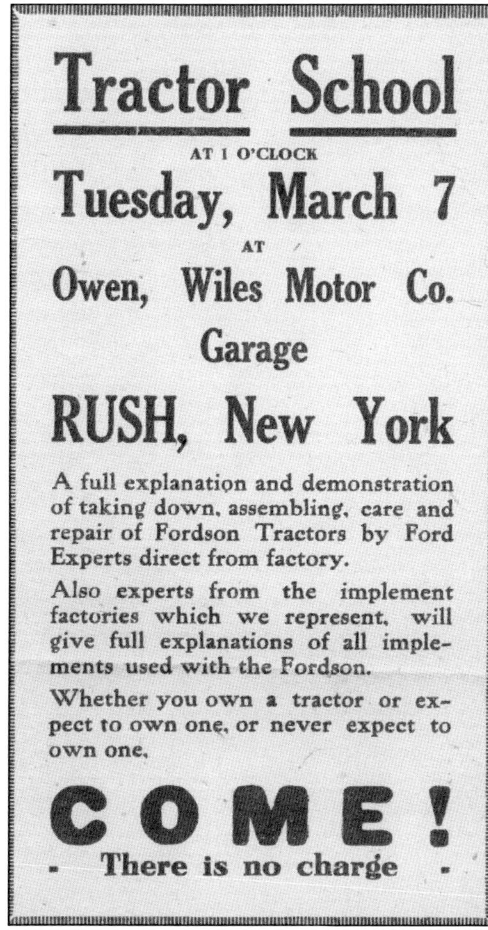

Tractor School

AT 1 O'CLOCK

Tuesday, March 7

AT

Owen, Wiles Motor Co. Garage

RUSH, New York

A full explanation and demonstration of taking down, assembling, care and repair of Fordson Tractors by Ford Experts direct from factory.

Also experts from the implement factories which we represent, will give full explanations of all implements used with the Fordson.

Whether you own a tractor or expect to own one, or never expect to own one,

COME!

There is no charge

The Wilson General Store was owned and operated by the Wilson brothers. They purchased their store from Nathaniel Mead and a Mr. Provost, who had first opened for business in 1893. The store was located on the east side of East Henrietta Road, north of the creek. The cover image shows the storefront with the mail wagon parked between the two buildings.

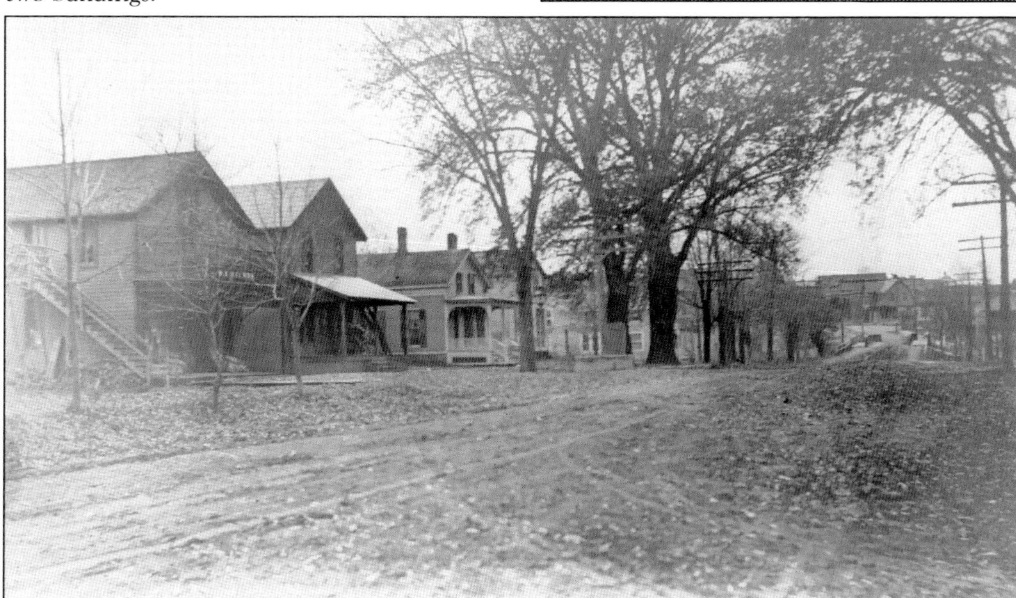

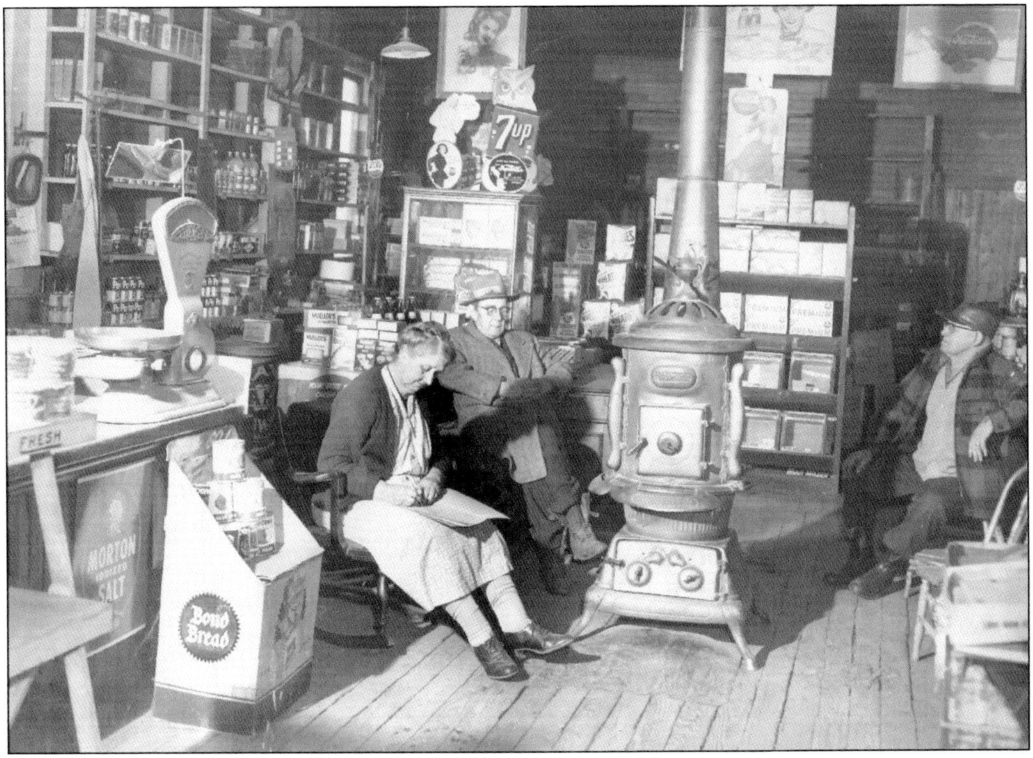

Dora Behnk began working at the general store located at 6008 East Henrietta Road in 1906. The store was owned by William Wilson at that time, but she and her brother Carl purchased it in 1909. In addition to the store, Carl peddled his wares by wagon and covered the countryside Mondays–Thursdays; his route traversed Rush and extended into Mendon and Henrietta. On Fridays, he would travel to Rochester to trade his goods for other stock. Carl died in 1936, and Dora continued running the store with help from her brother Philip. Dora finally closed the doors to her store in 1962, leaving a void for the local folks who regularly gathered there to catch up with one another. Pictured, from left to right, are Dora Behnk, H. Dean Kazmayer, and Frank Faugh. (Courtesy of Bertha and Vincent Woolaver family.)

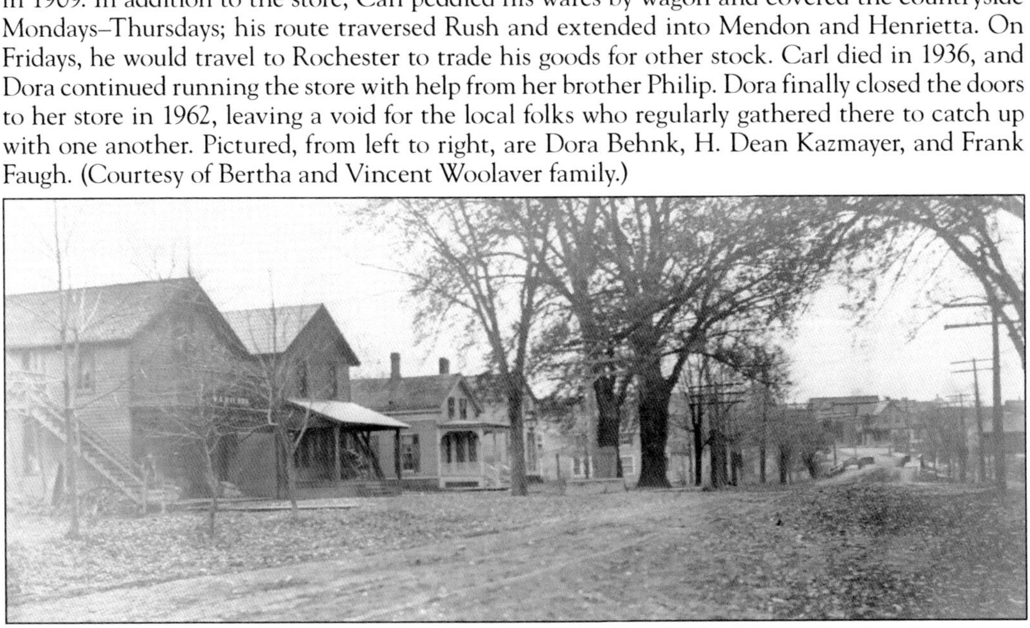

This view of the hamlet is facing south on East Henrietta Road. The Wilson Brothers' store is on the left, and the Price Hotel can be seen on the right over the bridge. Note the watering trough on the left side. (Courtesy of Eleanor Mason DeFreze.)

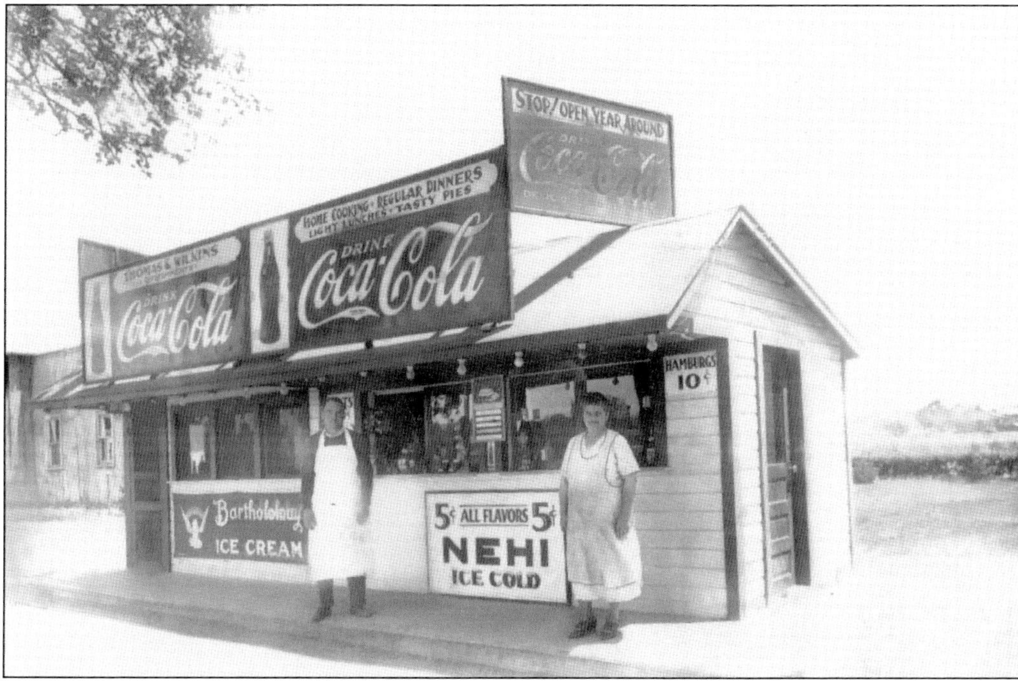

Friends and business partners Arthur H. Wilkins and Anna C. Thomas are outside their restaurant in 1925. Art's son Laverne "Jake" Wilkins and wife, Betty, took over the business in 1948. Located in the center of the hamlet, the restaurant was a popular social hub for the town for many years. Across the street, where the town hall is now located, Lucy Bock once operated an ice cream stand. The former Art and Annie's is now the home of Joelle Lane's Hair Design.

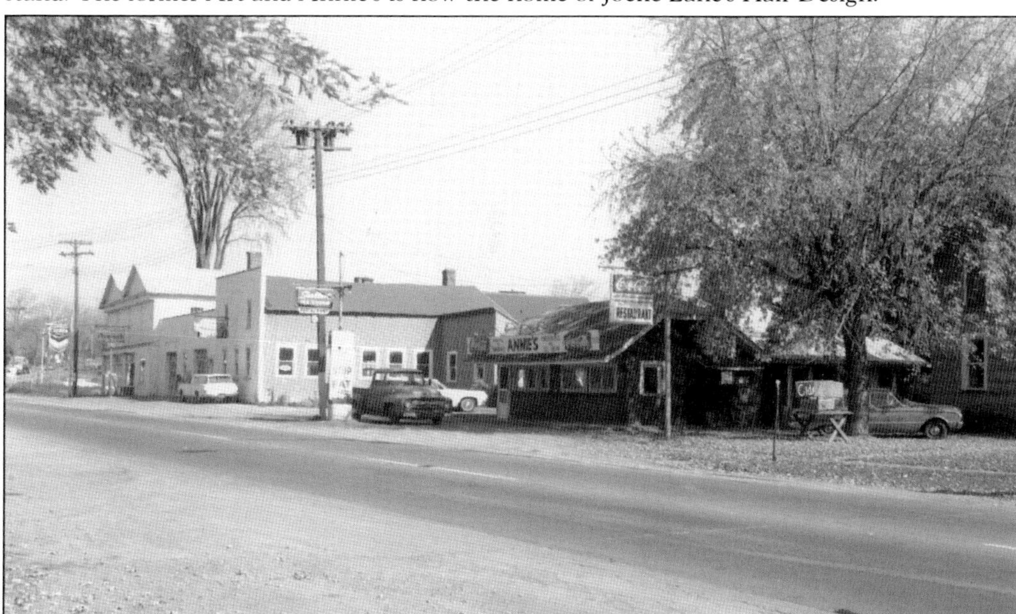

In a northward view on East Henrietta Road, Art and Annie's Diner is seen on the right-hand side, with Thitchener's Garage in sight just beyond the diner.

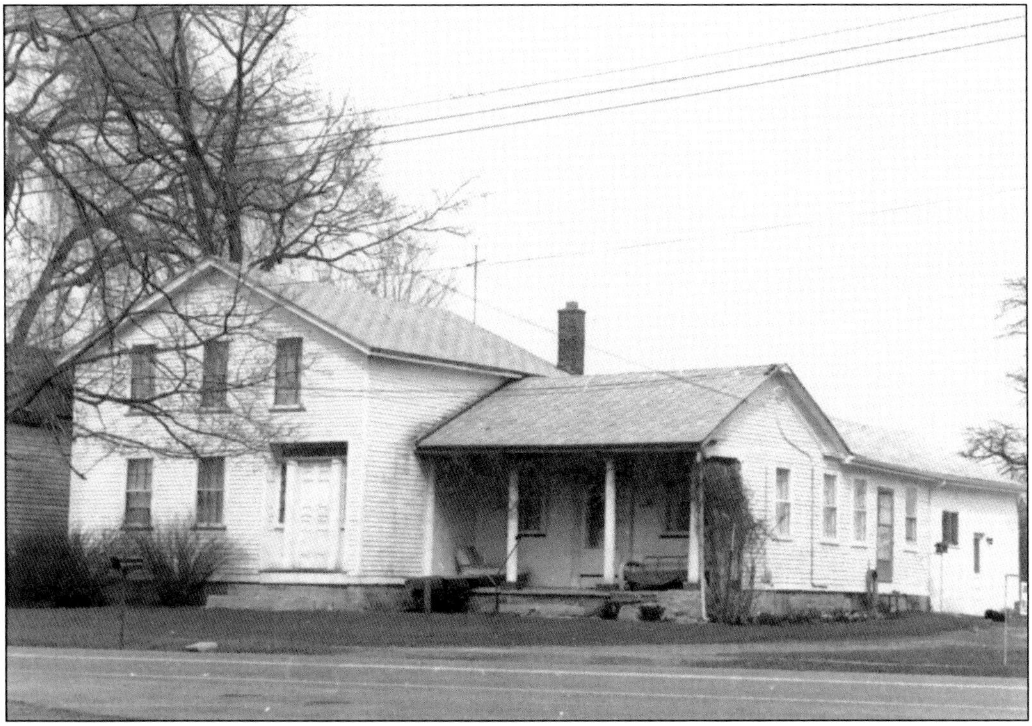

The Miller family home is shown here. This house, located at 6018 East Henrietta Road, has previously been home to the Thompson and Behnk families. The frame structure is noted for its Post-Colonial entrance, featuring an eight-panel door with a decorative transom window across the top.

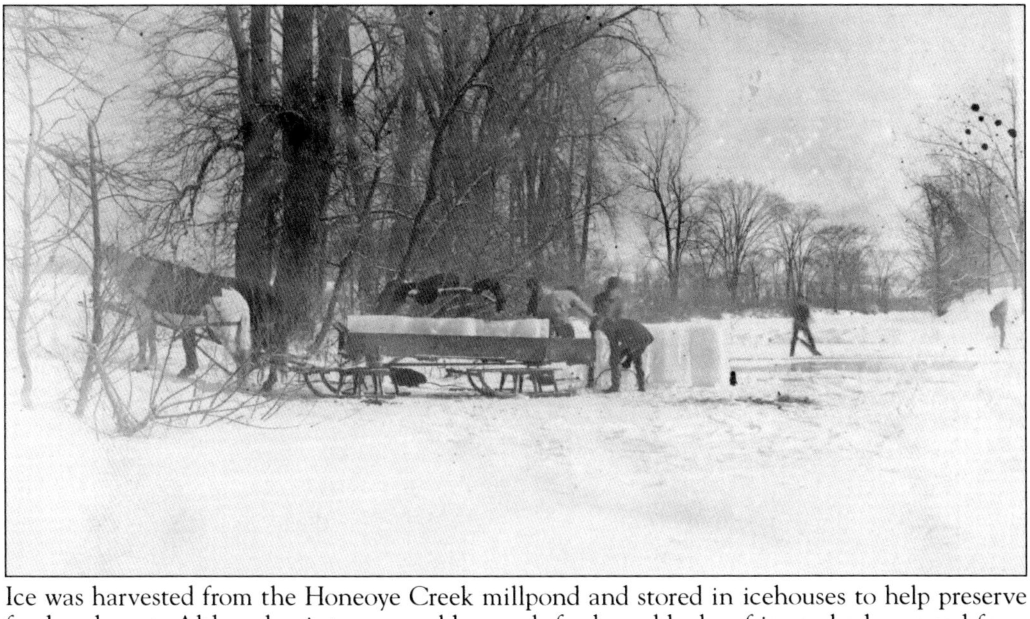

Ice was harvested from the Honeoye Creek millpond and stored in icehouses to help preserve food and meat. Although winter was cold enough for large blocks of ice to be harvested from the creek, the discarded jackets hanging from the trees provide a sense of how much effort was involved in this work. (Courtesy of Eleanor Mason DeFreze.)

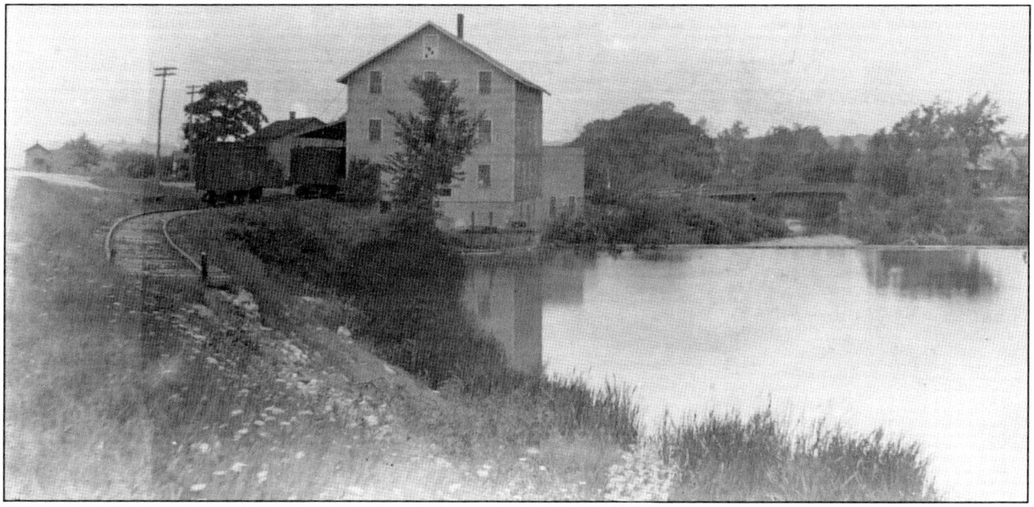

The first flour mill in East Rush was built by John Webster in 1810 on land purchased from James Wadsworth. In 1847, when owned by Benjamin Weaver, the mill burned. Weaver partnered with Warren Foote and rebuilt the mill. It operated as Weaver and Foote until 1884, when Hiram Smith purchased Foote's share, changing the name to Weaver and Smith. Ownership changes continued with Homer L.S. Hall, the Darrohn family, and J.R. Smith and Sons. The final owners, Tomkinson, Kenyon, and Tomkinson, leased the mill in 1904 and purchased it the following year. Roscoe and Samuel Tomkinson and Delia Kenyon also owned a mill in Honeoye Falls. After some financial struggles at the turn of the century, the mill thrived under the Tomkinson, Kenyon, and Tomkinson ownership until its demise from a fatal fire in September 1941. (Below, courtesy of Eleanor Mason DeFreze.)

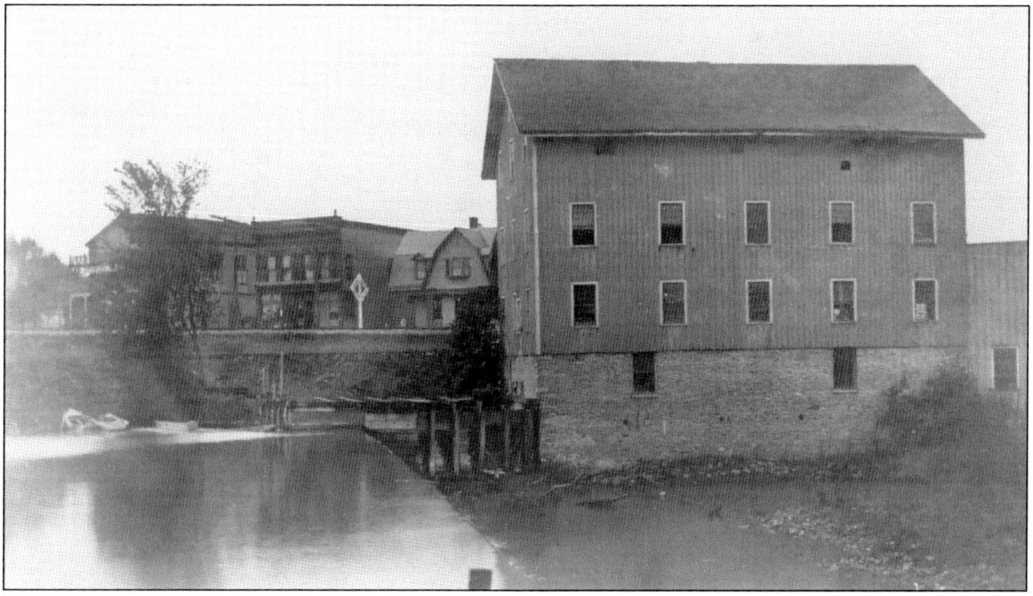

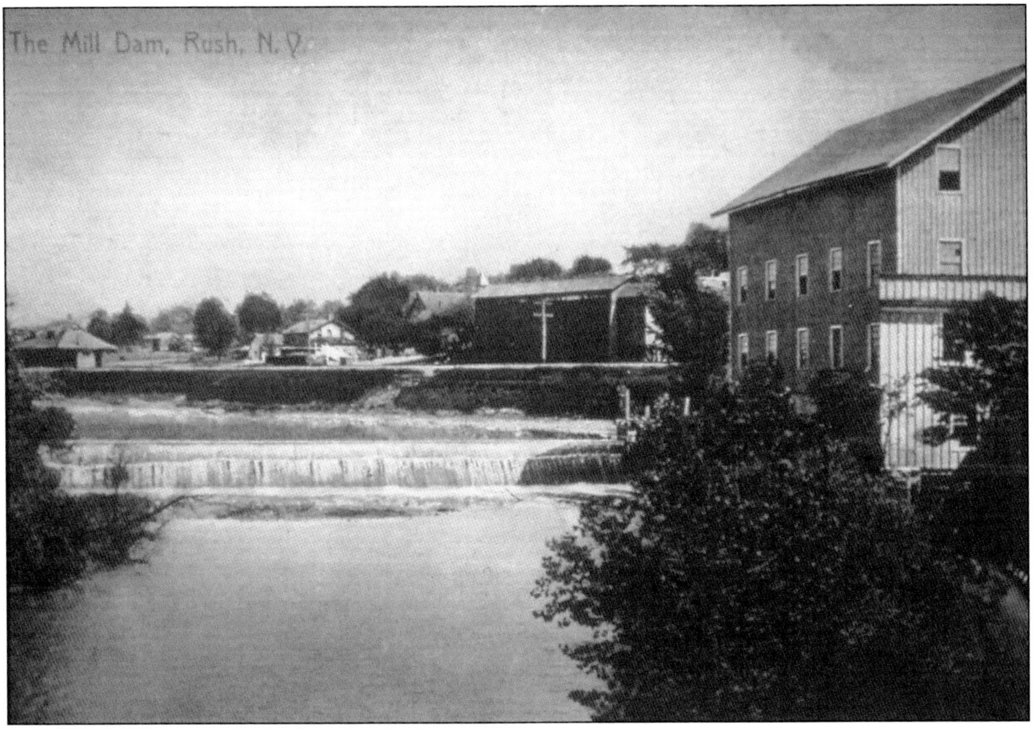

Taken around 1910, this photograph shows the Rush Mill Dam with the businesses and school backing up to the south side of the creek, before the silo was built. The coal trestle, school, and the train depot are at the far left.

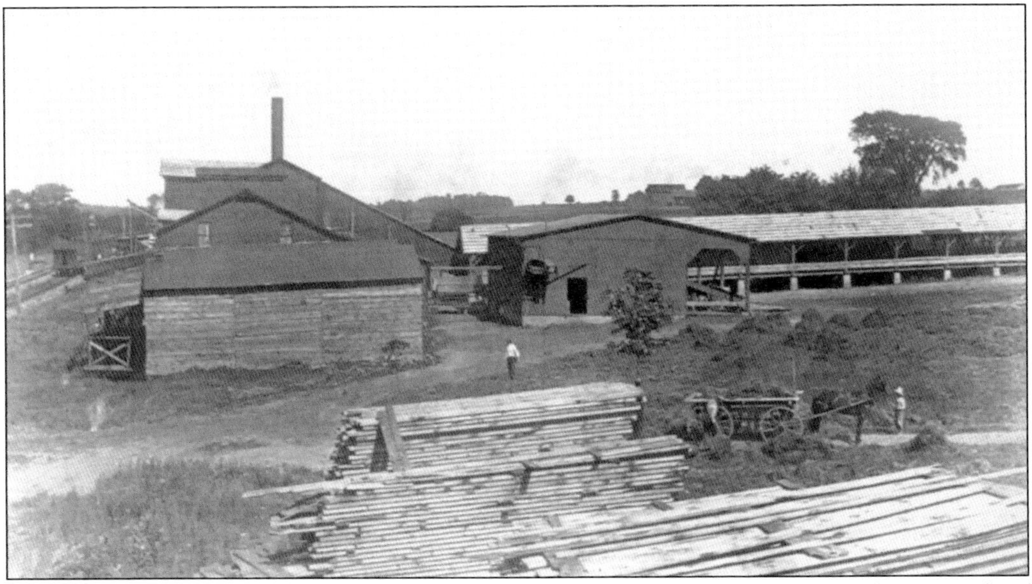
The lumberyard was situated south of the Lehigh Valley Railroad tracks and on the west side of the Canning Factory. Maps from the early 1900s identify the business as the Morris R. Darrohn and Son Coal and Lumber Company. Previously, Henry Sherman and Son owned the coal and fertilizer business before selling to Everett Darrohn. The Darrohn family also owned and operated the mill for a period of time. (Courtesy of Eleanor Mason DeFreze.)

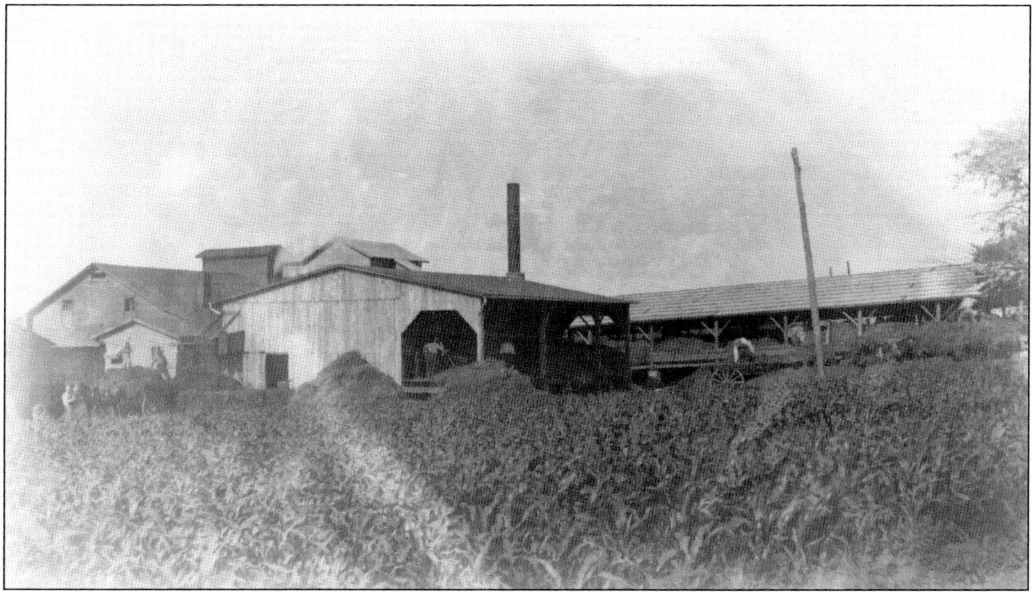

First named the Rush Preserving Company and later the Genesee Valley Preserving Company, the business was commonly referred to by the locals as the Canning or Bean Factory. The company began in Rush in 1900 and was located alongside the railroad, behind District School No. 10 (the present post office). Within the first year of its opening, the factory was operating day and night, processing corn and tomatoes, and employed approximately 70 local people. Although the canning factory had seemed to start off with good success, by the close of the decade it was said to be several thousand dollars in debt. A change in management revived its livelihood, and the year 1911 saw more than one million cans of vegetables packed at the Rush factory. Owners William Osborn and Sons moved the factory to Honeoye Falls a few years later. (Both, courtesy of Eleanor Mason DeFreze.)

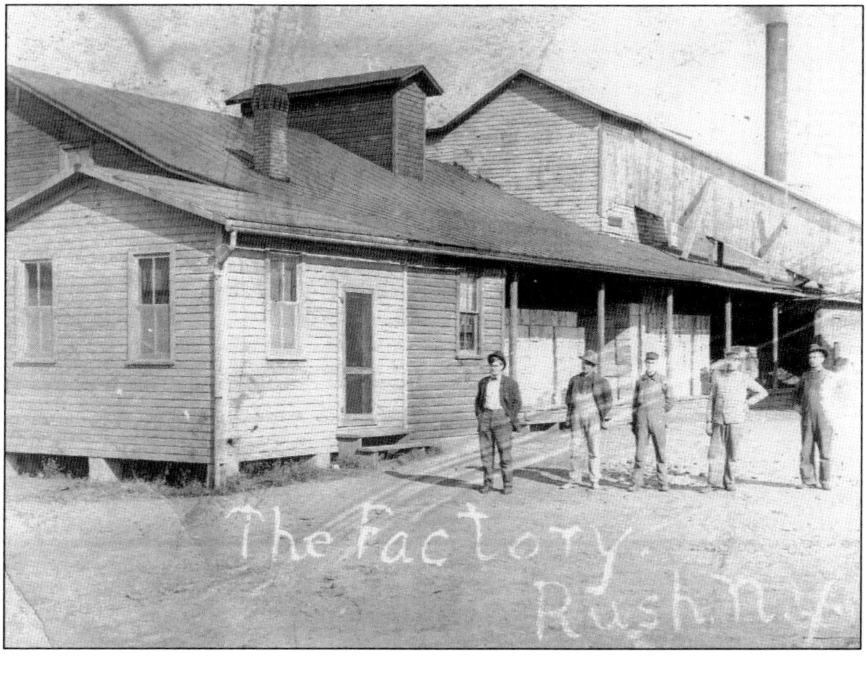

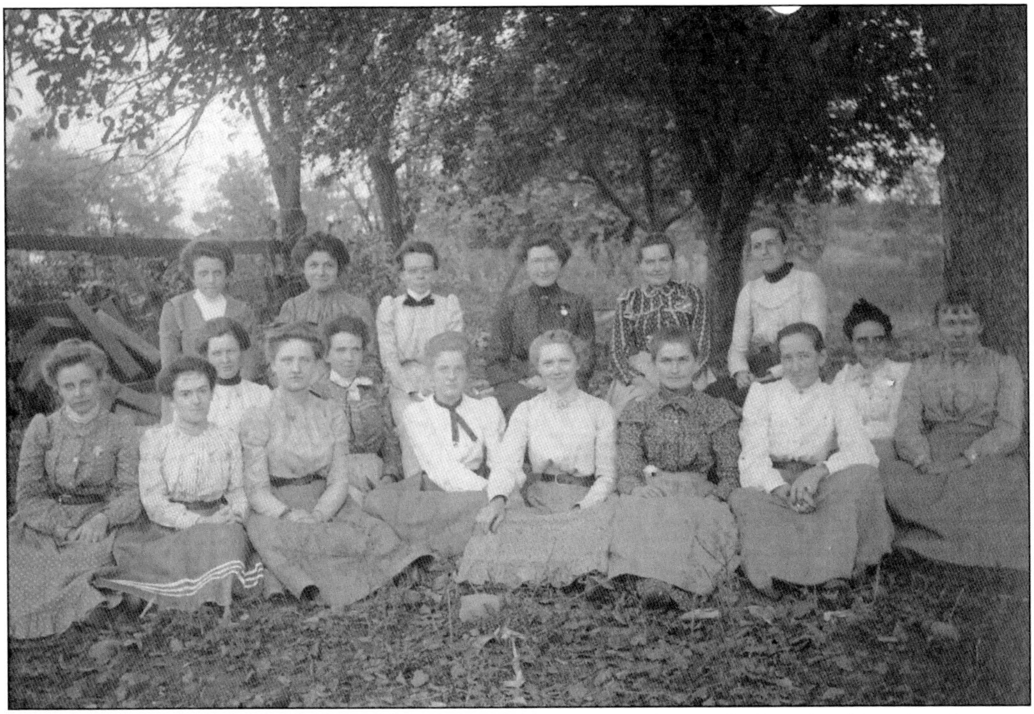

This October 1901 photograph is of a group of the women who worked at the Canning Factory.

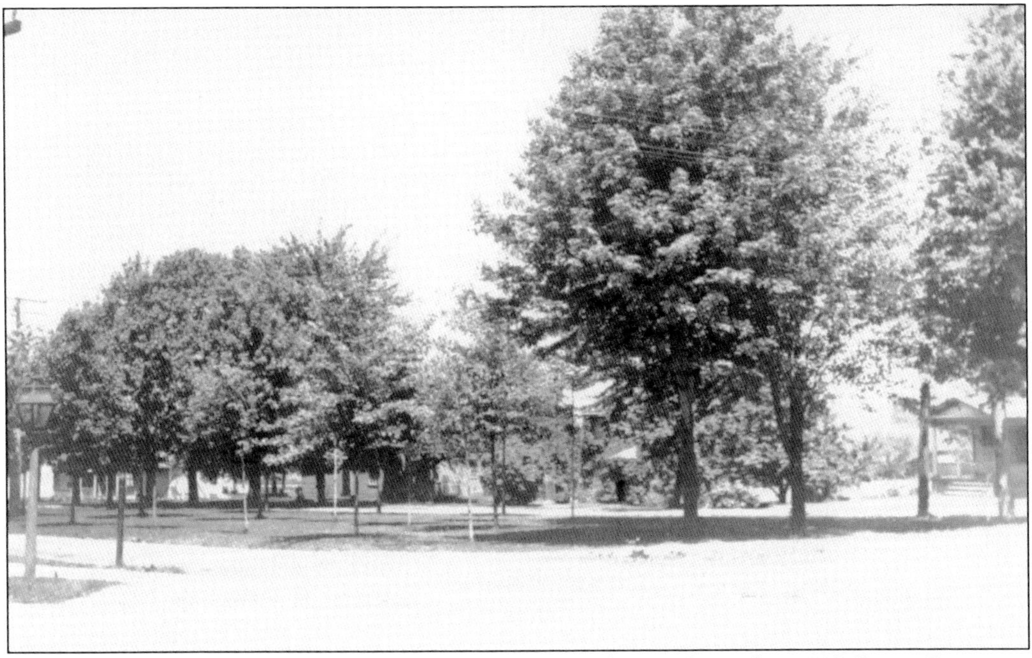

Plans to turn the Village Green, or Commons, into a park were formed in 1897. Byron Diver was named superintendent of construction at a planning meeting, and work was soon underway. The ground was leveled, driveways added on either side, and trees planted. Flowerbeds were eventually added as well. James Congdon, Frank Stull, and James W. Wiles were among those who dedicated time and effort to create a pleasant park for all to enjoy.

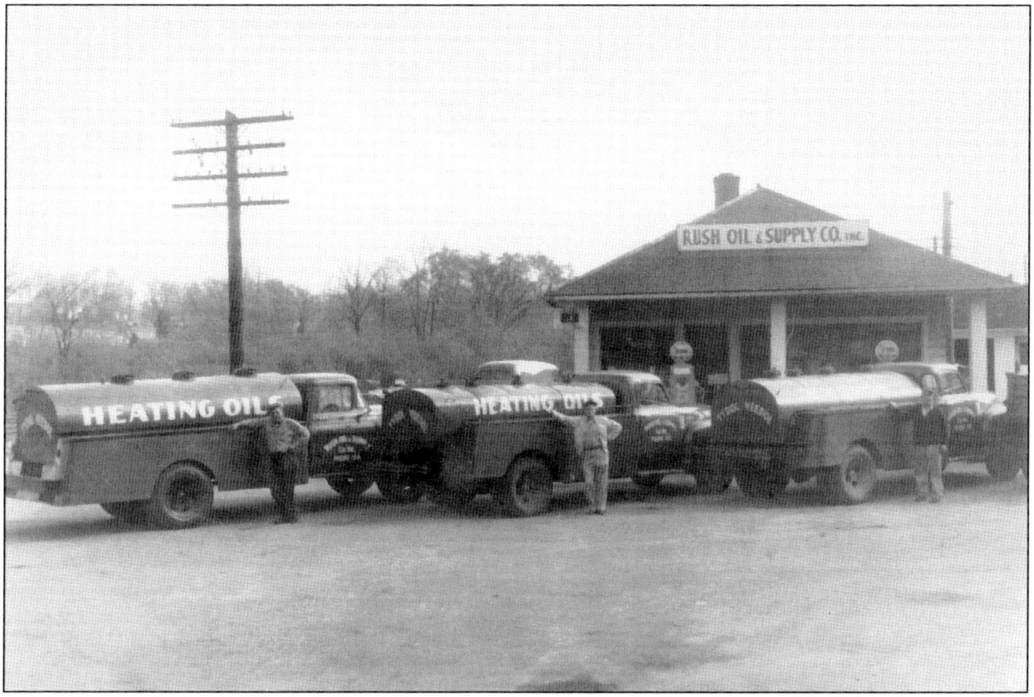

The Rush Oil and Supply Company, located at the current site of Montesano's Pizza at 2 Park Lane, was incorporated in 1930 with firm owners William Klick, George Sherman, and H. Grad Diver. The men in the photograph above are unidentified, but in the photograph below are, from left to right, William Klick; Klick's wife, Elsie Ward Klick; and Agnes McAvoy, the office secretary. The truck in this c. 1950s photograph is a 1940s Chevy Stepside. (Both, courtesy of Jim Klick.)

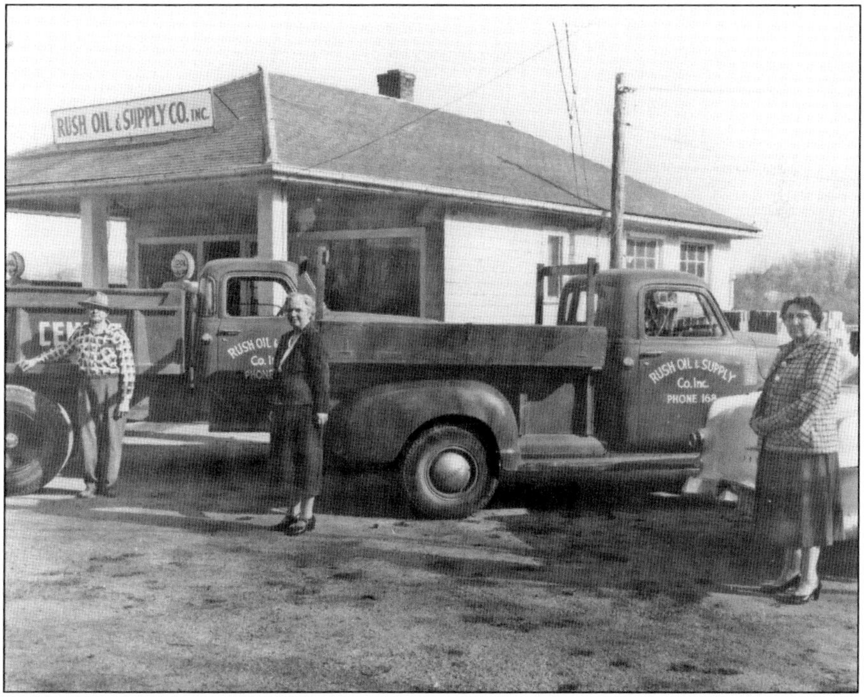

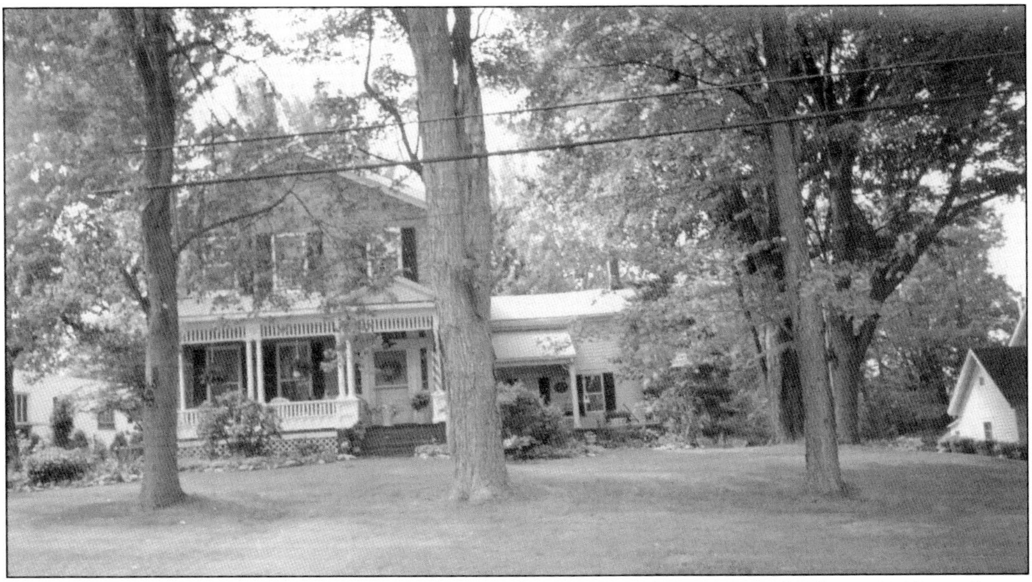

This home, known as Poplar Terrace, was located at 6123 Rush Lima Road. The c. 1840 residence was said to be built of fieldstone quarried from the Five Points area. Built by Matthew Stull, son of Jacob and Susannah Price Stull, the home had several additions over the years, and the small rear addition was once a dairy store and later a tailor shop.

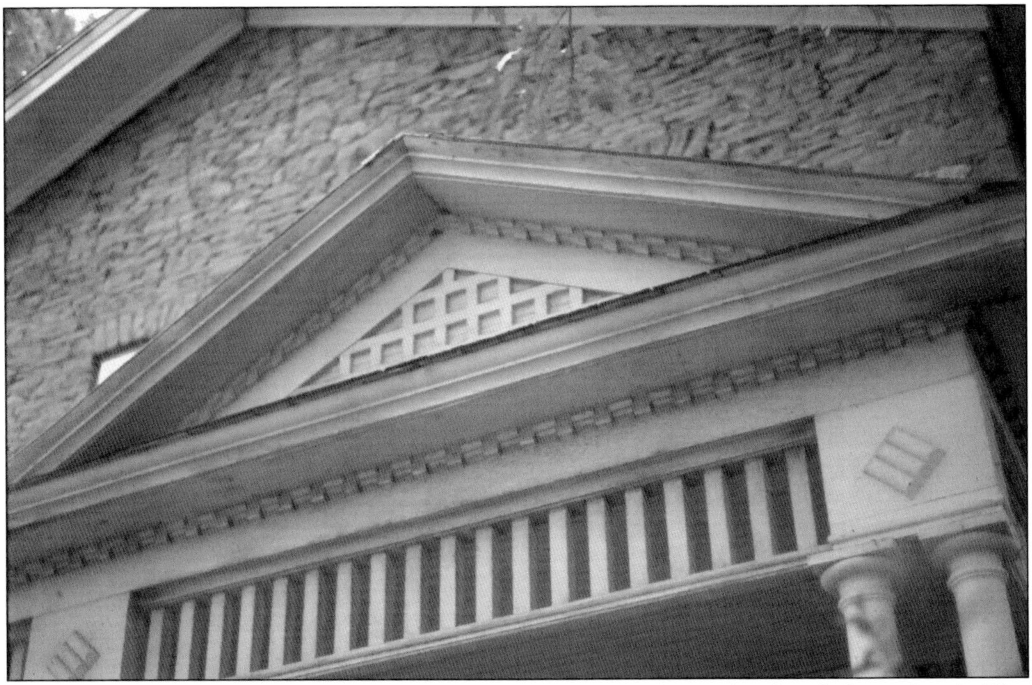

This close-up view of the front entrance of Poplar Terrace shows the detailed woodwork. The historic home once sat upon a small knoll between the Catholic and Methodist churches (now the Church of God). It had true divided-light windows, wide windowsills, pocket doors, an open staircase with curved banister, and ornately carved woodwork. The Stulls, Galentines, and Divers were among the early families of Rush to have lived here.

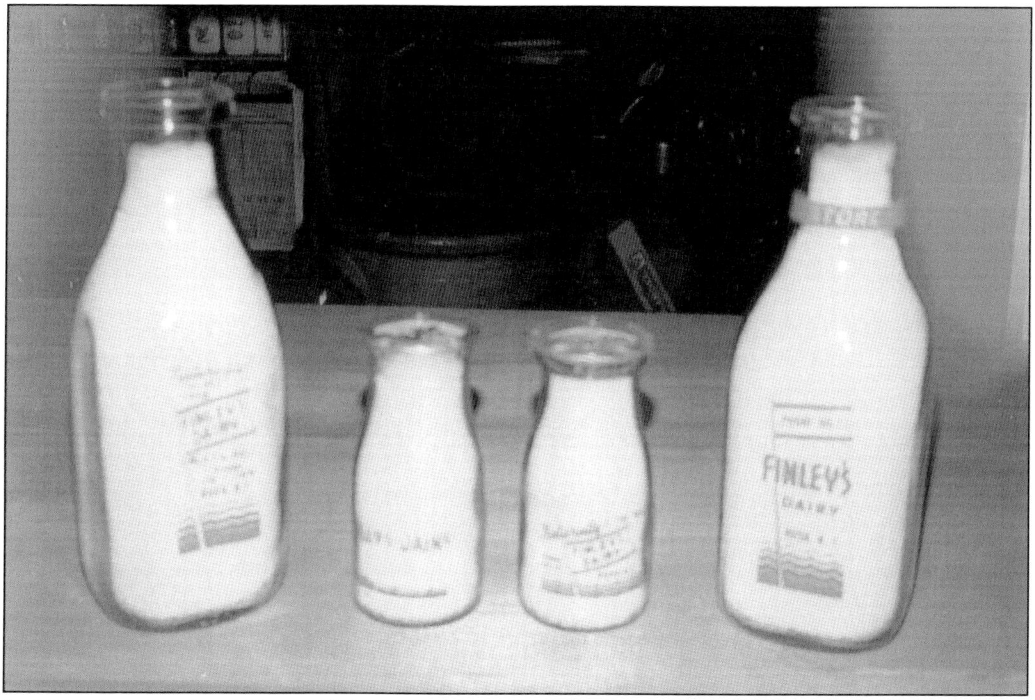

In 1940, Ray Bock sold his milk business to Frank Finley and his son William. Over the course of the next 20 years, the customer base expanded from 300 quarts daily to an output of 1,500 quarts on a daily basis. Arthur K. Dell was a partner with Finley for five years before Finley returned to sole ownership in 1959. Pictured here are bottles from the Finley Dairy. (Courtesy of Robert Page Collection.)

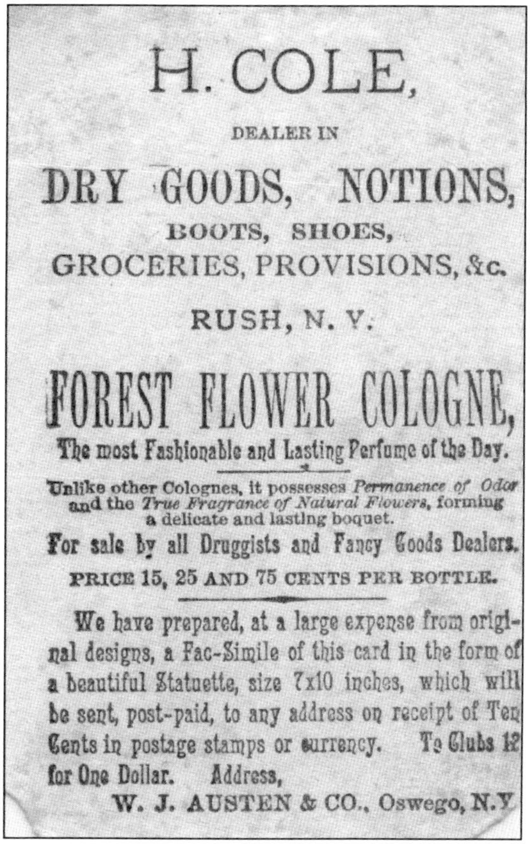

Shown here is an advertisement from the H.C. Cole General Store. Cole sold the building, along with its contents, to Samuel Kinsey in December 1885. Kinsey promptly began making repairs and updates to what became known as Kinsey Hall. In previous years, Kinsey had been in the sugarcane business in Rush. Along with raising his own cane, he had a mill and evaporators, and took in cane from other farmers.

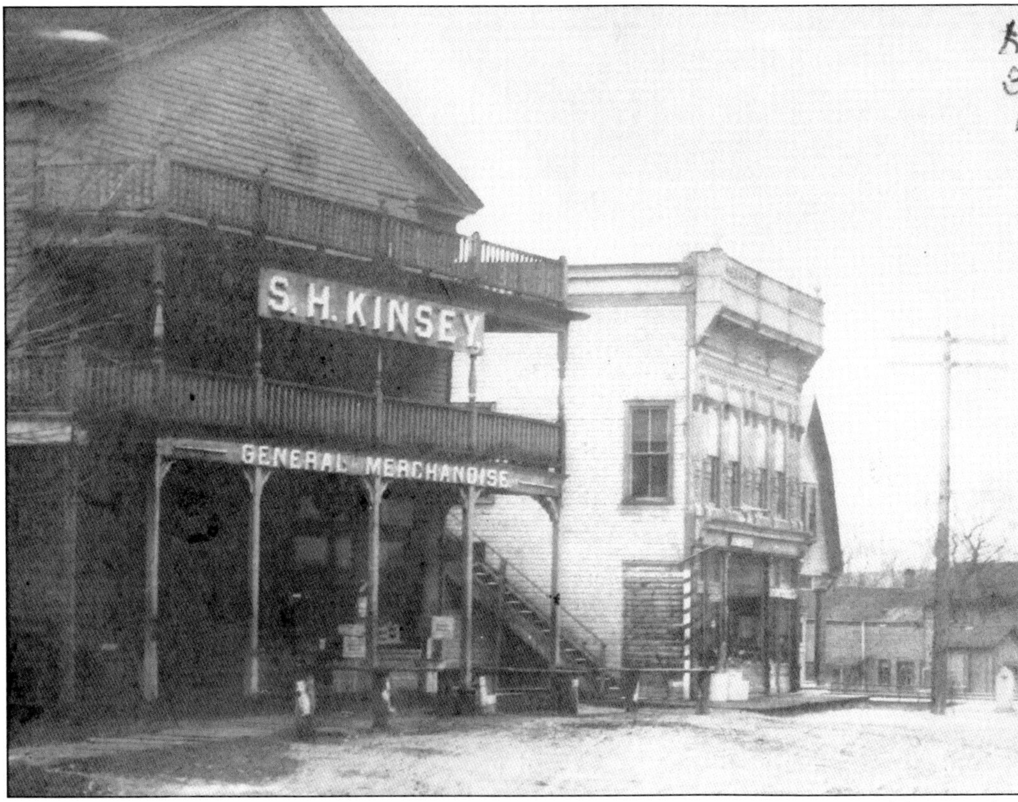

The "Big Fire" of Rush occurred in August 1892 and started in Kinsey's Store, quickly spreading to the Price Hotel and then across the driveway on the south to the Methodist church. At that time, the town clerk's office was in the store, and all records were lost to the fire. The Baptist church, at the site of present-day Montesano's Pizza, was no longer in use, so Samuel Kinsey purchased the church and moved it across the road. The first floor became the Kinsey Store and the second floor was used as the town hall for many years. The second floor also served as a dance hall, library, basketball court, and hosted many plays and lectures over the years. In 1907, Kinsey sold his grocery business to his son Maurice and C.F. Zeitler. Don Woods then operated a Red & White Store at this location from 1937 to 1956. (Above, courtesy of Pam Bock Ebersold.)

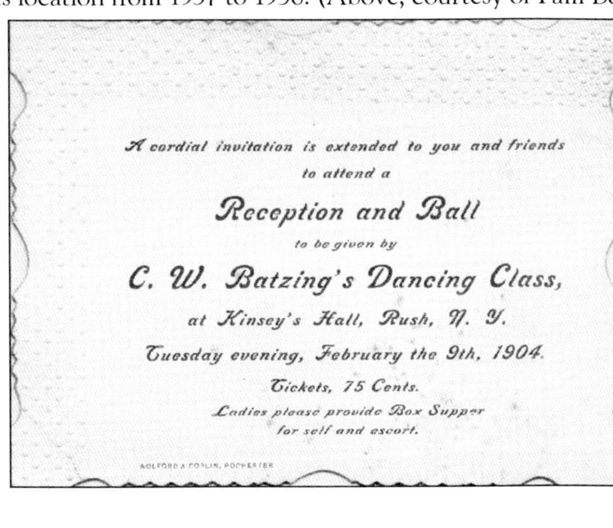

A cordial invitation is extended to you and friends
to attend a

Reception and Ball

to be given by

C. W. Batzing's Dancing Class,

at Kinsey's Hall, Rush, N. Y.

Tuesday evening, February the 9th, 1904.

Tickets, 75 Cents.

Ladies please provide Box Supper
for self and escort.

Born in 1871, Maurice E. Kinsey, the son of Samuel and Elizabeth Hart Kinsey, served his hometown in many ways. Upon his father's retirement, he operated the Kinsey Store for 50 years, served as town clerk, and then became Rush supervisor from 1904 to 1911. He later served as Rush postmaster from 1917 to 1922.

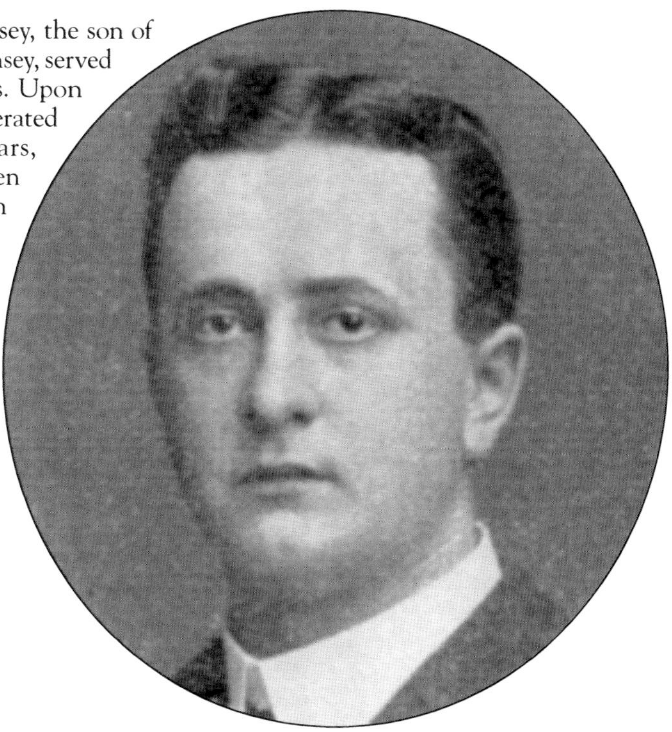

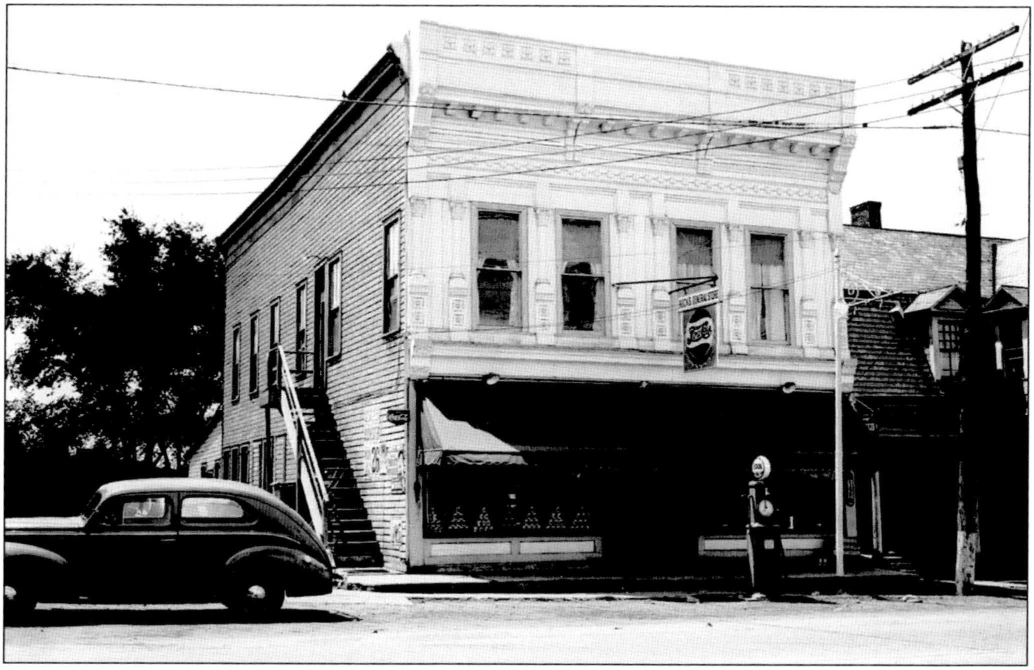

Mr. and Mrs. Harry Britton operated a grocery store for 15 years, from 1930 to 1945, when the building was sold to Raymond Bock. The store remained in the family upon Ray and Lucy's retirement with Bob and Ruth Bock continuing operation until 1994. The Bock's Supermarket served the people of Rush for many years—even providing home delivery of groceries. (Courtesy of Honeoye Falls-Mendon Historical Society.)

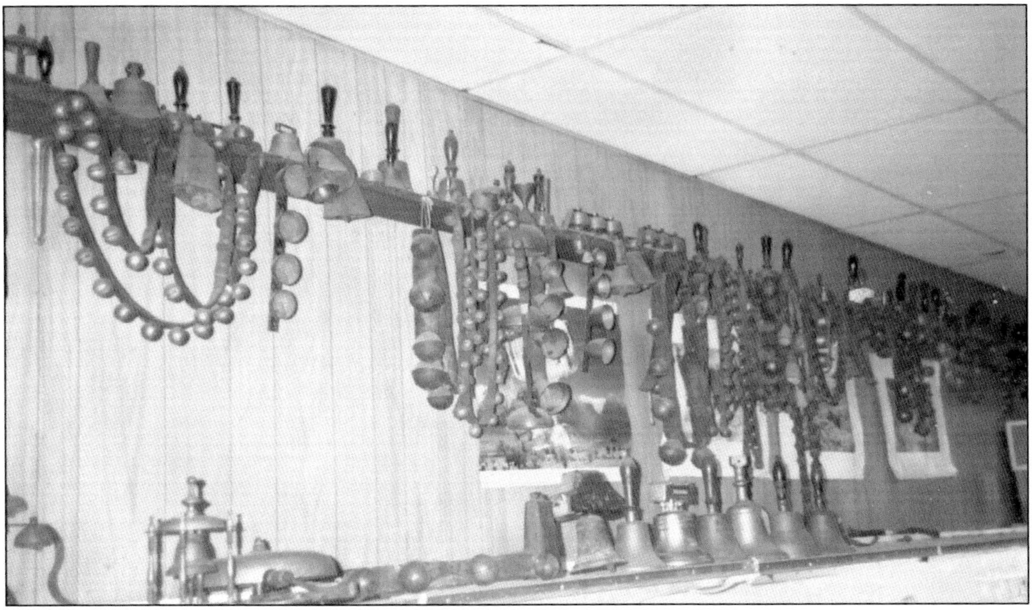

Anyone who remembers shopping at Bock's Supermarket surely remembers the collection of bells of every type and size throughout the entire store. Raymond Bock was an avid bell collector and displayed many of his bells in the store. (Courtesy of Bob Bock.)

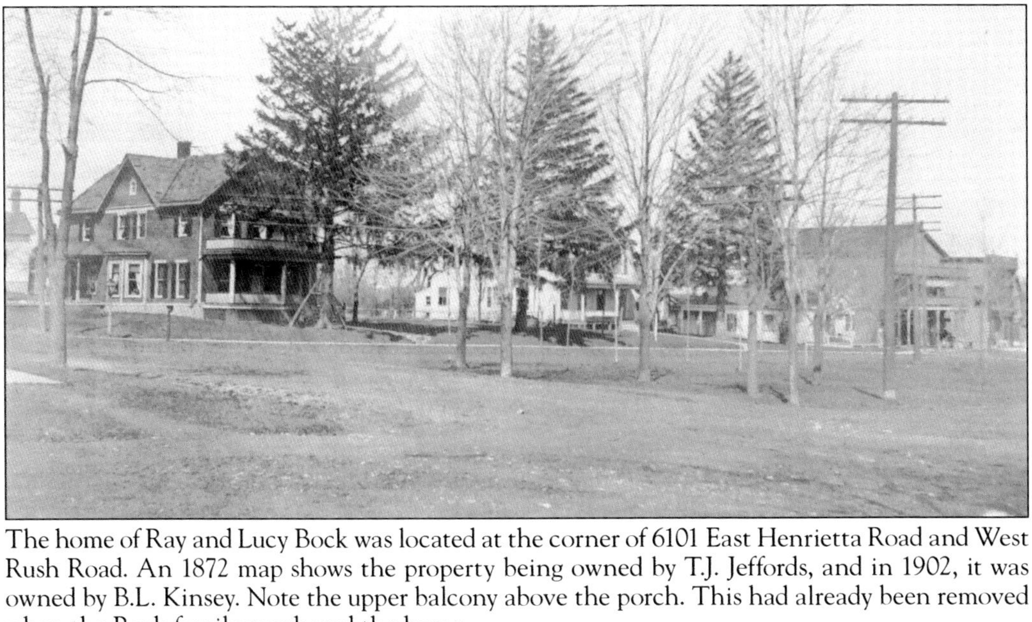

The home of Ray and Lucy Bock was located at the corner of 6101 East Henrietta Road and West Rush Road. An 1872 map shows the property being owned by T.J. Jeffords, and in 1902, it was owned by B.L. Kinsey. Note the upper balcony above the porch. This had already been removed when the Bock family purchased the home.

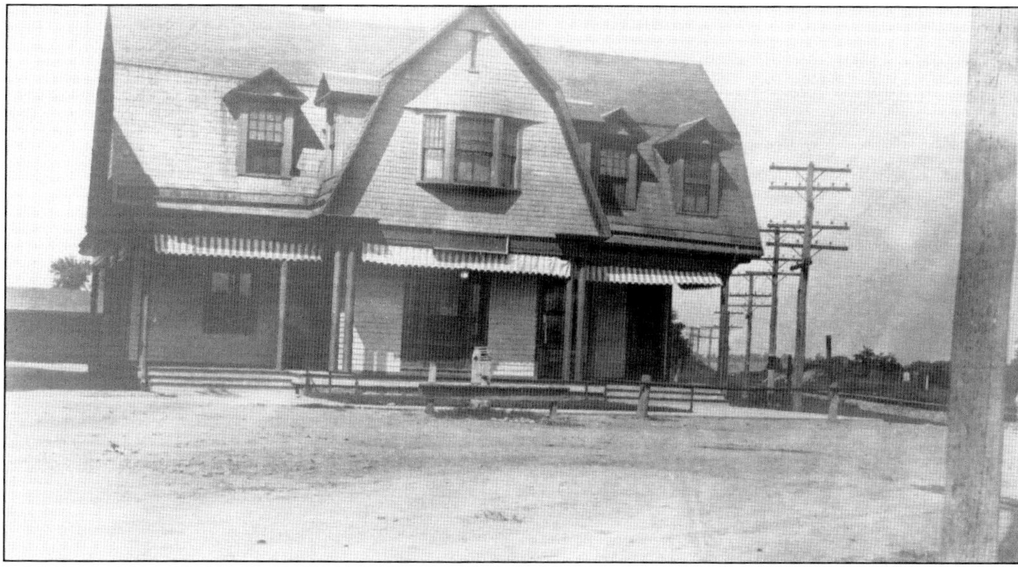

The Price House was founded in March 1891 by John C. Price, but it caught fire the following year, on August 9, 1892. Price was not to be deterred and shortly afterwards began making plans to rebuild. The Price House later became known as the Rush Hotel, the Landmark Inn, and today is the Creekside Inn, located at 6071 East Henrietta Road. Below is an invitation to an 1893 social event at the Price House.

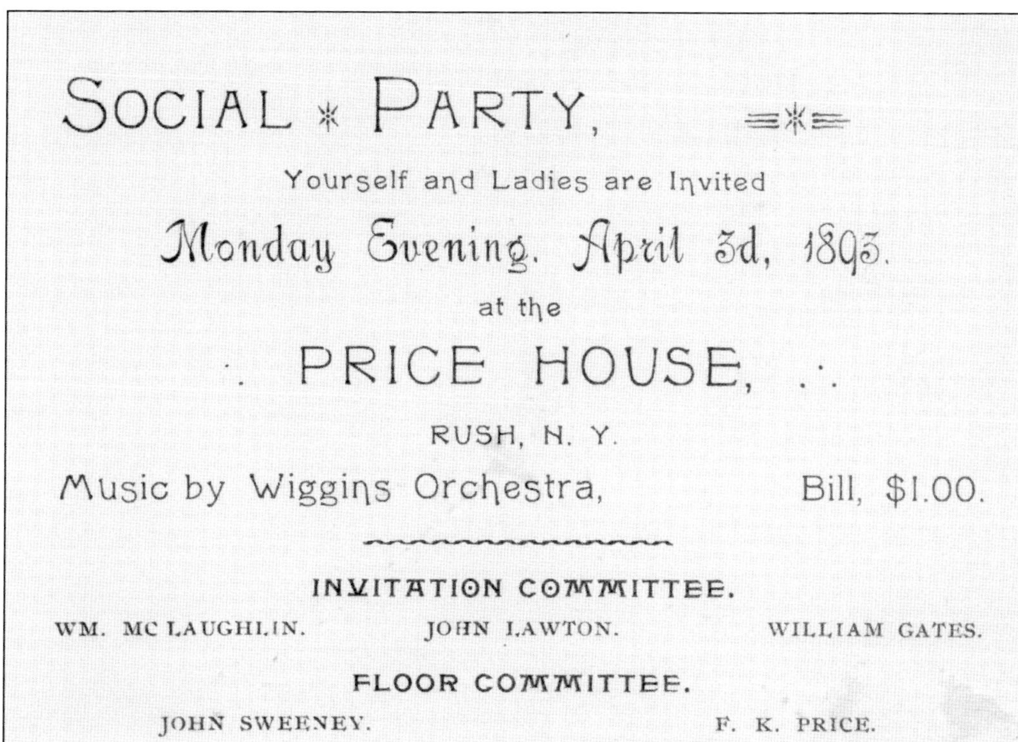

SOCIAL * PARTY,

Yourself and Ladies are Invited

Monday Evening, April 3d, 1893.

at the

PRICE HOUSE,

RUSH, N. Y.

Music by Wiggins Orchestra, Bill, $1.00.

INVITATION COMMITTEE.

WM. MC LAUGHLIN. JOHN LAWTON. WILLIAM GATES.

FLOOR COMMITTEE.

JOHN SWEENEY. F. K. PRICE.

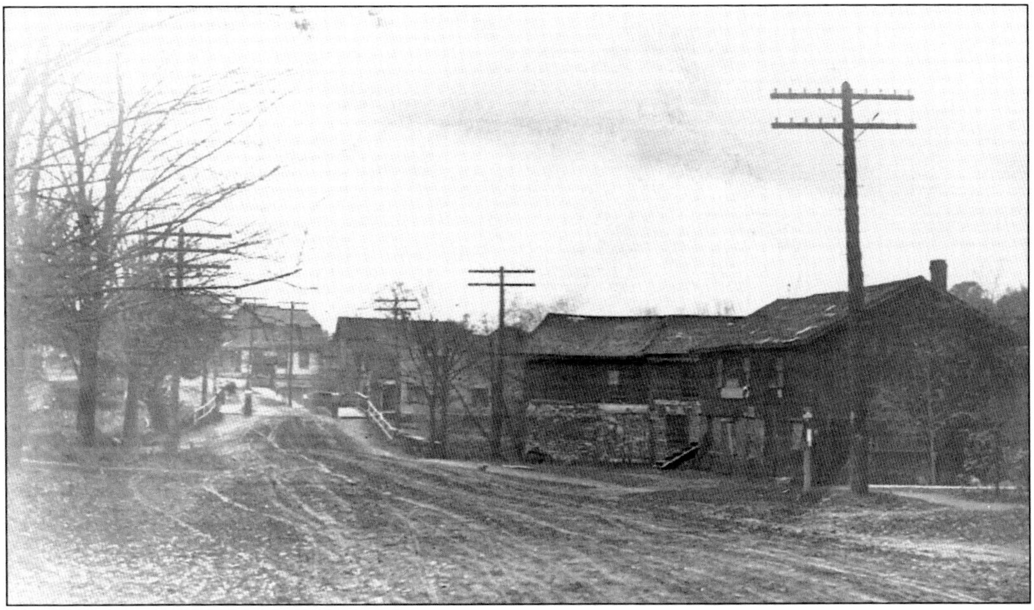

In the mid-1800s, H.L. Wilson owned property on both sides of the creek along the west side of East Henrietta Road. Wilson was a wagon- and carriage maker and a dealer in agricultural implements. Frederick Clayman purchased the property in 1874 and, along with John Nicholson, continued building wagons and operated a blacksmith shop. The blacksmith shop was a hub of activity during the construction of the Lehigh Valley Railroad through Rush.

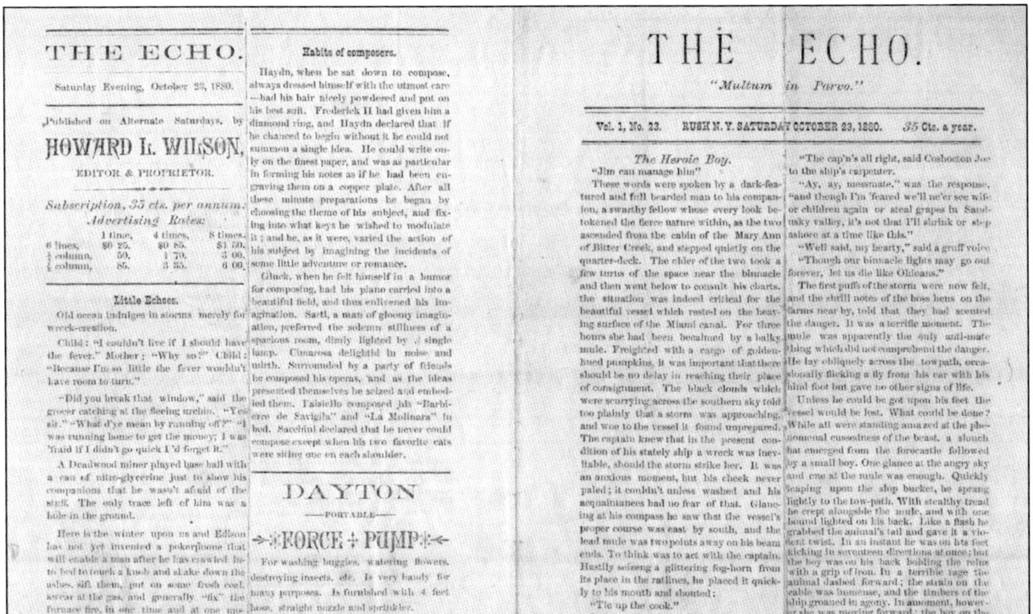

THE ECHO.

Saturday Evening, October 23, 1880.

Published on Alternate Saturdays, by

HOWARD L. WILSON,

EDITOR & PROPRIETOR.

Subscription, 35 cts. per annum.

Advertising Rates:

	1 time,	4 times,	8 times.
6 lines,	$0 25.	$0 85.	$1 50.
¼ column,	50.	1 70.	3 00.
½ column,	85.	3 35.	6 00.

Little Echoes.

Old ocean indulges in storms merely for wreck-creation.

Child: "I couldn't live if I should have the fever." Mother: "Why so?" Child: "Because I'm so little the fever wouldn't have room to turn."

"Did you break that window," said the grocer catching at the fleeing urchin. "Yes sir." "What d'ye mean by running off?" "I was running home to get the money; I was 'fraid if I didn't go quick I'd forget it."

A Deadwood miner played base ball with a can of nitro-glycerine just to show his companions that he wasn't afraid of the stuff. The only trace left of him was a hole in the ground.

Here is the winter upon us and Edison has not yet invented a pokerphone that will enable a man after he has crawled into bed to touch a knob and shake down the ashes, sift them, put on some fresh coal, swear at the gas, and generally "fix" the furnace fire, in one time and at one motion.—Boston Bulletin.

Habits of composers.

Haydn, when he sat down to compose, always dressed himself with the utmost care—had his hair nicely powdered and put on his best suit. Frederick II had given him a diamond ring, and Haydn declared that if he chanced to begin without it he could not summon a single idea. He could write only on the finest paper, and was as particular in forming his notes as if he had been engraving them on a copper plate. After all these minute preparations he began by choosing the theme of his subject, and fixing into what keys he wished to modulate it; and he, as it were, varied the action of his subject by imagining the incidents of some little adventure or romance.

Gluck, when he felt himself in a humor for composing, had his piano carried into a beautiful field, and thus enlivened his imagination. Sarti, a man of gloomy imagination, preferred the solemn stillness of a spacious room, dimly lighted by a single lamp. Cimarosa delighted in noise and mirth. Surrounded by a party of friends he composed his operas, and as the ideas presented themselves he seized and embodied them. Paisiello composed his "Barbiere de Savigila" and "La Molinara" in bed. Sacchini declared that he never could compose except when his two favorite cats were siting one on each shoulder.

DAYTON

—PORTABLE—

FORCE PUMP

For washing buggies, watering flowers, destroying insects, etc. Is very handy for many purposes. Is furnished with 4 feet hose, straight nozzle and sprinkler.

Call and see it. Howard L. Wilson Agt.

THE ECHO.

"Multum in Parvo."

Vol. 1, No. 23. RUSH N. Y. SATURDAY OCTOBER 23, 1880. *35* Cts. a year.

The Heroic Boy.

"Jim can manage him"

These words were spoken by a dark-featured and full bearded man to his companion, a swarthy fellow whose every look betokened the fierce nature within, as the two ascended from the cabin of the Mary Ann of Bitter Creek, and stepped quietly on the quarter-deck. The elder of the two took a few turns of the space near the binnacle and then went below to consult his charts. the situation was indeed critical for the beautiful vessel which rested on the heaving surface of the Miami canal. For three hours she had been becalmed by a balky mule. Freighted with a cargo of golden-hued pumpkins, it was important that there should be no delay in reaching their place of consignment. The black clouds which were scurrying across the southern sky told too plainly that a storm was approaching, and woe to the vessel it found unprepared. The captain knew that in the present condition of his stately ship a wreck was inevitable, should the storm strike her. It was an anxious moment, but his cheek never paled; it couldn't unless washed and his acquaintances had no fear of that. Glancing at his compass he saw that the vessel's proper course was east by south, and the lead mule was two points away on his beam ends. To think was to act with the captain. Hastily seizeng a glittering fog-horn from its place in the ratlines, he placed it quickly to his mouth and shouted:

"Tie up the cook."

It was a wise move. The cook was liable to have hysteries, and frequently tipped over the supper.

"The cap'n's all right, said Coshocton Joe to the ship's carpenter.

"Ay, ay, messmate," was the response, "and though I'm 'feared we'll ne'er see wife or children again or steal grapes in Sandusky valley, it's not that I'll shrink or step ashore at a time like this."

"Well said, my hearty," said a gruff voice "Though our binnacle lights may go out forever, let us die like Ohioans."

The first puffs of the storm were now felt, and the shrill notes of the boss hens on the farms near by, told that they had scented the danger. It was a terrific moment. The mule was apparently the only anti-mate thing which did not comprehend the danger. He lay obliquely across the towpath, occasionally flicking a fly from his ear with his hind foot but gave no other signs of life.

Unless he could be got upon his feet the vessel would be lost. What could be done? While all were standing amazed at the phenomenal cussedness of the beast, a slouch hat emerged from the forecastle followed by a small boy. One glance at the angry sky and one at the mule was enough. Quickly leaping upon the slop bucket, he sprang lightly to the tow-path. With stealthy tread he crept alongside the mule, and with one bound lighted on his back. Like a flash he grabbed the animal's tail and gave it a violent twist. In an instant he was on his feet kicking in seventeen directions at once; but the boy was on his back holding the reins with a grip of iron. In a terrible rage the animal dashed forward; the strain on the cable was immense, and the timbers of the ship groaned in agony. In amoment, however she was moving forward; the boy on the mule had saved her, and the captain said;

"That was the act of a statesman and diplomat" Who was the boy? James A. Garfield.

Seventeen-year-old Howard Wilson of East Rush was a very resourceful young man. The entrepreneur was said to have built his own printing press and then began publishing a biweekly, four-page newssheet called the *Echo*. The paper's header includes the Latin phrase *Multum in Parvo*, which fittingly translates to "much in little." The paper ran from 1879 to 1881.

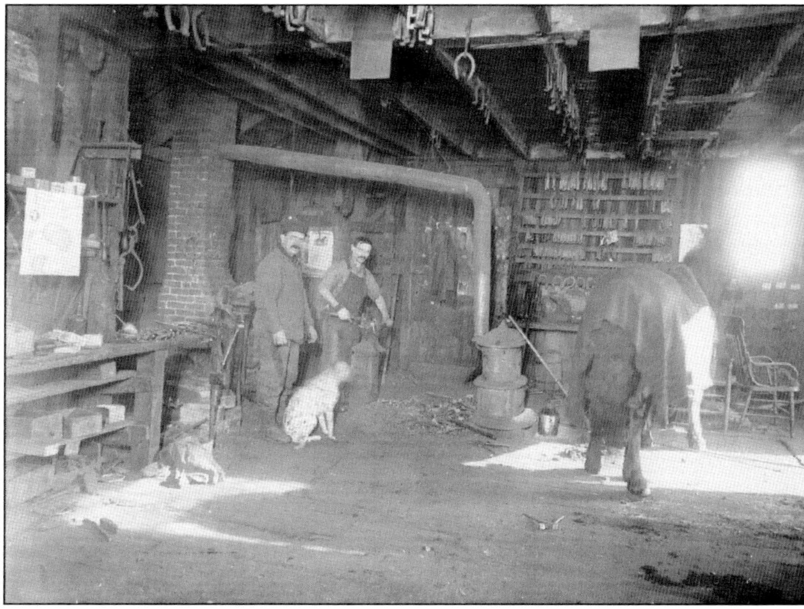

Rush blacksmith Frank Harding was born in England and arrived in Rush in 1911 at the age of 21. He first worked with fellow blacksmith Jacob Katzmeyer and then opened his own shop at 6017 East Henrietta Road in the barn behind. (Courtesy of Gwen Mack.)

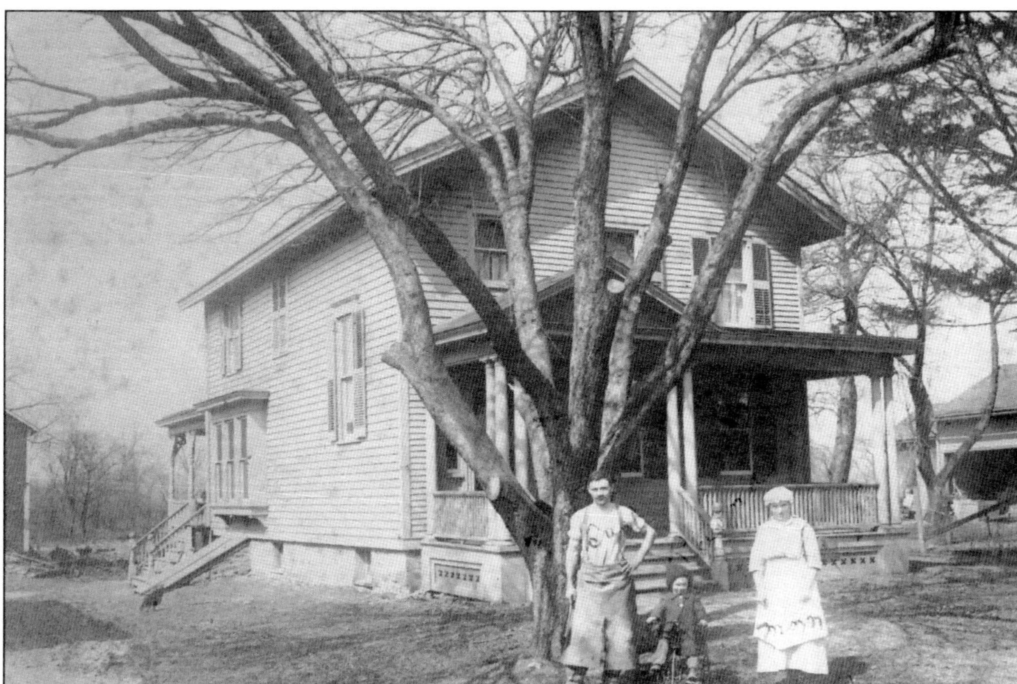

Pictured are smithy Frank Harding with his wife, Florence, and their young son, Ralph, in front of their East Henrietta Road home. Blacksmiths were considered the heart of the community because they kept the horses shod and also crafted hand tools. Francis Shearing learned his craft as an apprentice under Harding. Blacksmiths serving Rush over the years included James Courneen, George Frederick, Jacob Thomas, George Woods, F.P. Long, Fred Clayman, and Bub Thomas. (Courtesy of Gwen Mack.)

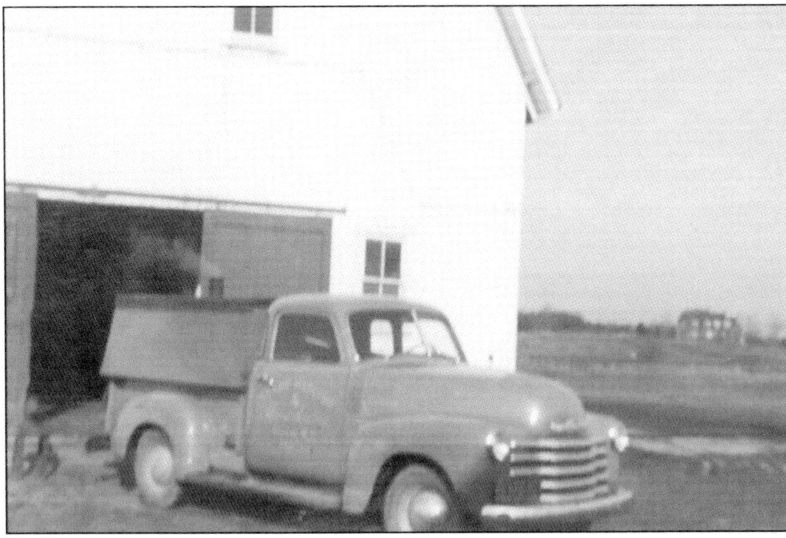

Frank Harding worked as a blacksmith for more than 50 years. In addition to his shop in town, he made the rounds caring for the horses at the Wadsworth Estates, Batavia Downs, and the Buffalo Raceway in Hamburg. (Courtesy of Gwen Mack.)

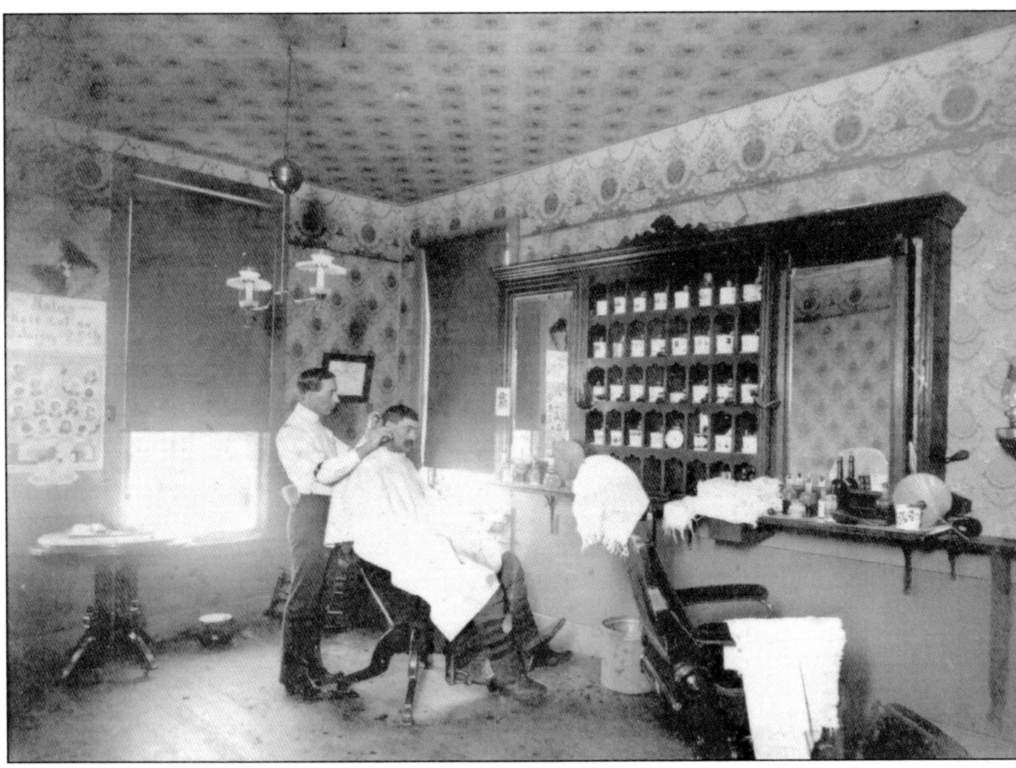

George Lonthair opened his barbershop in 1902 and continued to serve his hometown until shortly before his death on January 1, 1958. His first shop was on the second floor of the Bock's Supermarket location, and he later moved next door, to the first floor of the Red & White Store block. (Courtesy of Tina Lonthair Williams.)

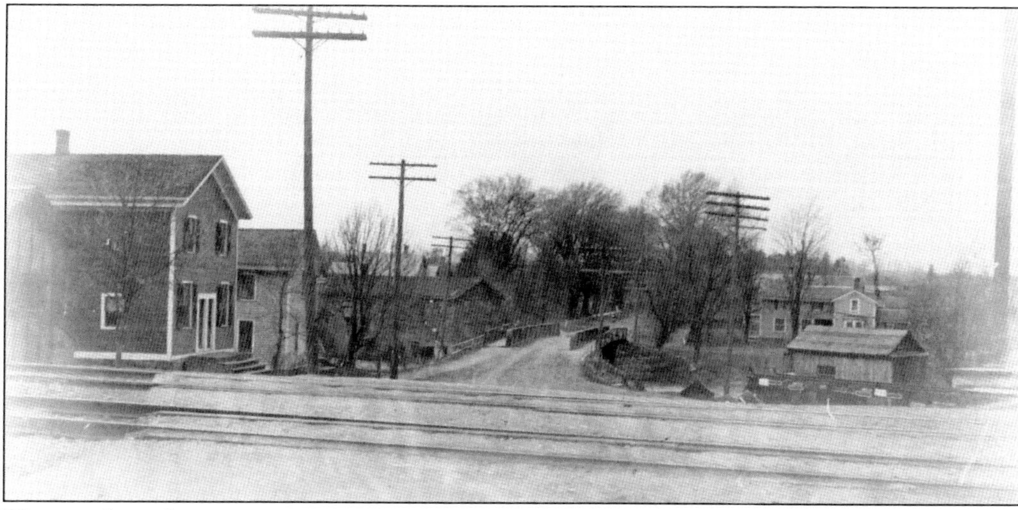

This northward view of East Henrietta Road from the Lehigh Valley Railroad shows the old bridge with the center for vehicle traffic and pedestrian lanes along both outside edges. Beloved town physician Dr. James Leary was the first person to drive across the new bridge in 1904. Retired highway superintendent Vince Behnk had the honor of riding in the first car over the newer bridge in 1992, a 1931 Ford Model A owned by Walt Bittner. (Courtesy of Eleanor Mason DeFreze.)

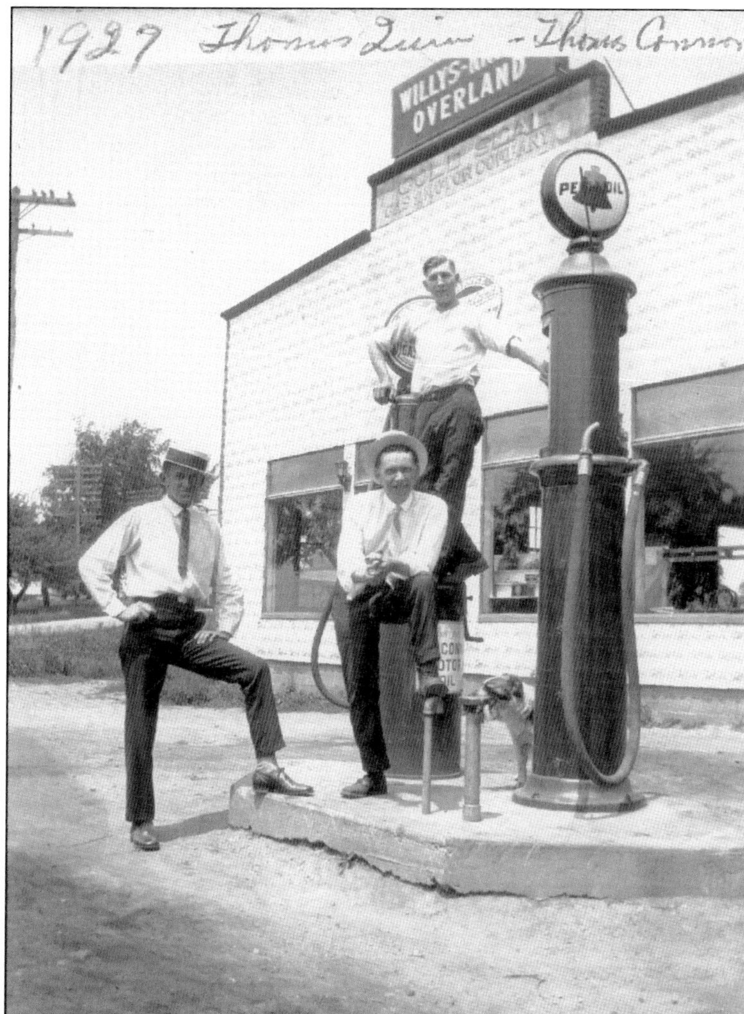

Vince Behnk and his friends are just hanging out at the local garage. From left to right in this c. 1927 photograph are Behnk, Thomas Quinn, and Thomas Connor. (Courtesy of Pam Bock Ebersold.)

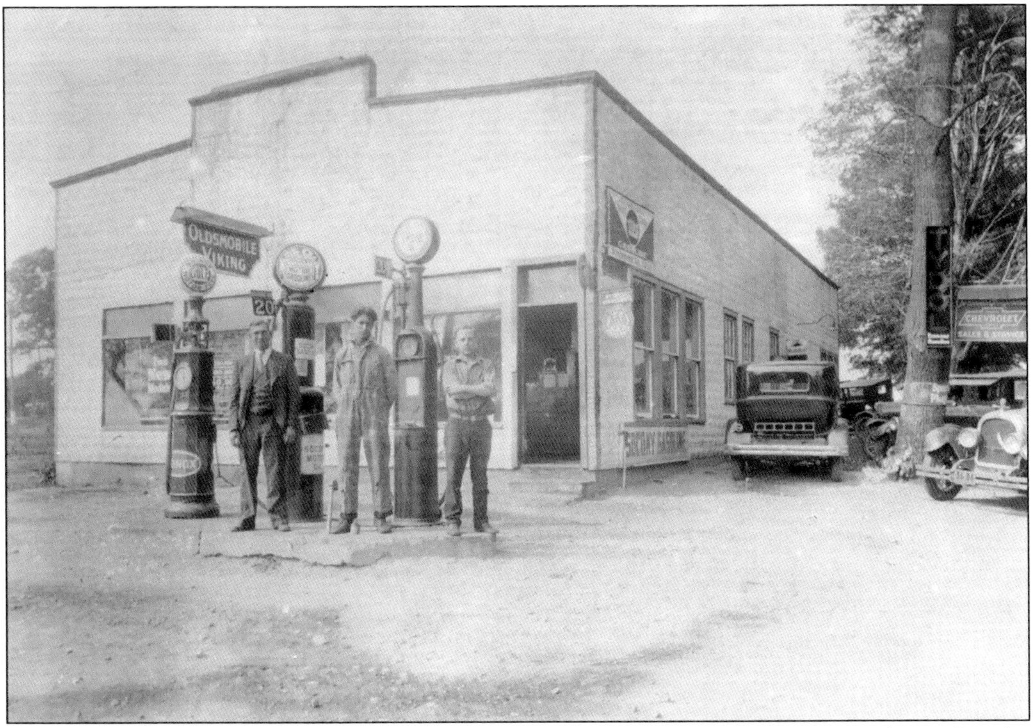

Quinn's Garage sold gasoline and was also an Oldsmobile dealership. Quinn's was located at the northwest corner of Rush-Scottsville and East Henrietta Roads, at the current location of the 7-Eleven convenience store. (Both, courtesy of Bob Bock.)

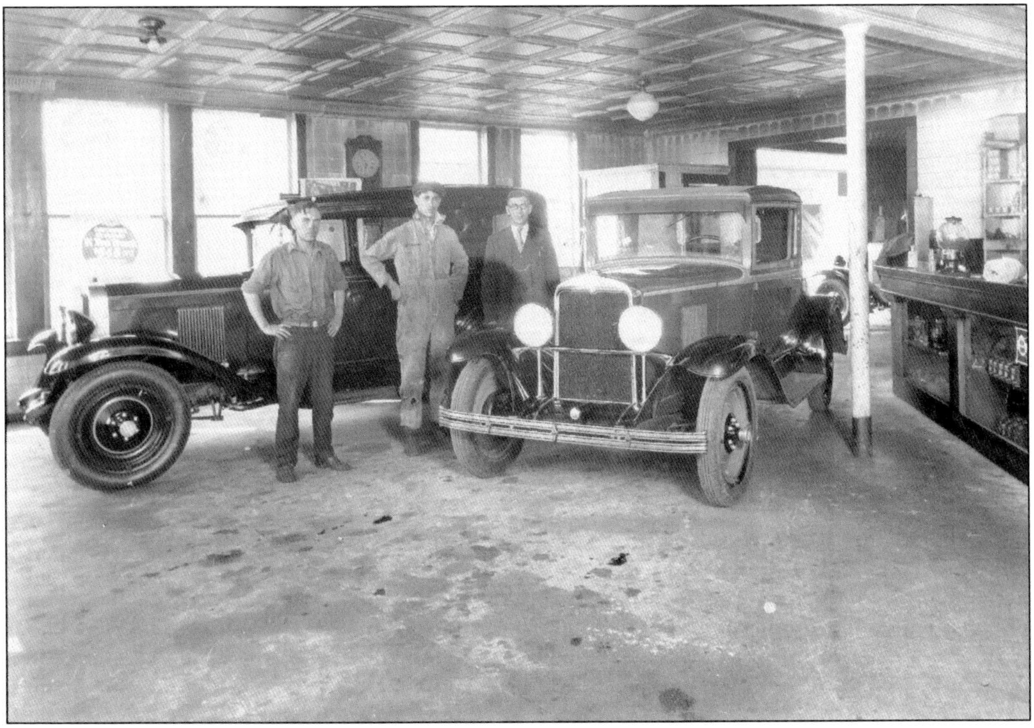

Three

West Rush

Brothers William and John Markham were the first permanent settlers of Rush, arriving in the 1790s. John founded what later became the hamlet of West Rush. In addition to his own home, he built the schoolhouse and the West Rush Hotel. The hotel was a stagecoach stop on the run between Rochester and Dansville. As a self-reliant community, West Rush had businesses including a blacksmith shop, a cobbler shop, a post office, general stores, and a cooperage. A church and a district schoolhouse were also once part of the West Rush landscape. In later years, car dealerships and repair shops emerged.

The 1869–1870 *Gazetteer and Business Directory of Monroe County* lists West Rush as having approximately 30 dwellings. In 1895, the population of the West Rush hamlet was about 200 people. The New York Central's Peanut Branch began its runs through West Rush in the early 1890s. This allowed West Rush to become a shipping point for locally grown produce, particularly large quantities of potatoes and cabbages.

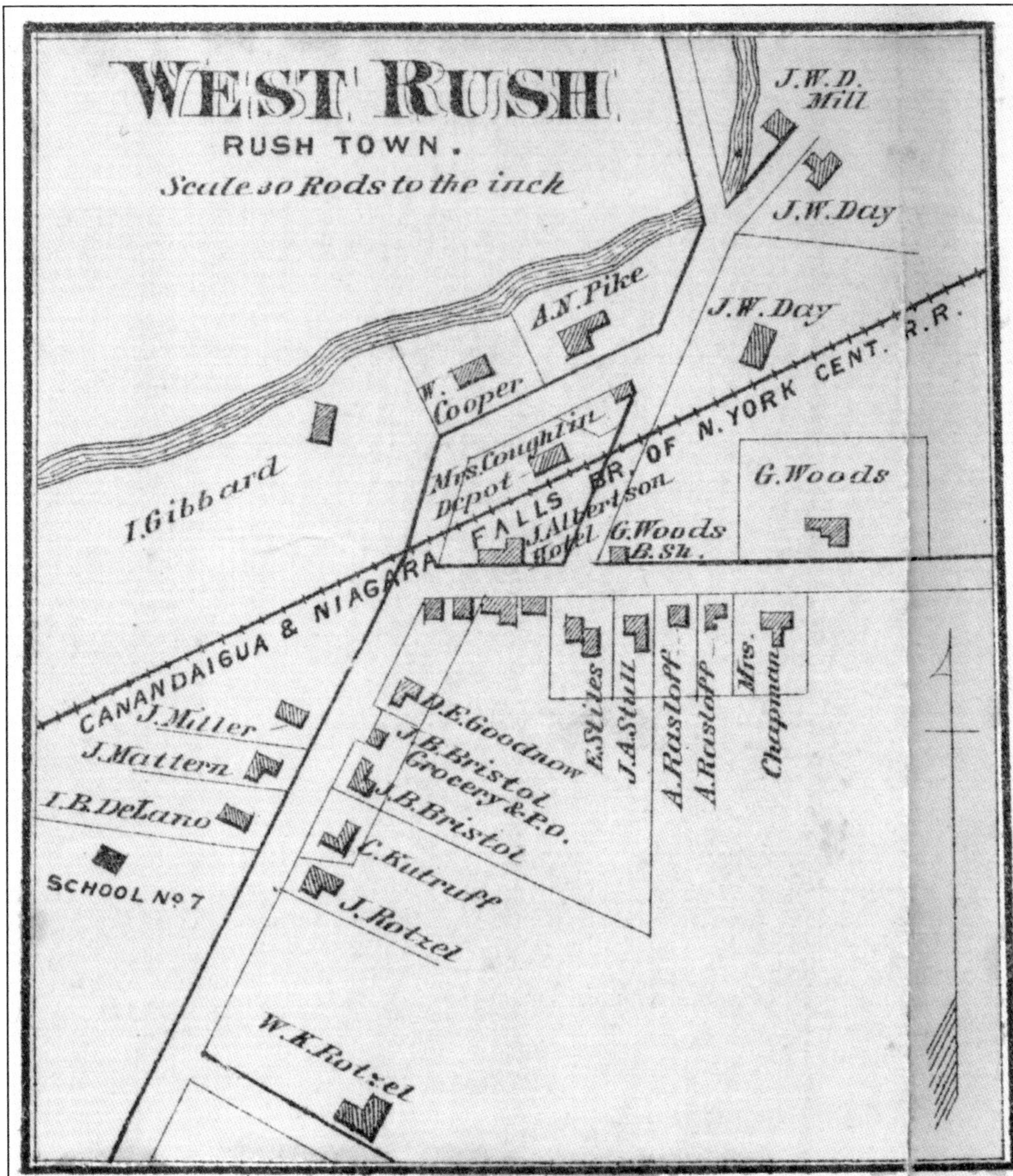

The F.W. Beers & Company map of the West Rush hamlet, of 1872, shows John B. Bristol as postmaster and grocer; J.B. Day as a miller, J.A. Stull as an attorney, and the West Rush Hotel owned by J. Albertson.

Addison Chapman was a well-known resident of West Rush. Born in Rochester, he moved first to West Henrietta and then to West Rush. He served as Rush town supervisor for one term in 1908 and was elected again in 1912, serving until 1921. He was also elected to the county board of supervisors. He resigned as town supervisor after being elected as the Monroe County treasurer and served two terms in this position. (Courtesy of *Honeoye Falls Times*.)

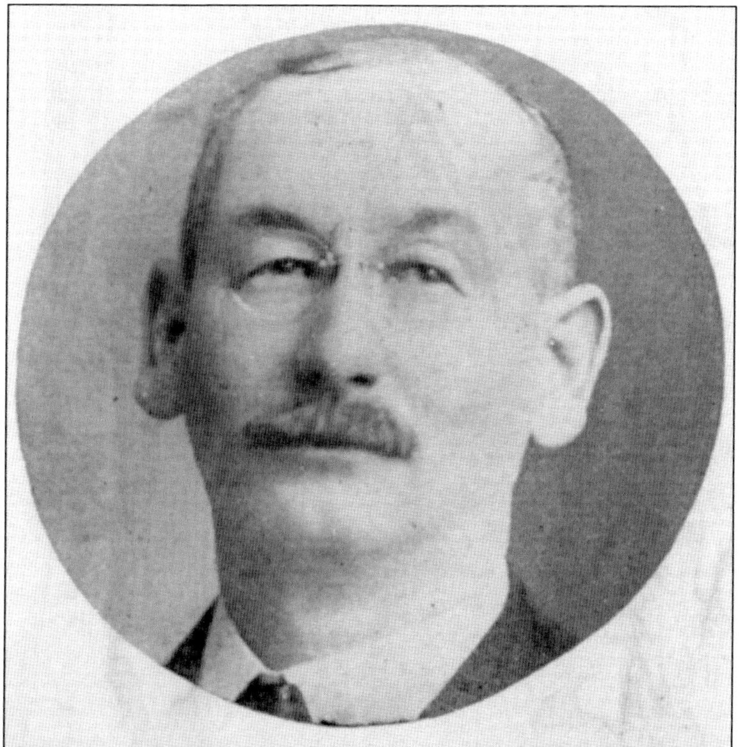

SUP. ADDISON D. CHAPMAN, Rush.

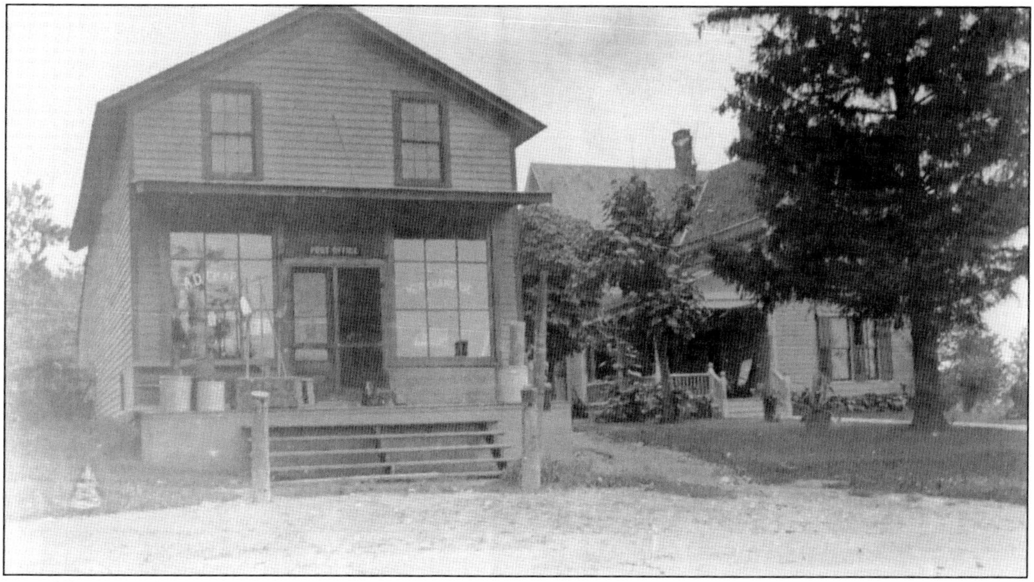

In addition to his public service work, Addison Chapman operated a general store in West Rush. He opened his store at the age of 17 and also served as the West Rush postmaster for 30 years. Chapman Road was officially dedicated in 1954 but had existed before that date. (Courtesy of Eleanor Mason DeFreze.)

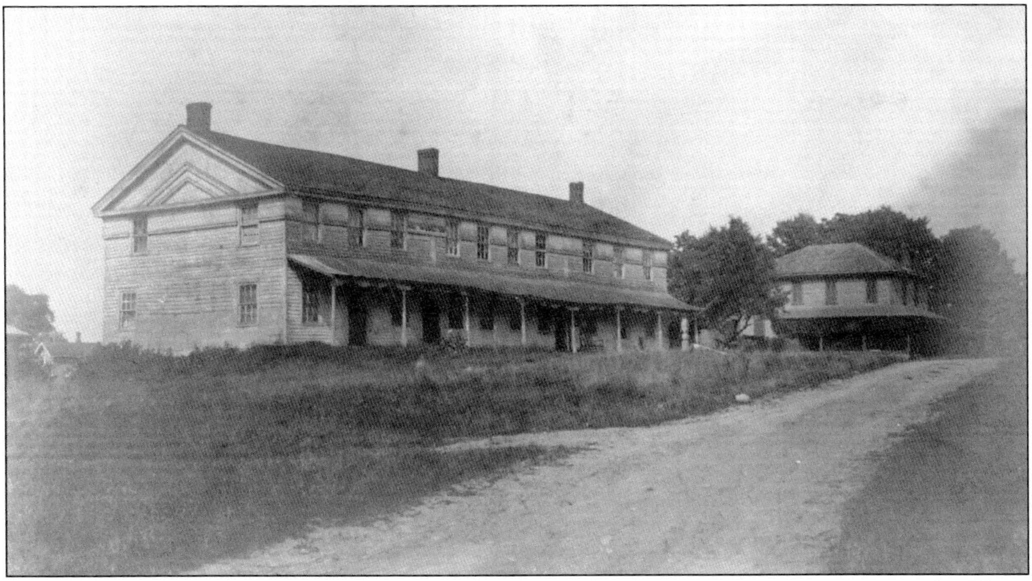

The West Rush Hotel was built in 1826 by John Markham. It was a large, two-story building, with an 80-foot ballroom on the second floor. The hotel burned on Halloween night 1931 and the West Rush firehouse now stands in that location.

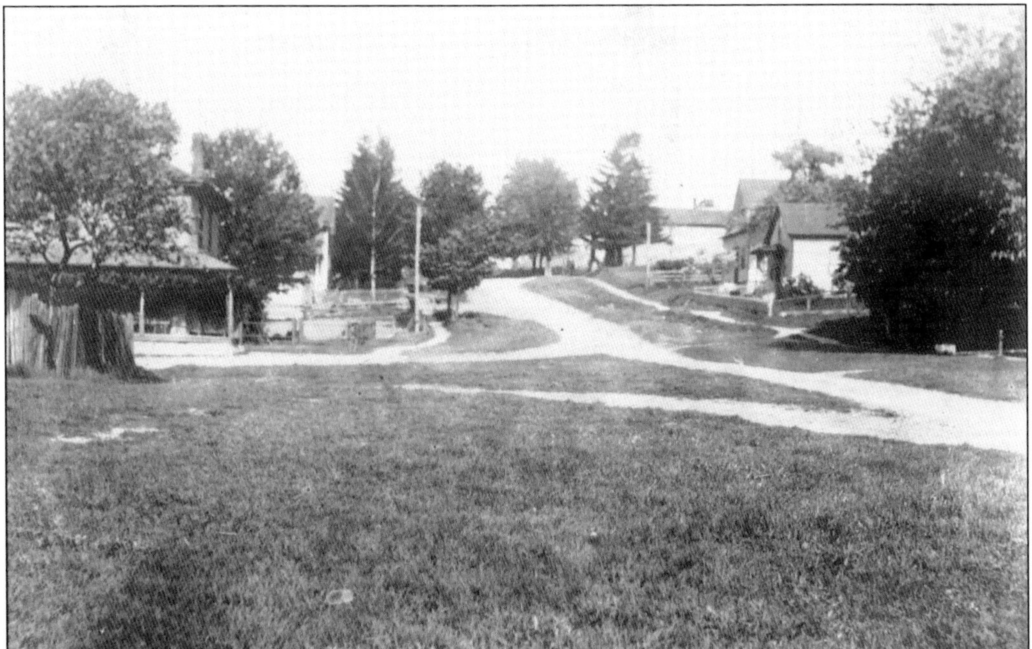

This is a view looking eastward at the West Rush hamlet. The West Rush Hotel would have been located at the far left of this picture. (Courtesy of Carolyn Swanton.)

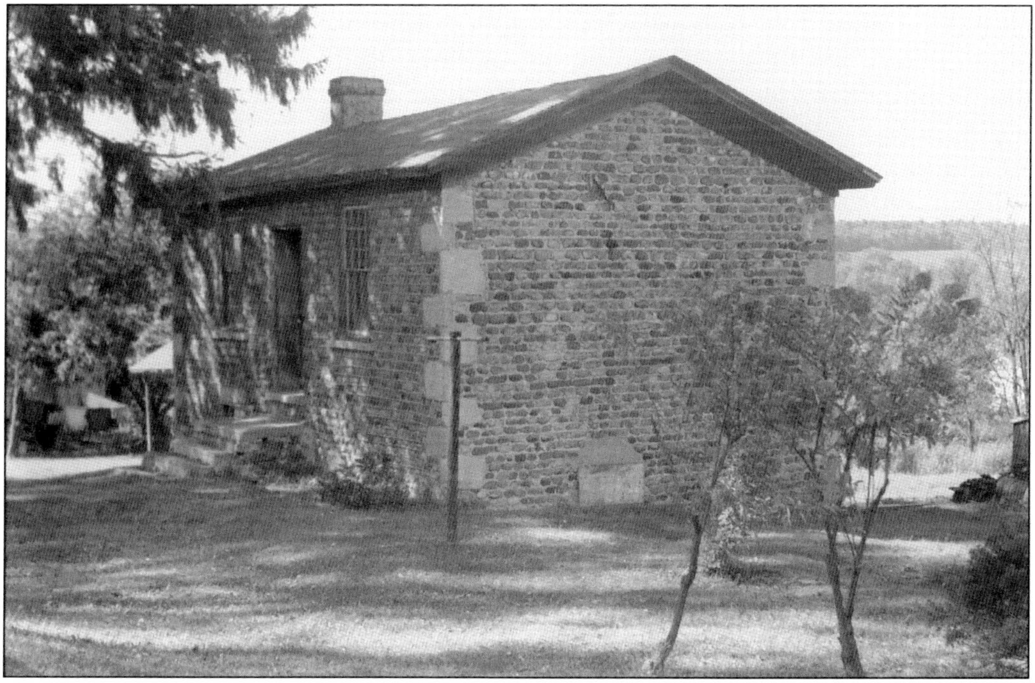

Built by John Green in 1826, the Bacchus cobblestone house is located at 42 Rush-West Rush Road. In the early 1900s, Mr. Bacchus was the gardener at Meadowood and also a correspondent for the *Honeoye Falls Times*. The house was the West Rush post office at one time as well.

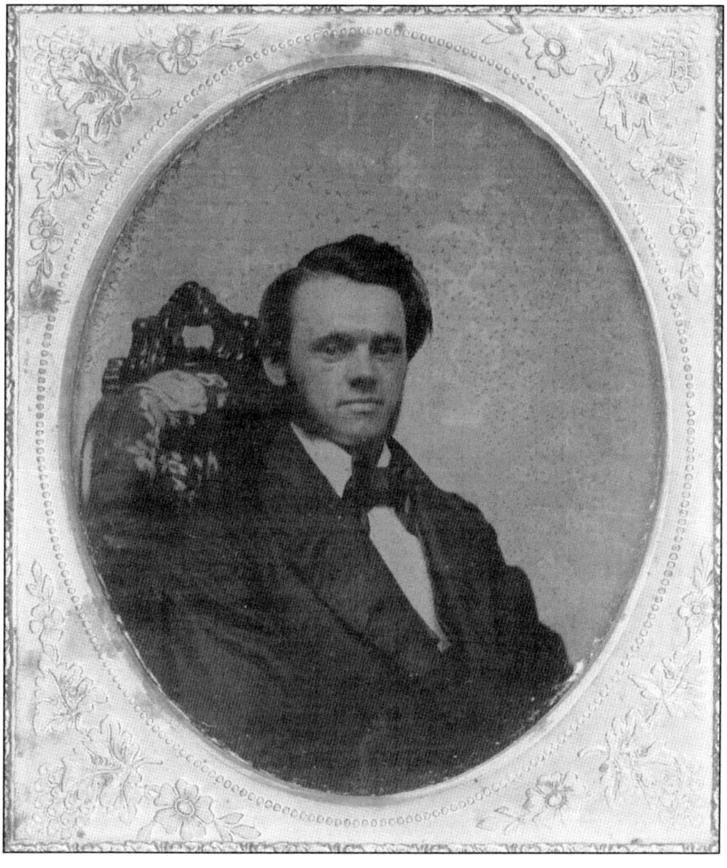

Born in 1833 in Padbury, Buckinghamshire, England, Rev. Isaac Gibbard married Louisa Smith, the only daughter of Dr. Socrates Smith and Matilda Markham, in 1859. Isaac and Louisa had four daughters who lived to adulthood.

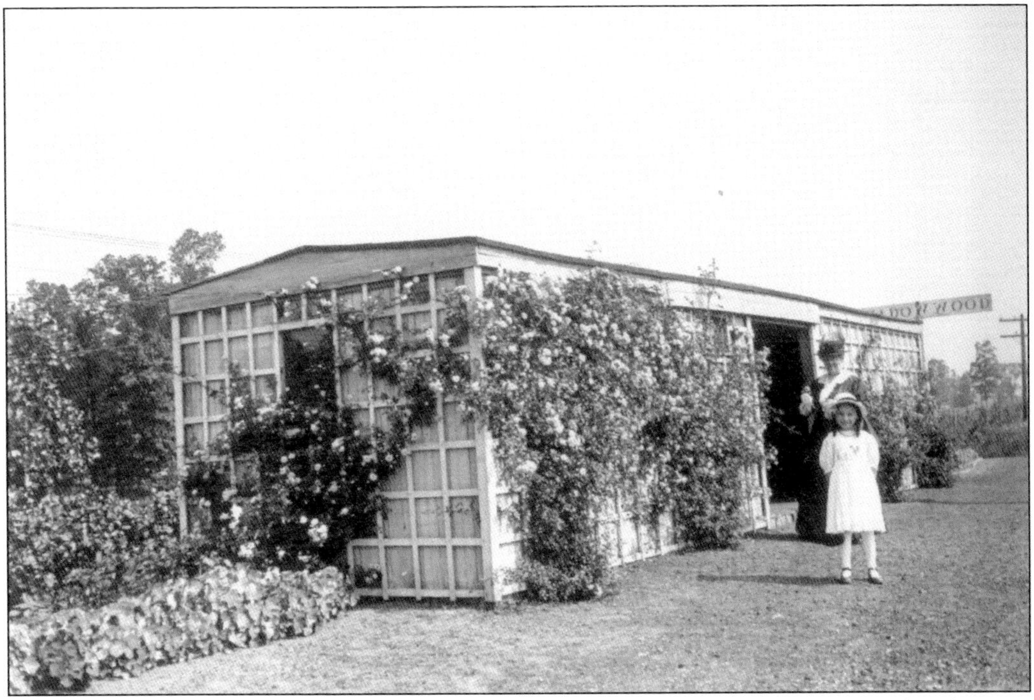

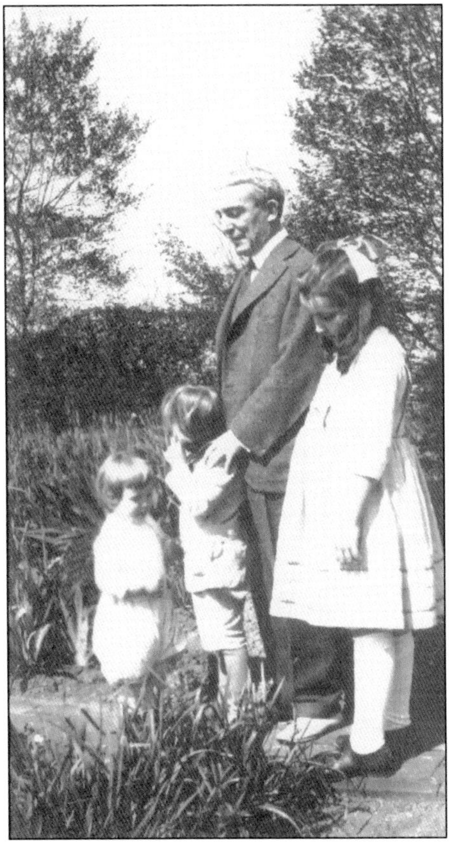

The Rochester and Genesee Valley Railroad built this line in the 19th century, which ran through Rush along the Genesee River. This converted boxcar at Meadowood made it possible for Meadowood residents to take the train to Rochester for work or to attend church. Some workers came out on the train to provide services to Meadowood families. Lois Warner Wray is shown here with her grandmother Cornelia Martin Wray. (Courtesy of Susan Swanton.)

The Stull family was a pioneering Rush family. Golah Road is partly named for the Stull family, whose large farm extended to the south of Stull Road, which leads to Meadowood. John Stull married Mary Wray of the Henry Wray & Sons Foundry on Mill Street and built the first home on Stull Road. He is pictured here with Mary's nephews Charles and Delos Wray Jr. and her niece Irene Wray. (Courtesy of Susan Swanton.)

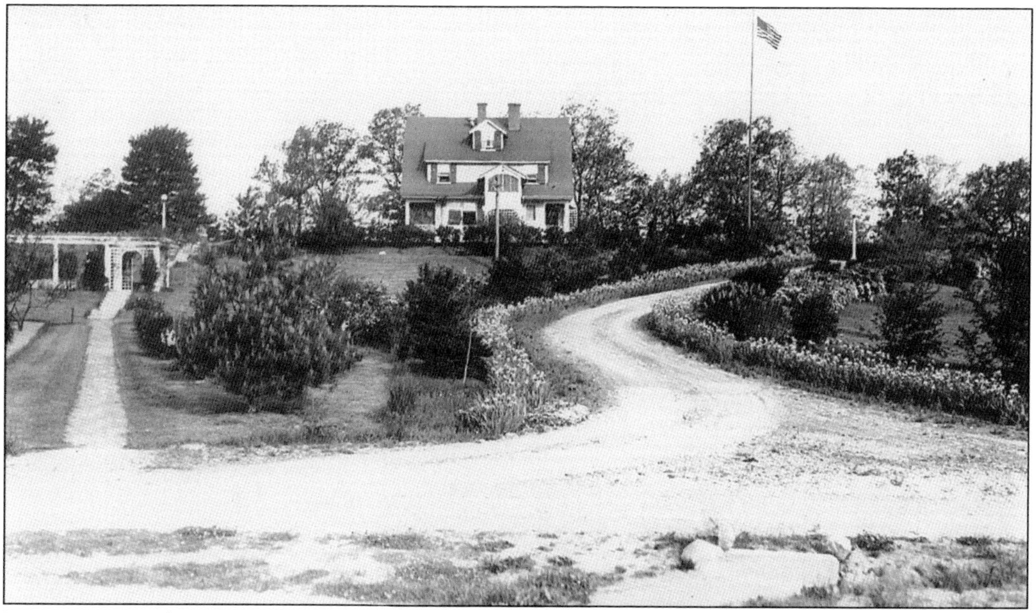

In 1912, Cornelia Martin Wray, widow of Henry Wray Jr., sold her city residence to move to Meadowood where her daughter, Mary, and John Stull were building their home. Noted Rochester architect Claude Bragdon designed this home and two others on the site. John and Mary lived north of this home. "Mother" Wray lived in the house pictured, with her youngest son, Delos, his wife, Irene, and four children. (Courtesy of Susan Swanton.)

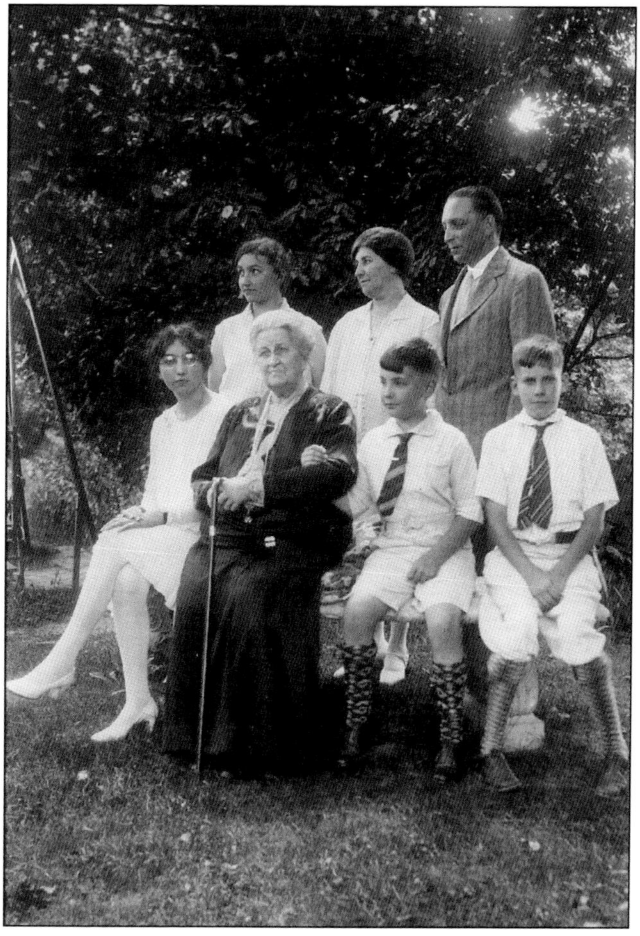

The Wray family is shown in the late 1920s. From left to right are (seated) Lois, "Mother" Wray, Charles, and Delos Jr.; (standing) Irene, Irene Warner Wray, and Delos Wray. Lois, the eldest, first taught at the West Rush one-room school; Irene became a geologist, but later was a local librarian. Delos Jr. worked at the foundry, and Charles became a noted local archaeologist whose Seneca tribe research is featured at the Rochester Museum and Science Center. (Courtesy of Susan Swanton.)

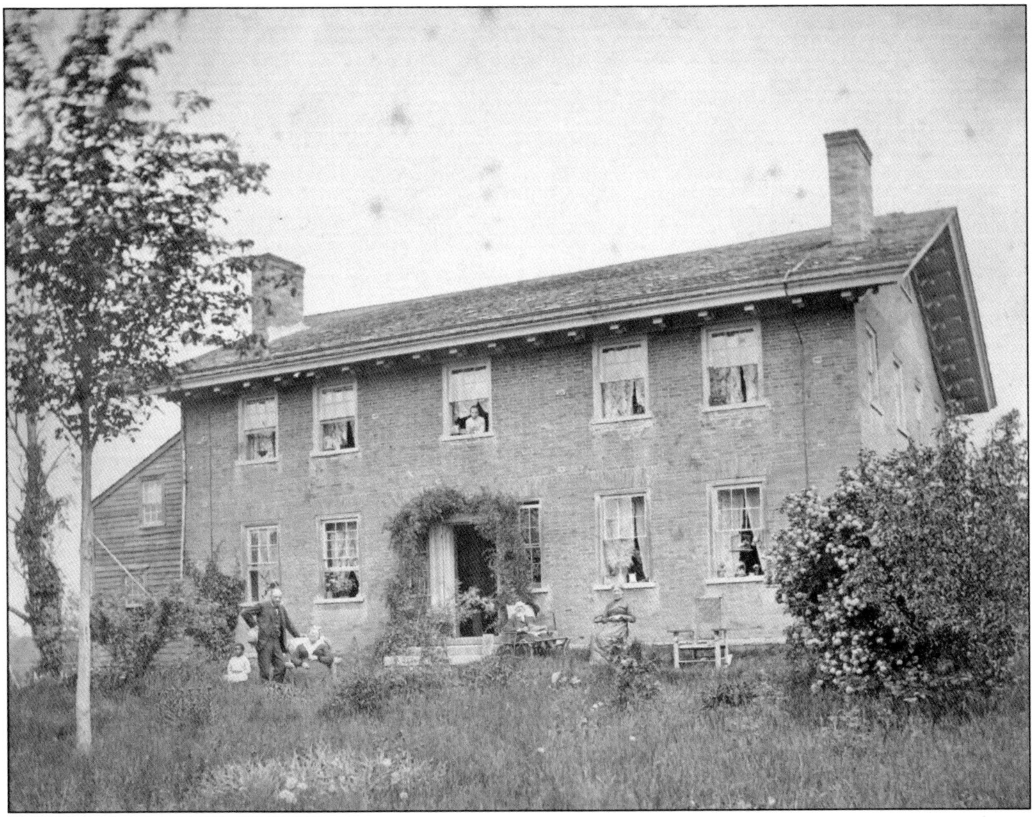

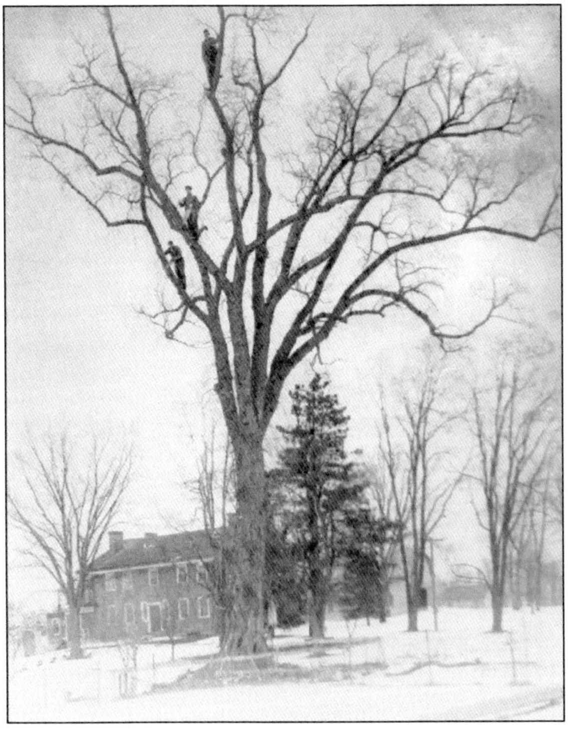

Col. William Markham III came to the Genesee Valley in 1789. He was the first permanent settler in Rush, living in a log cabin, and in 1804, he moved into the brick homestead pictured here. In 1818, Colonel Markham, seen standing to the left of the front door, became the first supervisor of the town of Rush. (Courtesy of Karen Hopkins.)

There were many elm trees on the farm known as Elm Place. The trees were huge, as portrayed here. The elm tree for which the Markham Farm was named stood on the flats west of the house near the river. In its prime, the circumference of the trunk measured 45 feet. Unfortunately, none of the original elms remain today, having fallen prey to disease, ice damage, lightning, and campfires. (Courtesy of Karen Hopkins.)

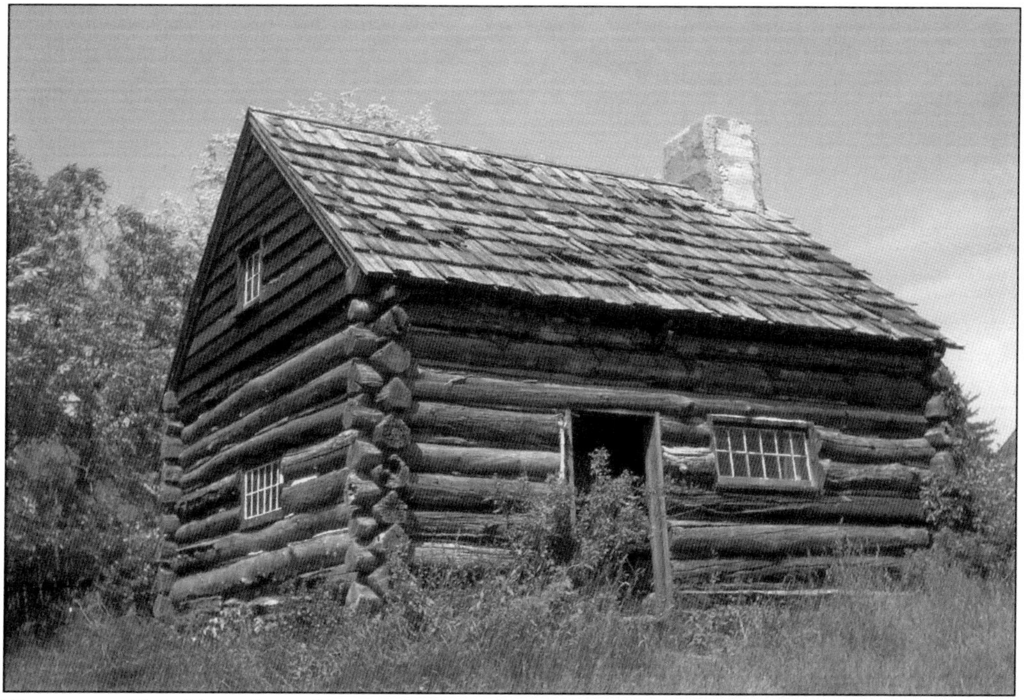

The original Markham log cabin was built in the early 1790s. Soon, it became too small for the growing family, and a second log cabin was built next to the original and connected by a covered passage. The current log cabin, pictured here, is a replica constructed in 1890 to celebrate 100 years of success for the Markham family at Elm Place. The replica log cabin became a "local" museum of pioneer artifacts. The cabin was visited by many local schoolchildren and their families from the 1890s to the 1980s, when the artifacts were sold as the final generation of Markhams at Elm Place left. (Courtesy of Karen Hopkins.)

In 1804, a kiln was built on the west lawn, and construction of the first brick house in the Genesee Valley began. The family moved into the home in 1805. Since that time, there have been many additions, with the residence more than doubling in size. Family members, including the Markhams, Puffers, and Seldens, lived in the home generation after generation until 1986. (Courtesy of Karen Hopkins.)

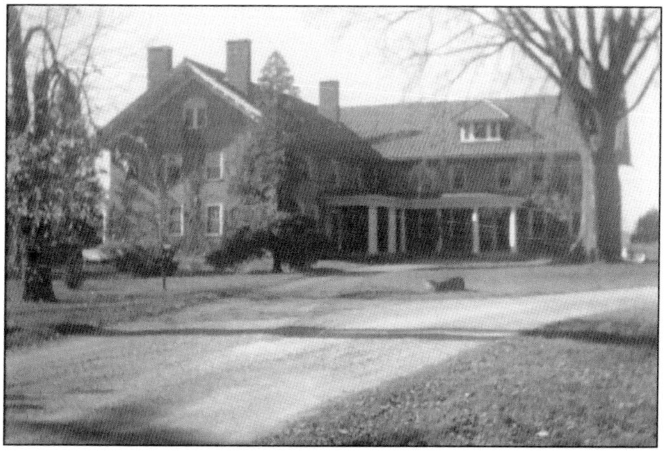

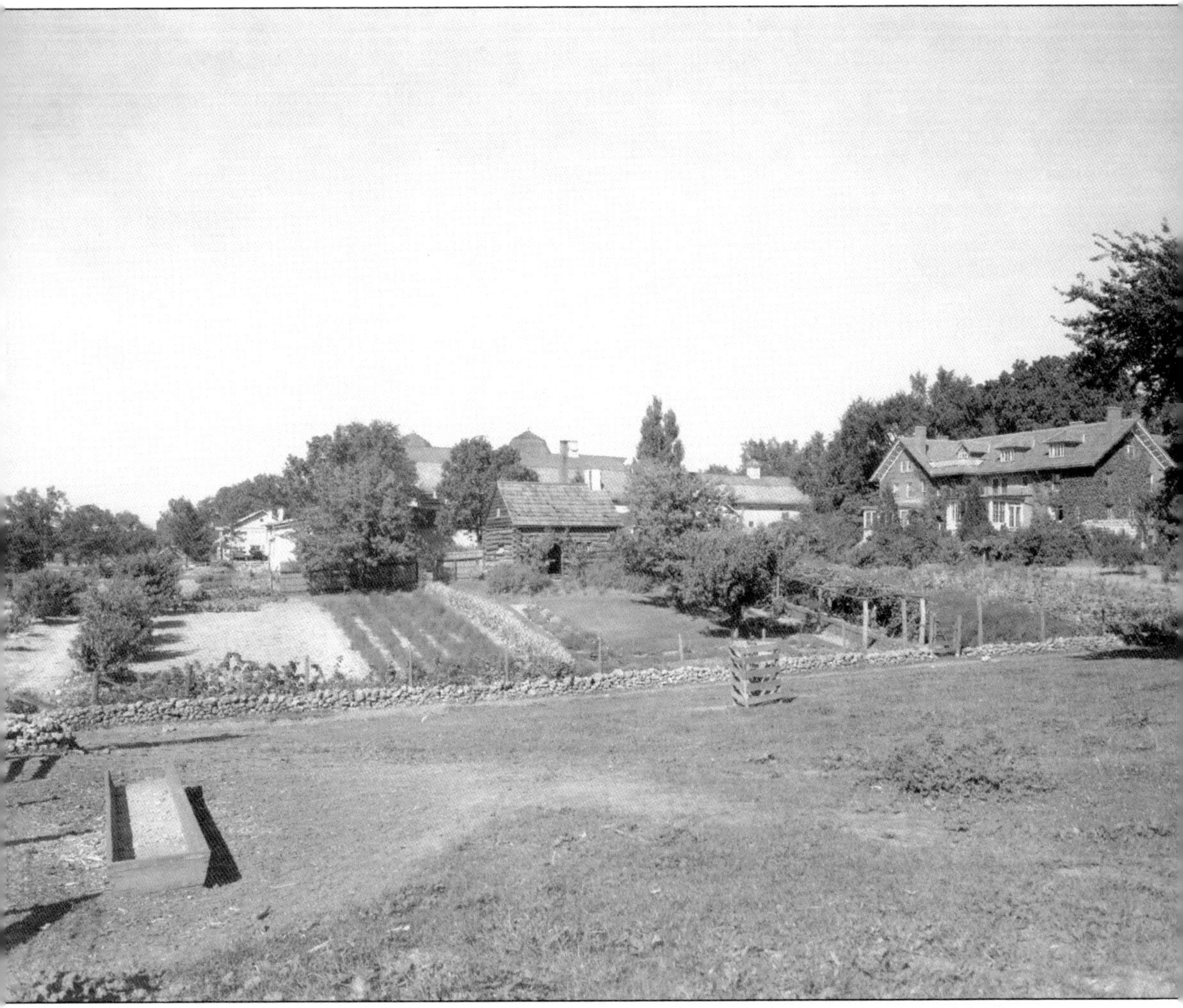

William Guy Markham, grandson of Col. William Markham, was well respected for his success in breeding American Merino sheep. He was also instrumental in the development of a sterilization process to create "certified milk." This helped improve the milk quality and decrease the risk of illness. This photograph of Elm Place, from around 1900, shows the enlarged house, replicated cabin, multiple barns, tenant houses, and well-tended grounds. (Courtesy of Karen Hopkins.)

Four

North Rush

The area surrounding the intersection of Rush-Scottsville and East River Roads is known as North Rush. It was originally called Sibley's Corners and then Hart's Corners. Joseph Sibley arrived in the area in 1804 from Rensselaer County and his brother Elisha followed in 1810. Elisha built his home and a distillery at the corner of East River and Fishell Roads and also a tavern on the northeast corner of East River and Rush-Scottsville Roads.

Daniel and Elizabeth Hart moved to Rush in about 1810, building their home on the southeast corner of East River and Rush-Scottsville Roads. They had three sons and two daughters. Daniel died in 1815, but Elizabeth stayed and raised their family. Two of their sons, Henry B. Hart and Daniel, lived their lives in Rush. It was Henry B. who built the house on the northwest corner, and Daniel was known as "Saddler Dan."

The settlement of North Rush had its own school, church, store, and post office. The North Rush Cemetery on Rush-Scottsville Road is the final resting place of many of the early residents from this area of town.

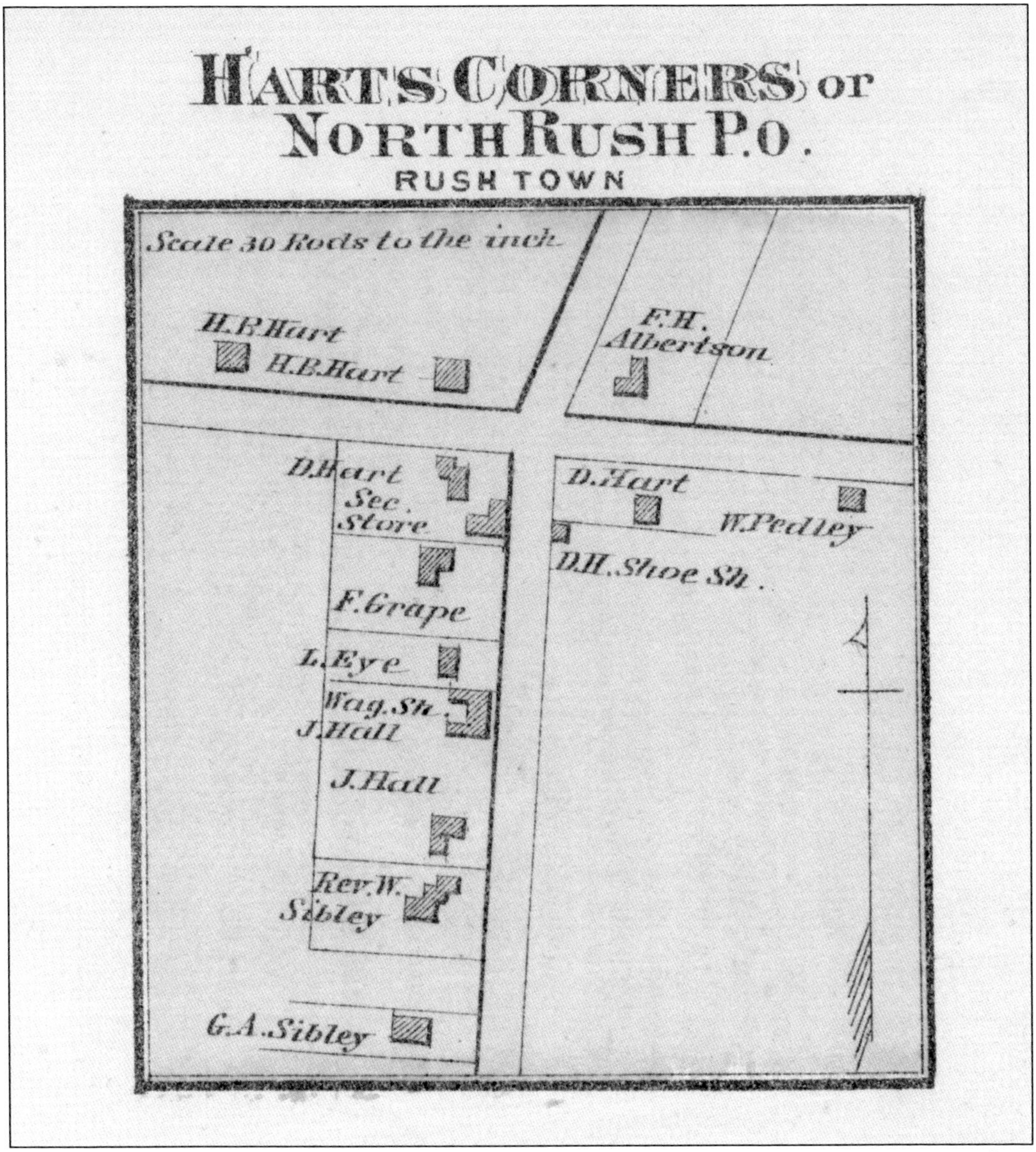

The F.W. Beers & Company 1872 map of North Rush, known as Hart's Corners, shows members of the Hart family occupying three corners and F.H. Albertson on the northeast corner. The home of Reverend Sibley is shown south of the intersection, on the west side of the road. The Sibley home later became the parsonage for the North Rush Church.

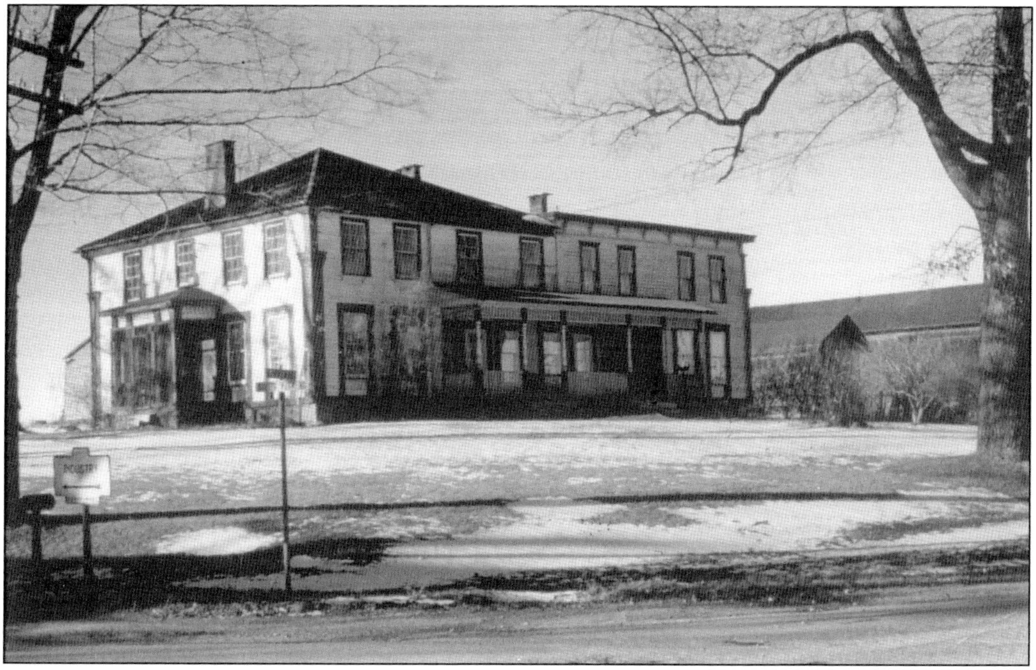

Shown above is the former home of Henry B. Hart located at 6809 East River Road. The large square house, built in the mid-1850s, is located on the northwest corner of Rush-Scottsville and East River Roads. The residence was designed and built by Henry Hart, with functionality and details carefully planned with his wife and her household work in mind. The kitchen, pantry, stairs, and even the closets, of which there were 11, were all designed with efficiency, space, and saving steps at the forefront. The house took second place in a national contest for farm homes in 1959. The photograph below shows the original barn and house on the Hart property. The house was still standing into the 1980s, but both structures are now gone. The property is currently owned by Jerry and Sandy Tallo.

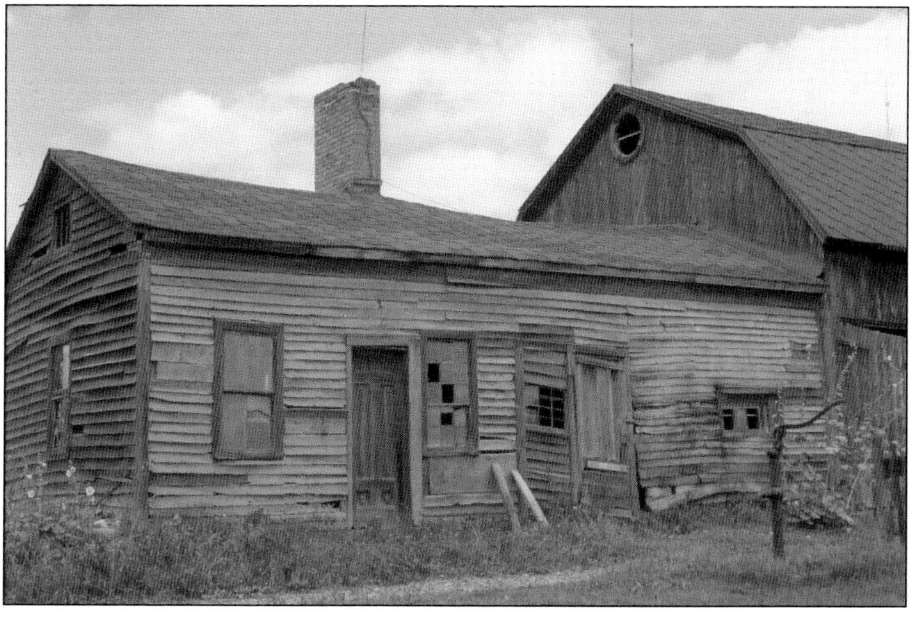

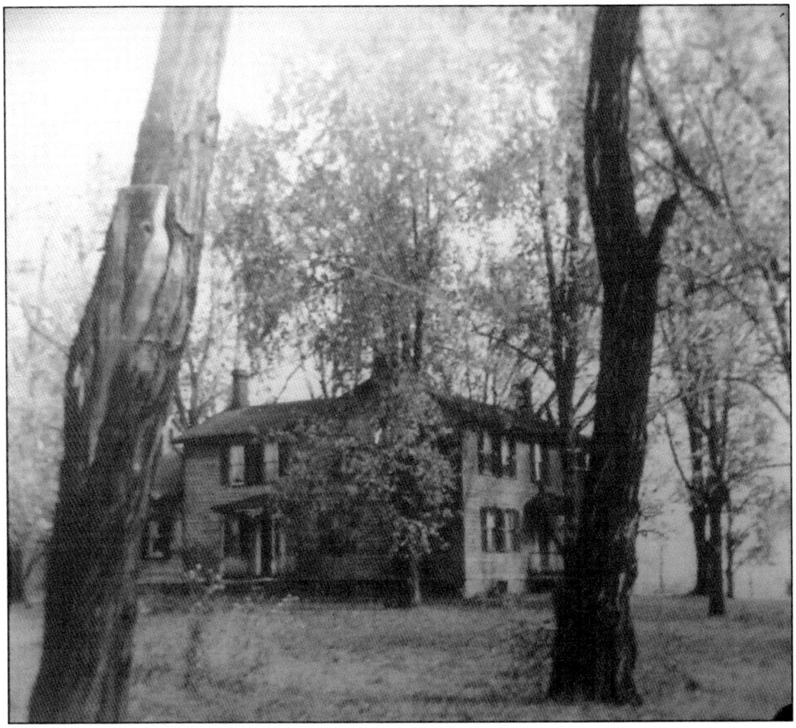

The structure at 550 Rush-Scottsville Road was originally a tavern owned by Elisha Sibley and dates to the early 1800s. Federal census records from 1860 indicate the property was then owned by Isaac Albertson, and he apparently operated a horse-breeding farm. The property later changed hands to Caroline Barker and then to Robert and Alice McKay. John R. Cherry is the present owner.

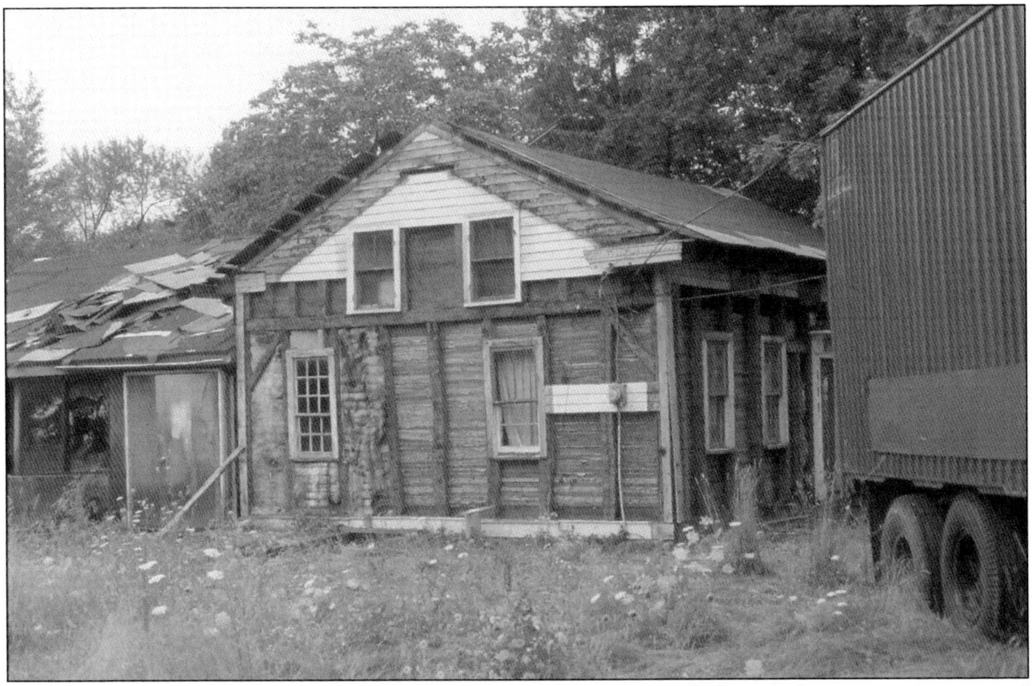

The 1830s home of "Saddler Dan" Hart sat at 549 Rush-Scottsville Road, the current location of the Mary Cariola Children's Center. Saddler Dan was known for his fine leather craftsmanship. In 1980, the house was carefully dismantled and removed to the Genesee Country Village and Museum where it now houses the museum's costume department.

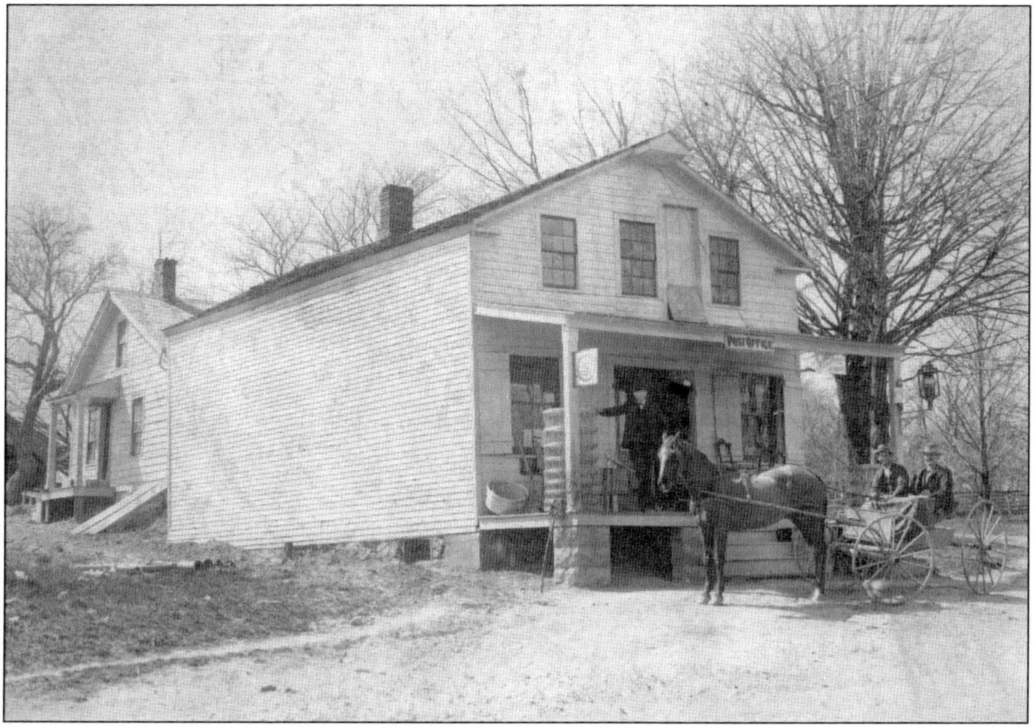

Enoch Arnold and Thomas J. Jeffords opened a store on the southwest corner of Rush-Scottsville and East River Roads in 1835. It also served as a post office. Over the years, it changed ownership a number of times.

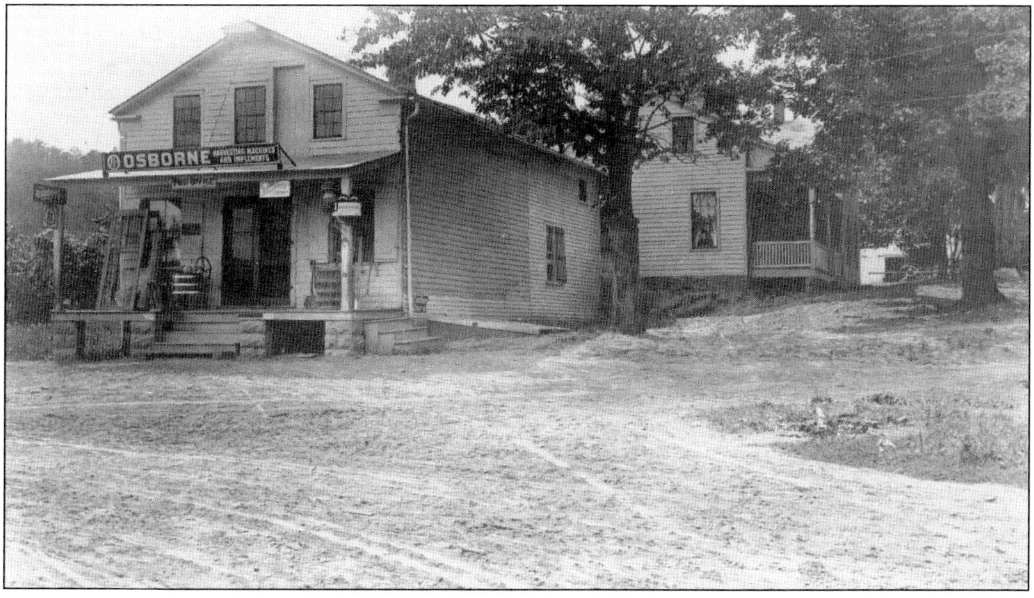

By the early 1900s, the Eugene Barker family owned the store and lived in the house behind it. The Barker Store served the North Rush community until 1959. This photograph was taken around 1907.

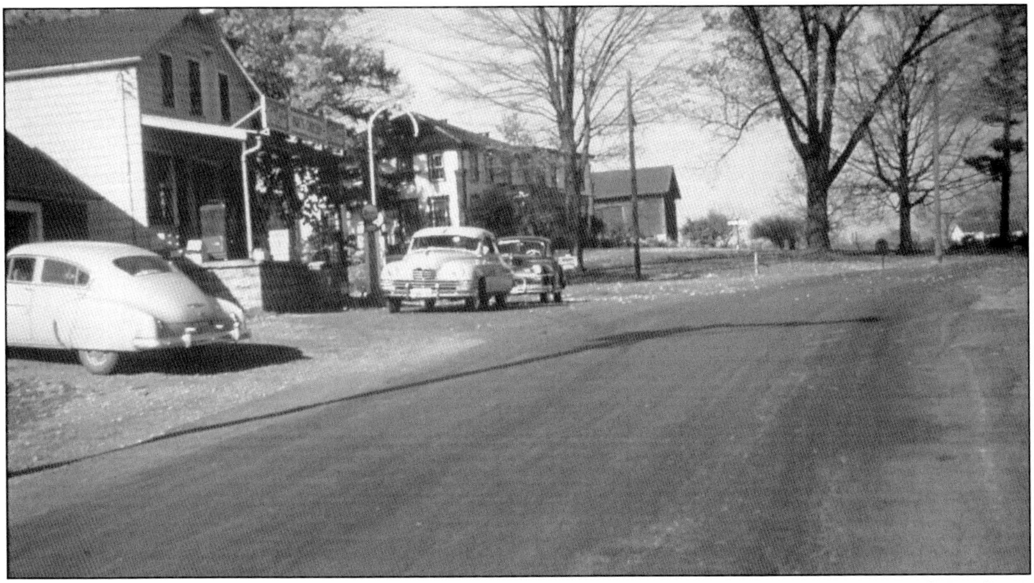

This photograph of Hart's Corners is dated November 1949. North on East River Road, Barker's Store and the Hart house are on the left. Just beyond the Hart house is a barn that is no longer standing.

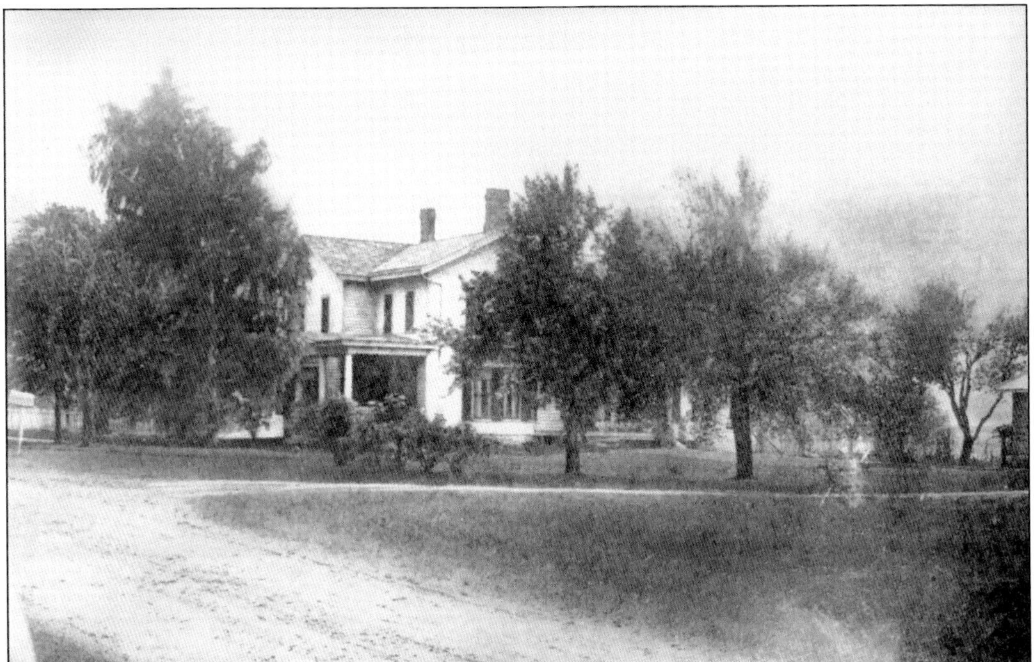

Built in 1848, 1131 Rush-Scottsville Road was once the farm and home of Eugene and Emma Runner Green. Emma often helped out at the Mann's Corners school providing music instruction. The farmhouse has been the home of Bernie and Diane Hemmerick since April 1969.

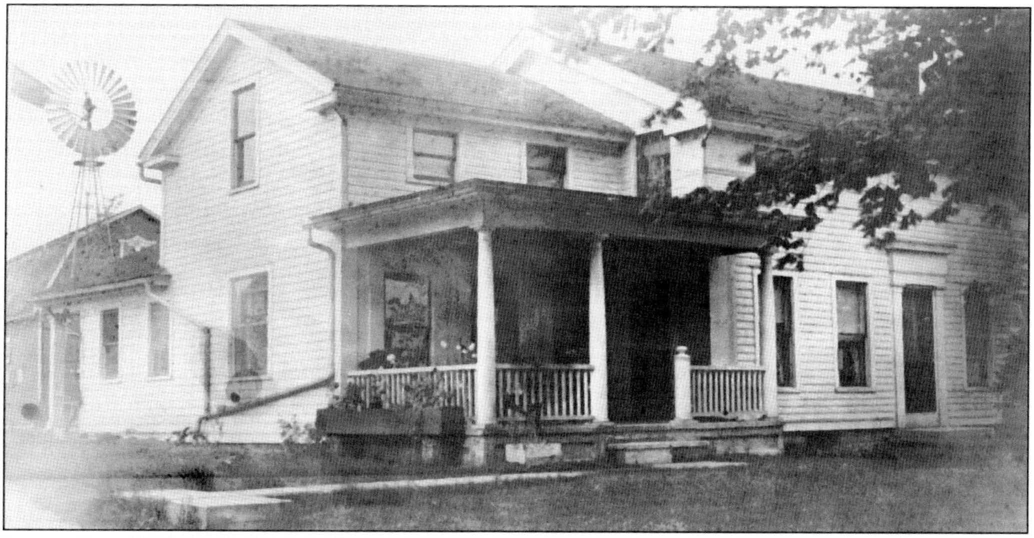

Located at 1215 Rush-Scottsville Road, Cedarcrest Farm was originally owned by Roswell and Clarissa Blood in the mid-1800s and conveyed to Martin Norris in 1868. Martin was married to Ellen Louise Sherman, a daughter of Hallaway Sherman and Augusta Stull Sherman. Upon Ellen's death in 1900, her sons, Dean Sherman Norris and Lloyd Harvey Norris, inherited the farm. (Courtesy of Eleanor Mason DeFreze.)

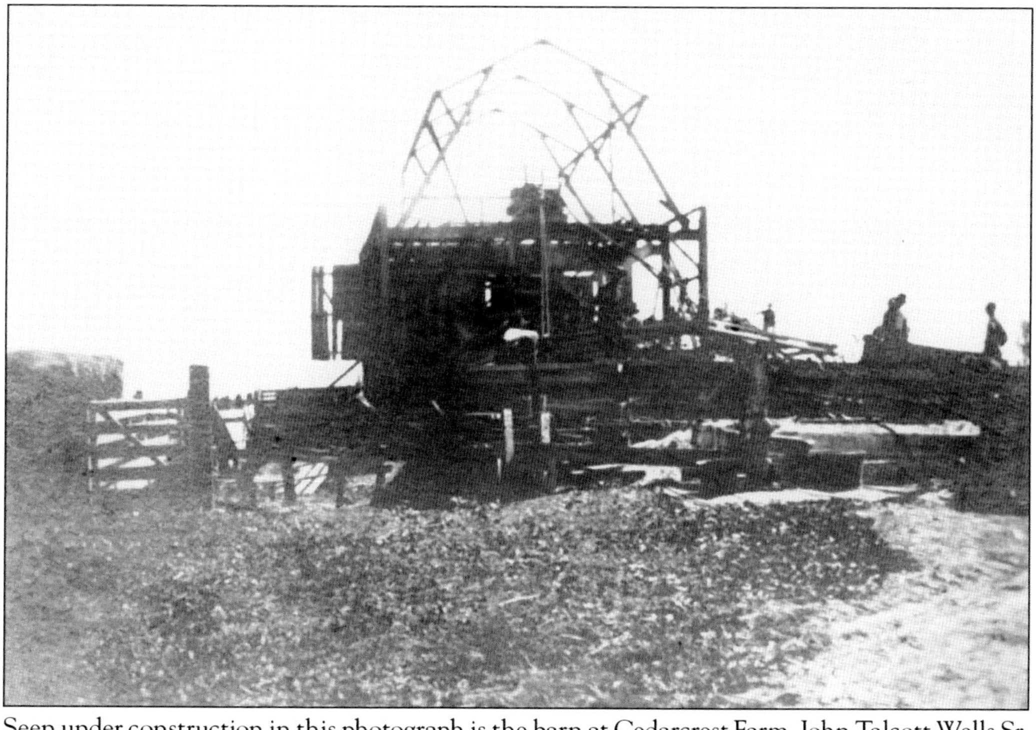

Seen under construction in this photograph is the barn at Cedarcrest Farm. John Talcott Wells Sr. of Wheatland invented a truss design that eliminated the need for supporting posts and beams and also opened up the interior storage space of the barn. The Wells family firm built nearly 200 Wells barns in New York, Ohio, Pennsylvania, and Canada, with more than 50 constructed in western New York. The Cedarcrest barn was lost to fire in 1962. (Courtesy of Eleanor Mason DeFreze.)

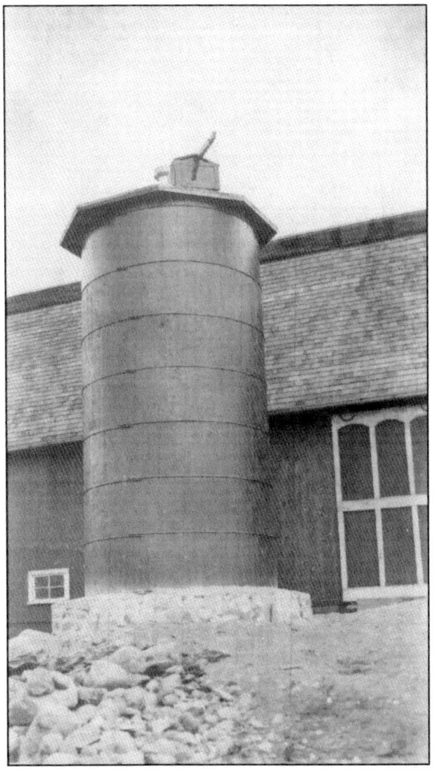

A Unadilla silo was built next to the barn. Unadilla silos are wooden, with a tongue-and-groove construction. Two roof styles were offered; one was conical and the other was gambrel. Founded in 1906, the company is still in existence today. It is now called Unadilla Laminated Products, or Una-Lam, and remains family owned. Unadilla now manufacturers arches, beams, and rafters and its products are used in large-building construction. (Courtesy of Eleanor Mason DeFreze.)

Pictured here are Dean Sherman Norris and Ruth Martin on their wedding day, March 21, 1901. Dean was the official photographer for Rush in the early 1900s. He was a Rush justice of the peace and town board member. His brother Lloyd was the director of the Monroe County Farm Bureau and a member of the National Grange. Both brothers also sang in the Norris Brothers Quartet. (Courtesy of Eleanor Mason DeFreze.)

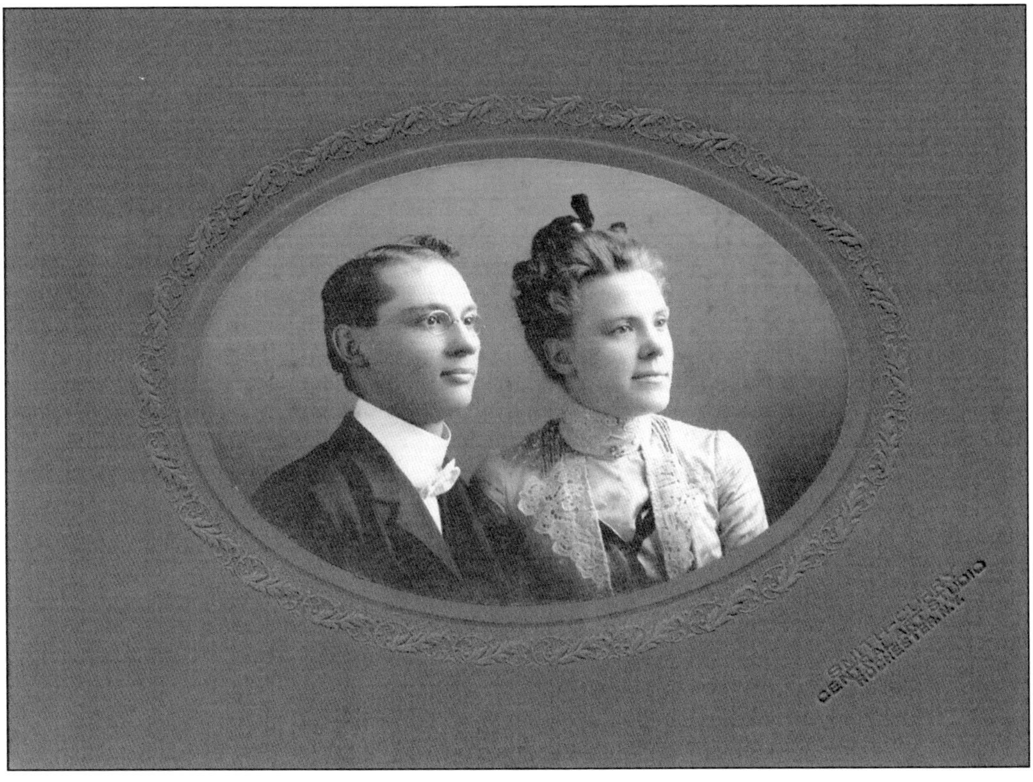

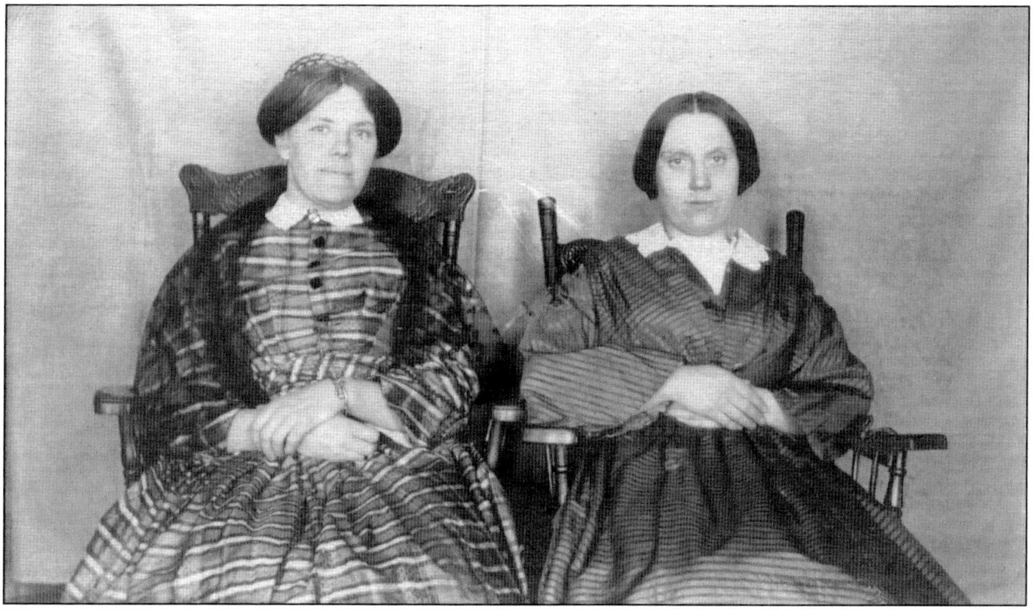

The Martins and Shermans were among the early pioneer families of Rush. Ruth Norris (left) was the daughter of Roxa Bushman Martin and Marcus J. Martin. Her childhood home was at the corner of Telephone and Martin Roads, not far from Cedarcrest. With her in this photograph is cousin Emma Sherman, daughter of Fitz James Sherman and Lavina Ellen Martin. (Courtesy of Eleanor Mason DeFreze.)

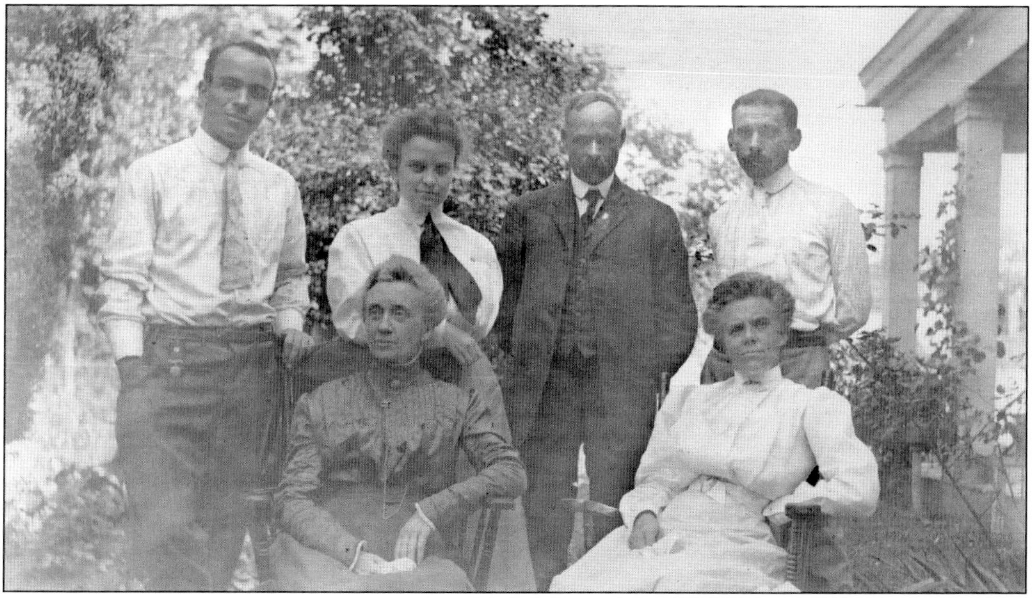

The Rotzel name goes back many years in West Rush. Jonas Rotzel was born in Pennsylvania but had settled in Rush prior to 1840. Pictured are, from left to right, (standing) Jonas's great-grandchildren, Clare and Grace Rotzel; grandson, Warren Rotzel; and Lloyd Norris; (seated) Alice Sherman Rotzel, daughter of Hallaway Sherman and Augusta Stull Sherman; and Ruth Martin Norris. (Courtesy of Eleanor Mason DeFreze.)

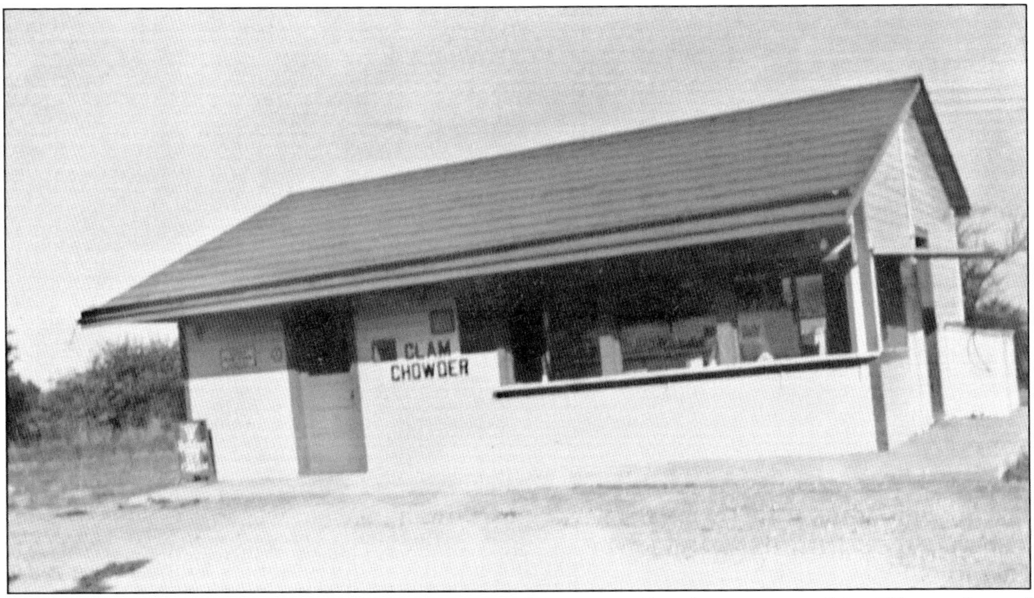

Wasson's Store, formerly located at 7262 West Henrietta Road, was owned by Ellsworth and Flora for many years. Some longtime residents recall stopping late at night for a bite to eat. The penny candy counter was a favorite among the children right up until the store's closing in the early 1990s.

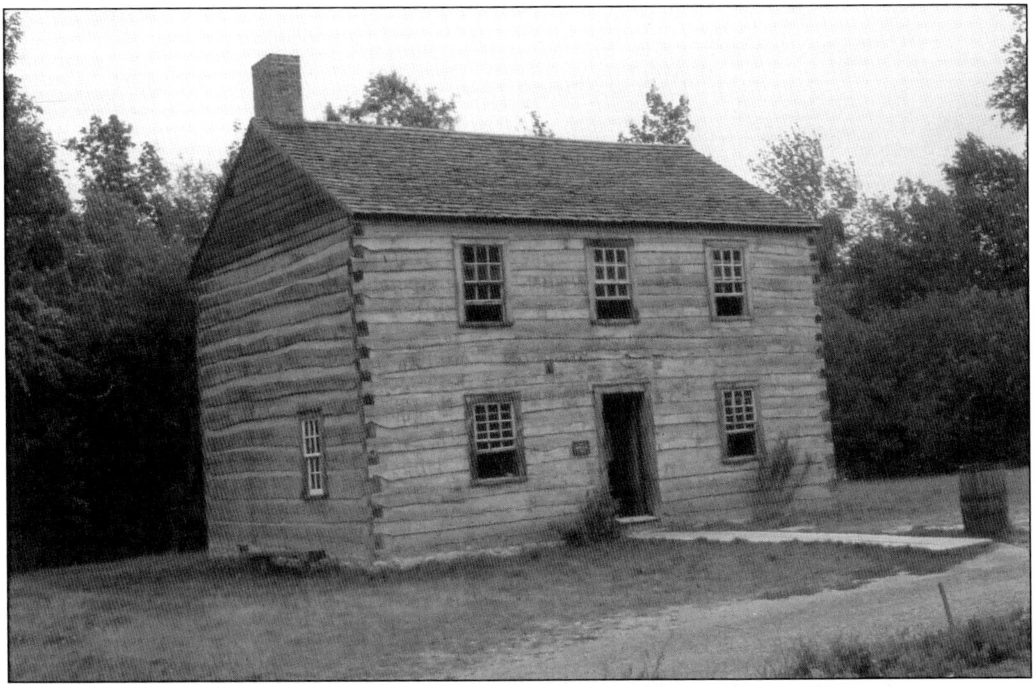

The Martin Kieffer house, from around 1814, is a two-story building utilizing a dovetail construction technique favored by early-19th-century Pennsylvania Germans. Both the interior and exterior walls were covered many years ago, which protected the original structure. During construction of Interstate 390, the original age and structure was discovered, and the house was carefully dismantled and relocated to the Genesee Country Village and Museum.

Five

Homes, Farms, and Family

Photographs in this chapter attempt to capture and represent a time and place in the town's past by showing some of the homes, the daily work, and the people. Rush has always been a small, rural farming community. What that means has changed over the years. In 1858, a total of 318 families were living in Rush with 14,837 acres reported as improved land. The 1870 statistics reported 219 farms, and by 1950, the number of farms had decreased to 139. By the end of that same decade, the number of farms in Rush was 84, with an average of 161 acres per farm. Similar to the fate of the small family farm across America, the number of small farms in Rush has also decreased.

Today, Rush still maintains a strong agricultural base, but there has also been an introduction of new homes and families. Improved roads and automobiles make the commute to Rochester and other areas fairly quick and easy.

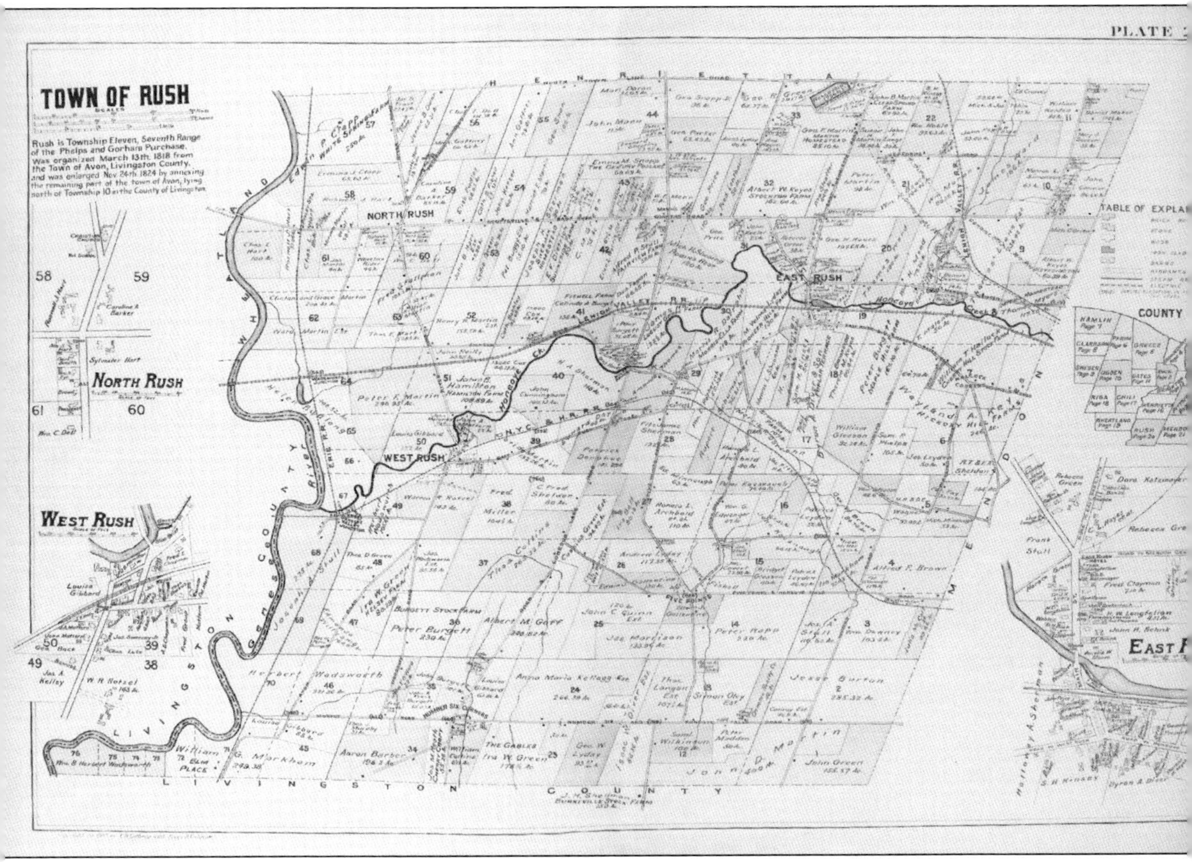

This 1902 map of Rush is included in the *Plat Book of Monroe County*, published by J.M. Lathrop and Co. The map shows the individual farms and the acreage of each one.

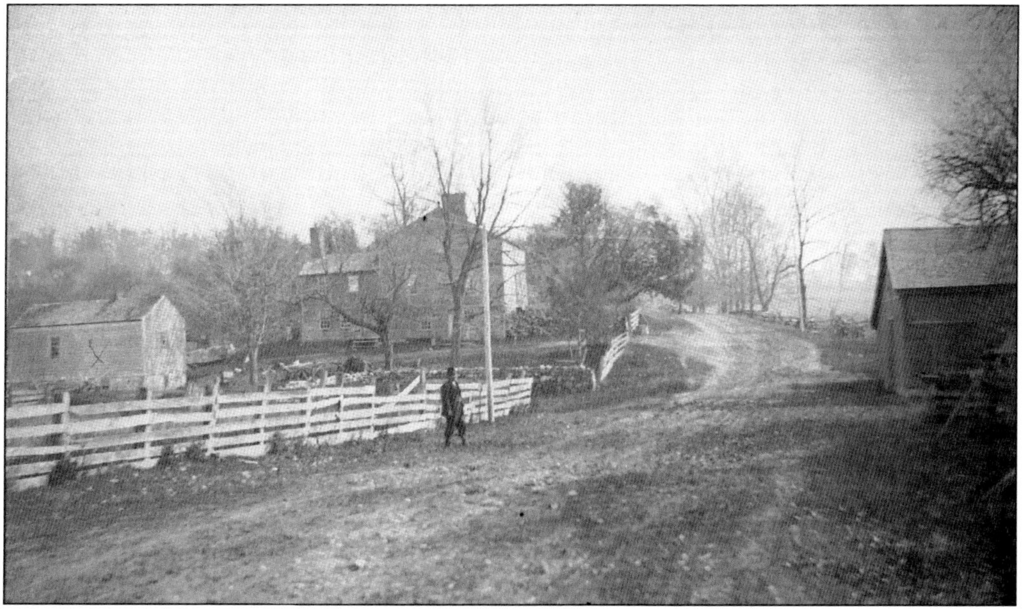

Born in Hagerstown, Maryland, in 1748, Peter Myers served in the Revolutionary War and settled in Rush in 1805. He purchased 600 acres on the north side of Honeoye Creek and by 1808 had built a house at 2608 Rush-Mendon Road. Descendants of Peter and Elizabeth Hoover Myers are the Martins, Stulls, and Divers. Believed to be the oldest frame house in Rush and Mendon, the home is currently owned by Harold Carter Jr. and his wife, Elise.

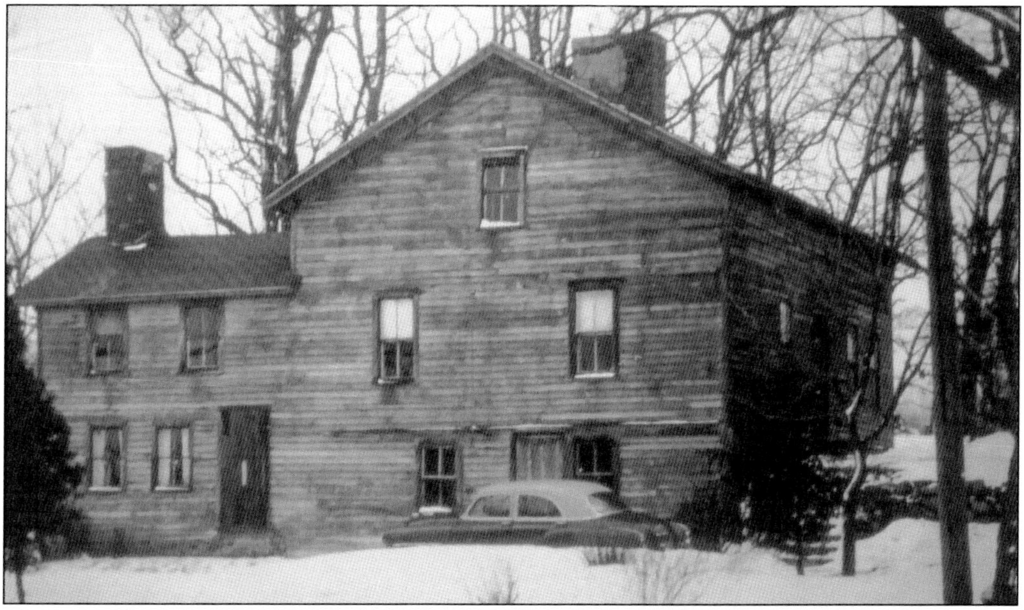

This 1947 photograph of 2608 Rush-Mendon Road shows the Peter Myers home prior to restoration. Graeme Bonham Carter purchased the property from James Reeves in 1969. Over the next six years, the Carter family made extensive renovations to the home. First among improvements were a bathroom, furnace, septic system, and cleaning out years of unwanted accumulation. Further restoration revealed multiple fireplaces that had been covered over. (Courtesy of Harold and Elise Carter.)

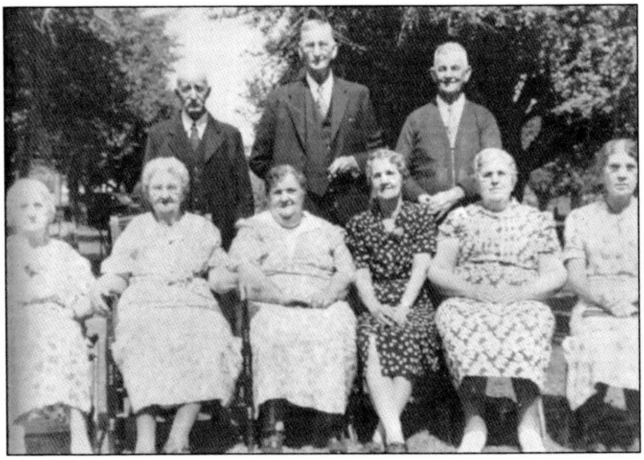

The children of George W. Lyday and Elizabeth Ward Lyday are shown at their 1939 family reunion. The Lydays had nine children, including two sets of twins. Pictured, from left to right, are (seated) Mary Darron from Walworth, Anna Goff from Rush, Jennie Darron from Niagara Falls, Harriet O'Day from Avon, Louise Howard from Avon, Alice Green from Avon; (standing) John Lyday from Avon, Cyler Lyday from Honeoye Falls, and Lewis Lyday from Avon.

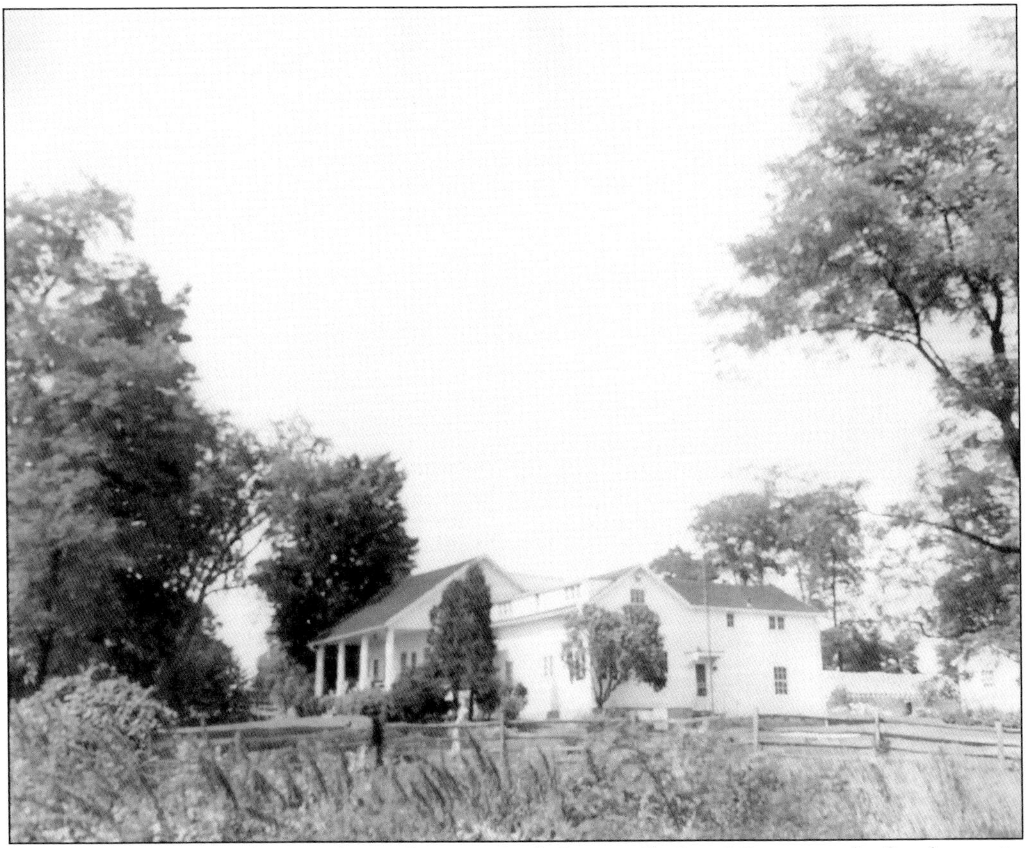

The c. 1911 Peter Price house is located at 1426 Rush-Scottsville Road. Price was the first lawyer in Rush in addition to serving in several elected positions. He was the son of early settlers Philip Price and Susannah Layman and married Rebecca Jeffords in 1809. The home has fireplaces at either end and an open porch facing south. It is currently owned by Matthew and Jean Schwasman.

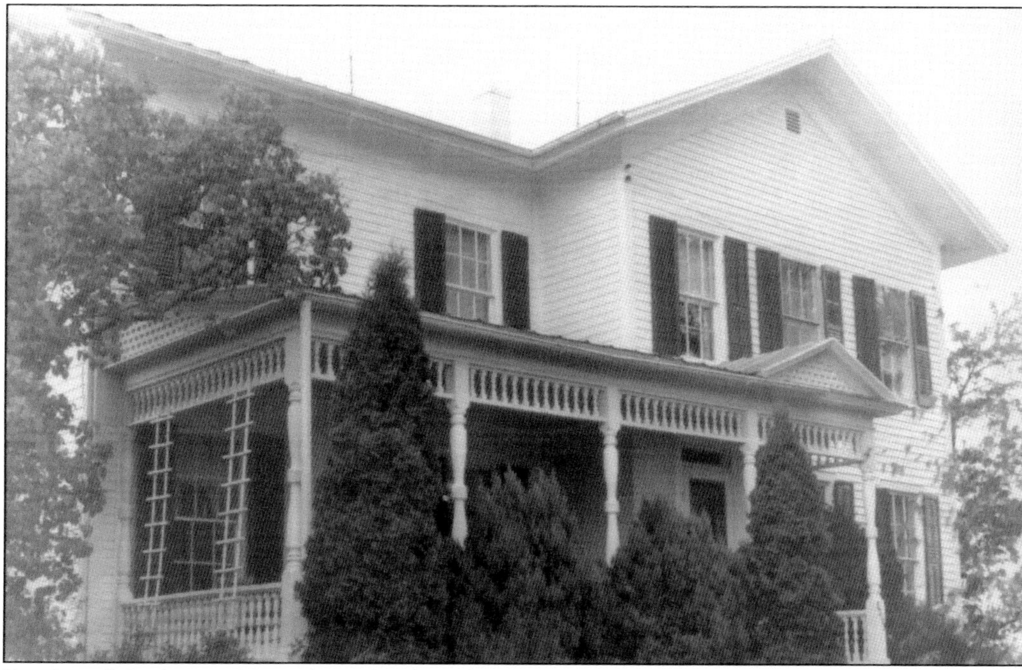

Frank and Catherine Mann brought their family from Pennsylvania in the mid-1800s and built their farm at the northwest corner of Rush-Scottsville and West Henrietta Roads. Their son Frank later owned this farm and his elder brother John owned the Stull/Shearing Farm on the southeast corner. The Albert Fleig family owned the farm for many years following the Manns. In order to make way for the Genesee Expressway, the farmhouse was moved through the fields to 534 Fishell Road in the mid-1970s.

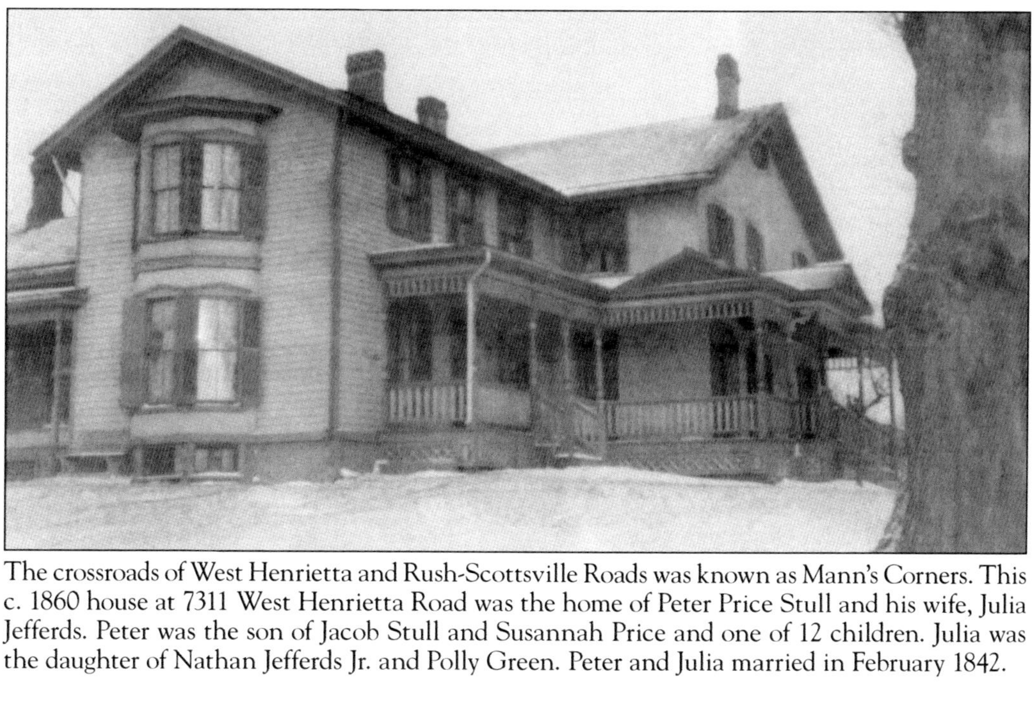

The crossroads of West Henrietta and Rush-Scottsville Roads was known as Mann's Corners. This c. 1860 house at 7311 West Henrietta Road was the home of Peter Price Stull and his wife, Julia Jefferds. Peter was the son of Jacob Stull and Susannah Price and one of 12 children. Julia was the daughter of Nathan Jefferds Jr. and Polly Green. Peter and Julia married in February 1842.

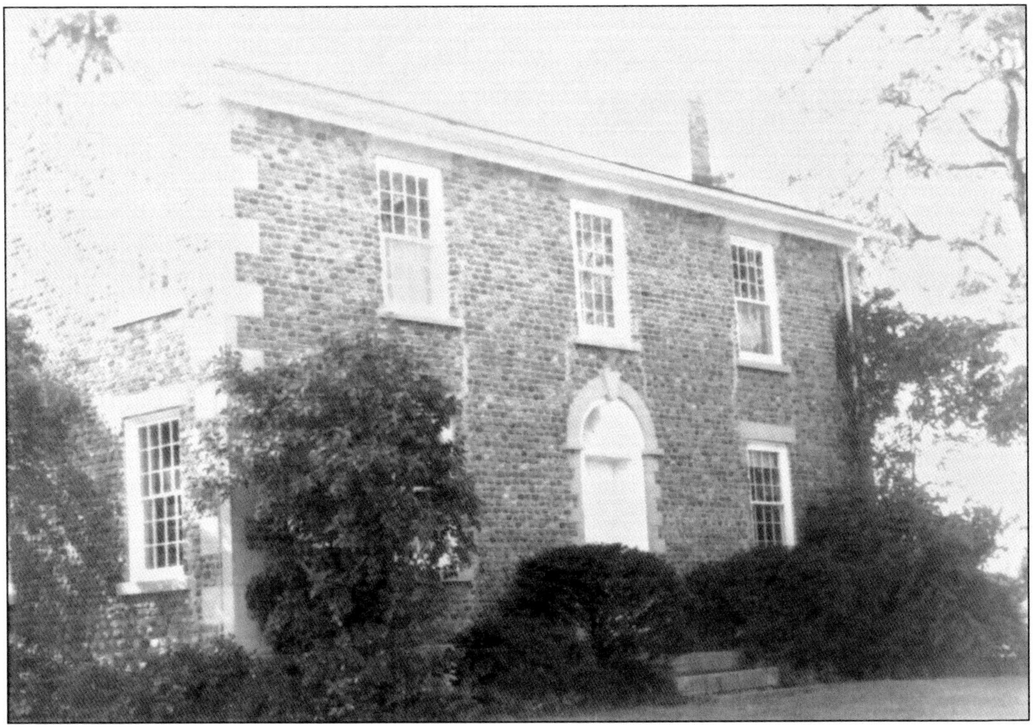

This cobblestone home is believed to have been built by John Hartwell in about 1830. It is located on Hartwell Road off of West Henrietta Road, south of the Honeoye Falls No. 6 Road. Born in Alstead, New Hampshire, Hartwell was a minuteman in the American Revolution. Mary Bugbee Hartwell was his third wife, and they had one son, John B., who became a physician and later worked as a druggist in Lockport, New York.

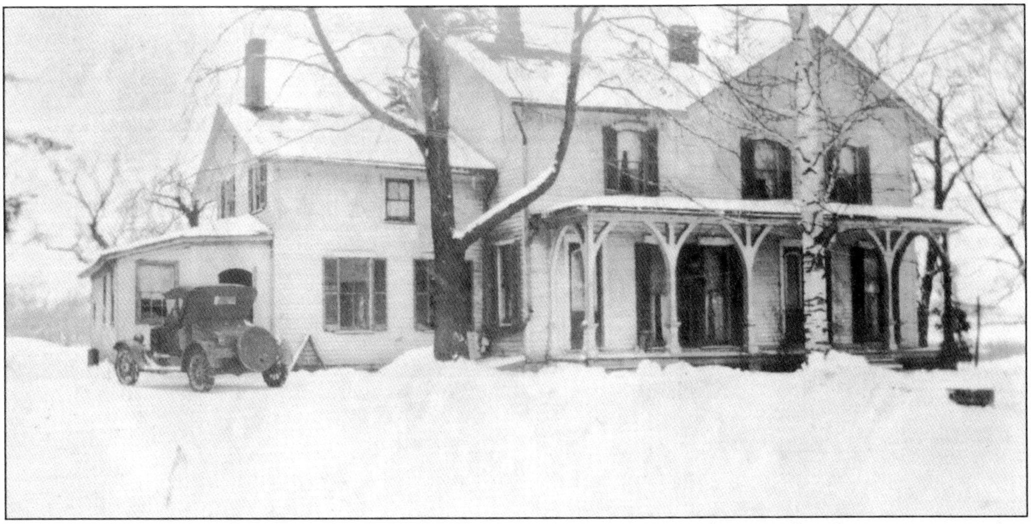

Jacob Martin, a friend of the Stull and Price families from Frederick, Maryland, came to visit his friends and the Genesee Country he had heard much about. Notably impressed, he returned to Maryland to sell his farm and bring his family to Rush in 1809. He bought four farms, one for each son, and built a new cabin for himself. The house presently standing at 5433 East Henrietta Road is the third Martin home on the site. (Courtesy of Robert Martin Kuhls.)

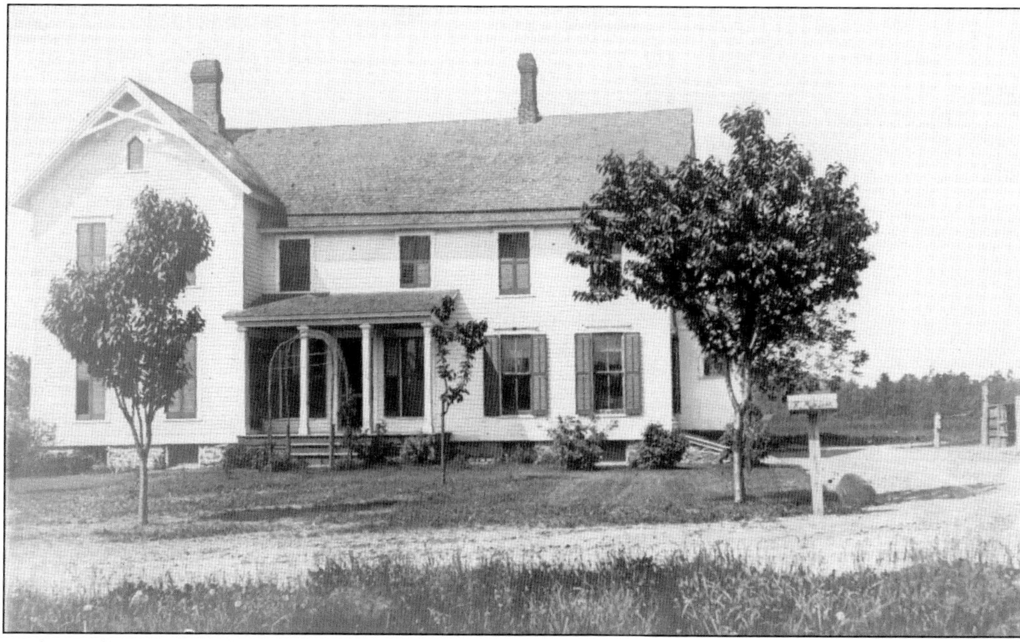

In the early 1800s, Killian Martin Sr. and his wife, Millicent Sibley Martin, were living in Rensselaer County with their young family. In 1814, at the age of 43, Killian died, leaving Millicent a young widow with 11 children to raise on her own. She took in weaving to pay the family debts and provide for her children. Five years later, their son James K. and his wife, Fanny Bristol, along with three younger Martin siblings, journeyed to the Genesee Country. Over the next two years, the remaining family, including Millicent, was eventually reunited and settled in Rush, with James K. purchasing 100 acres of land at the west end of Martin Road in 1825. James and Fanny had 13 children, and it became James's practice to purchase an area farm for each child as he or she married. The farm pictured here belonged to James's and Fanny's son Killian Martin. (Both, courtesy of Eleanor Mason DeFreze.)

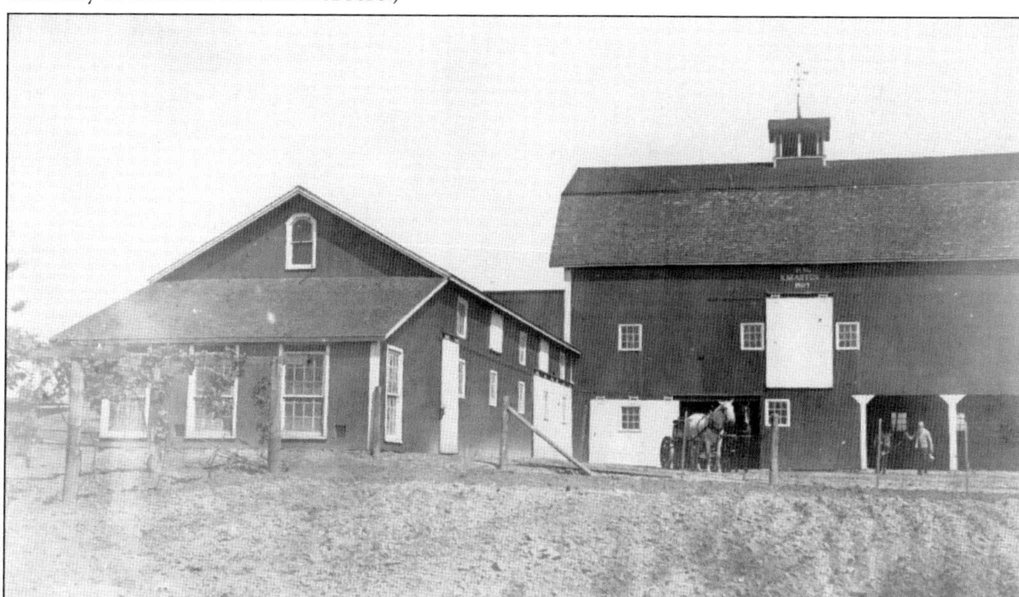

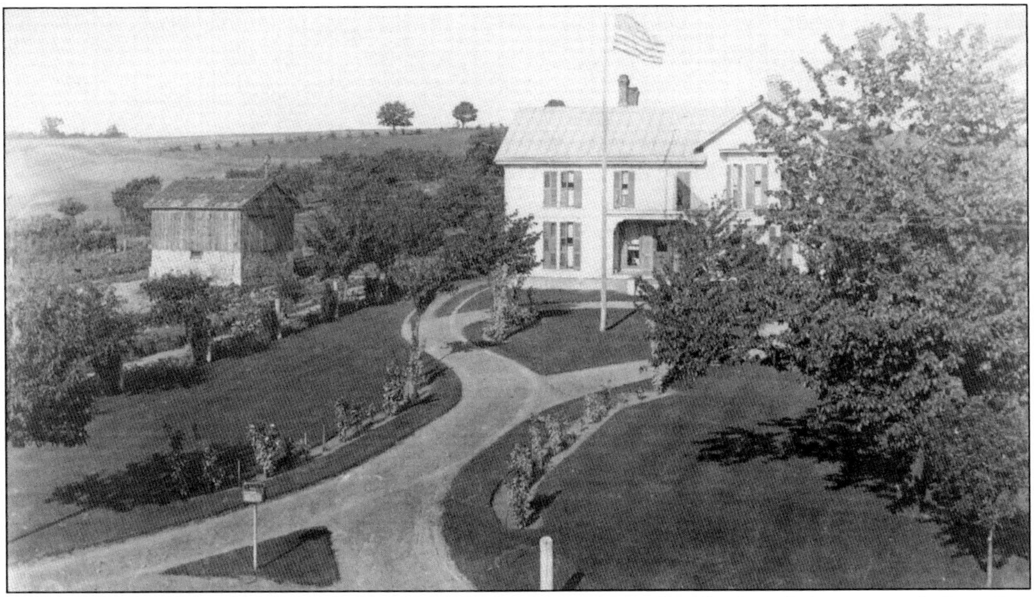

Ward Martin, the youngest son of James and Fanny, remained at the family homestead. Another son, Henry Ryan, had a farm at the corner of Fishell and East River Roads, which is presently owned by the Hacker family. Thomas Eugene Martin acquired Killian's farm at 7168 East River Road (shown here), which later passed to his daughter Della and her husband, Russell Warner Martin. The house was lost to a fire on July 4, 1978. (Courtesy of Sharon Hacker.)

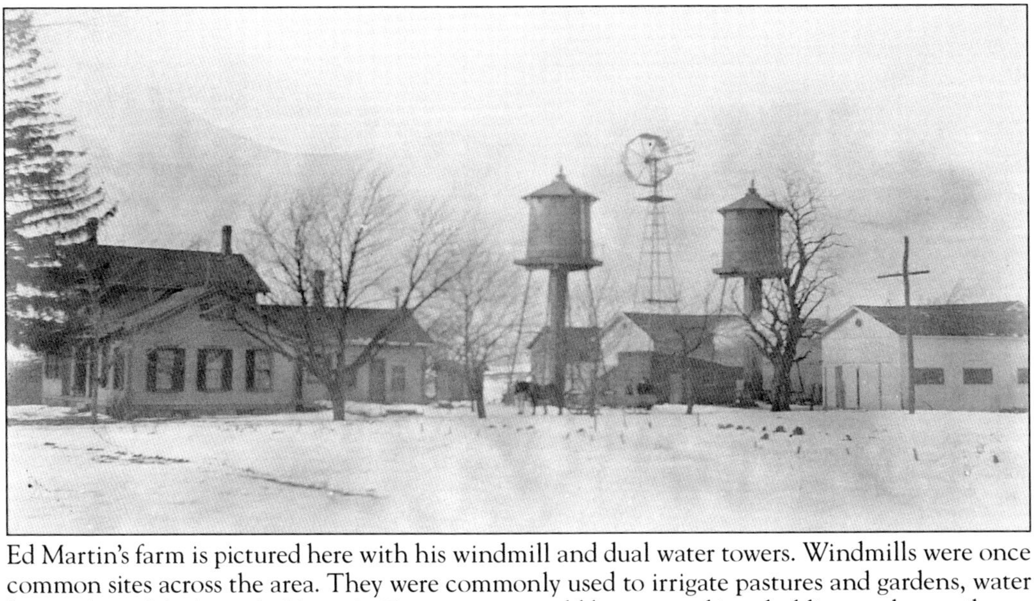

Ed Martin's farm is pictured here with his windmill and dual water towers. Windmills were once common sites across the area. They were commonly used to irrigate pastures and gardens, water livestock, and for household needs. Excess water could be reserved in a holding tank on stilts, or a water tower, as shown in the photograph. The elevated tank provided enough pressure to be on tap for household use. (Courtesy of Eleanor Mason DeFreze.)

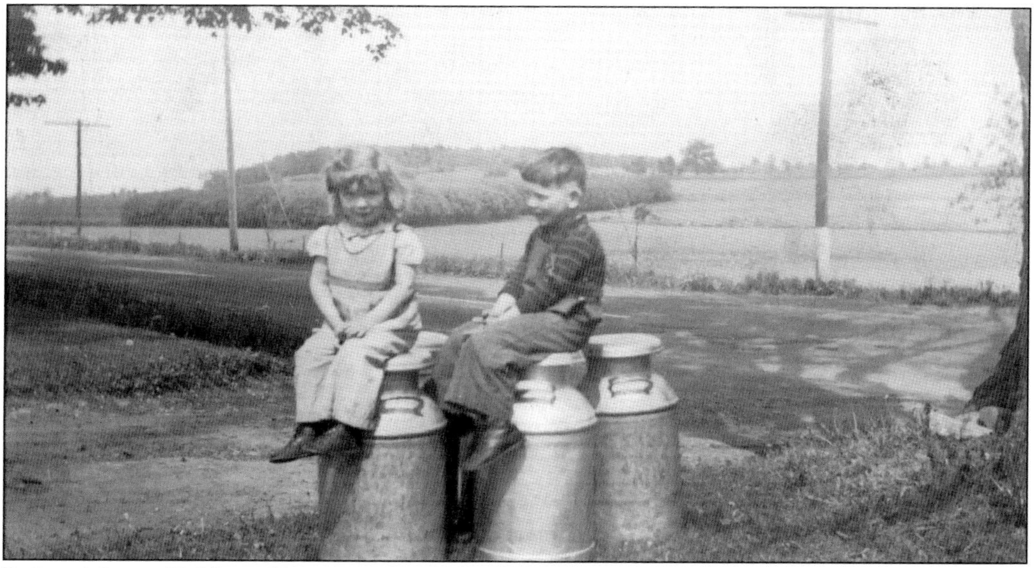

Robert Martin Kuhls and his sister, Janet, are relaxing atop old milk cans at the Martin farm on East Henrietta Road around 1944. (Courtesy of Robert M. Kuhls.)

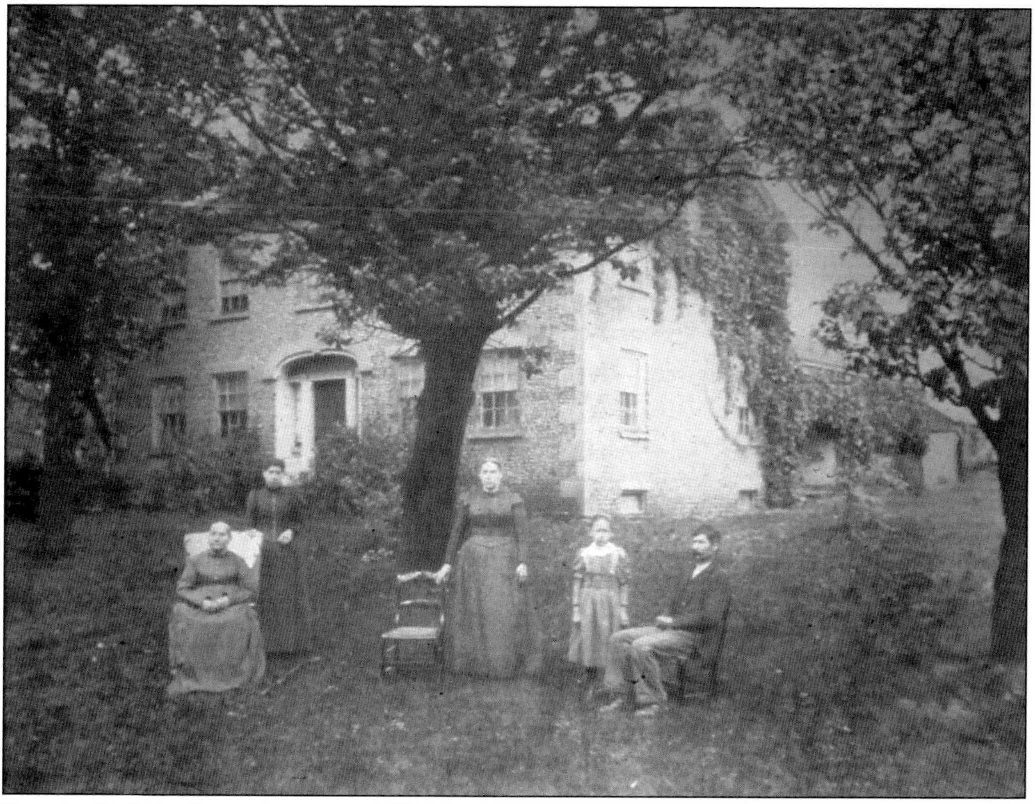

Born in Carlisle, Pennsylvania, in 1761, Henry Fishell moved his family to Rush in 1808. His son John built the fieldstone house at 512 Fishell Road in 1838. John was married first to Sarah Bell, and after her death, to Mary Fishell. In total, he raised a family of 21 children. Family members are not identified in this photograph, but the Fishell family held annual reunions for many years.

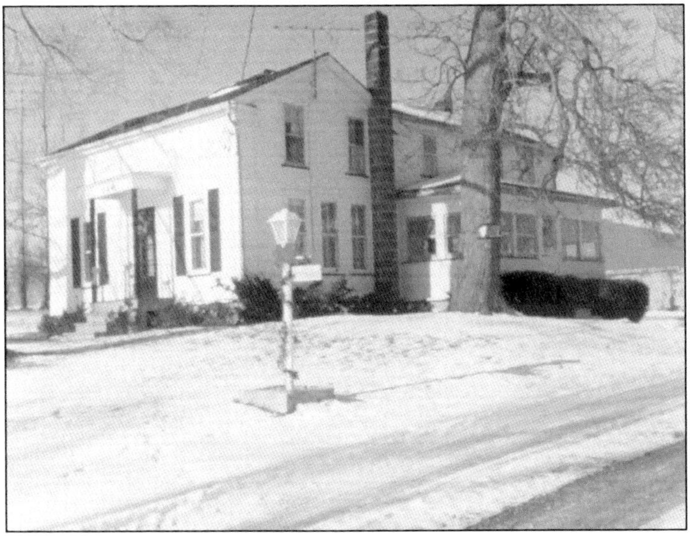

An 1852 map shows the farm at the bottom of the Fishell Road hill was the Blood farm. Isaac Cox later owned it. Earlier maps and family histories also indicate that Elnathan Perry and Jacob Thomas had log cabins in this same area, located some distance back from the road. Walter and Barbara Bittner purchased the Cox farmhouse in 1967 and sold it to Stanley and Sharon Scott in 1999. (Courtesy of Walter and Barbara Bittner.)

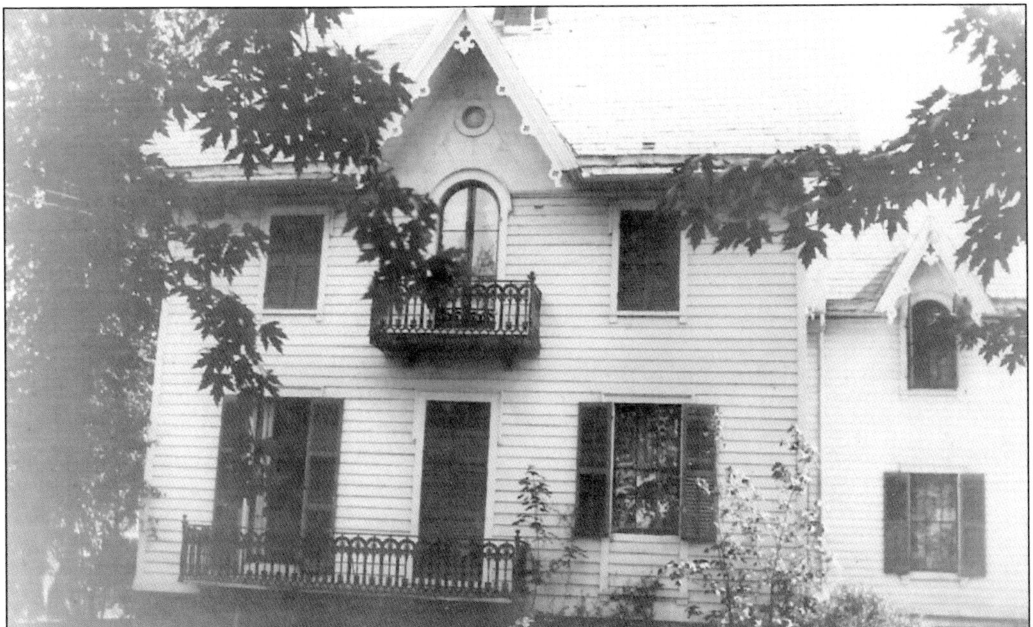

Ira Wesley Greene's farm, the Gables, consisted of over 175 acres by 1902. The farm was a productive produce and sheep farm. The 1860 agriculture reports indicate Greene had 214 sheep and produced 270 bushels of wheat, 500 bushels of corn, and 300 bushels of oats. His sheep produced 710 pounds of wool. 787 Honeoye Falls No. 6 Road is the childhood home of Marilyn Walters Chase and is currently owned by Nathan and Kelly Hatch. (Courtesy of Marilyn Chase.)

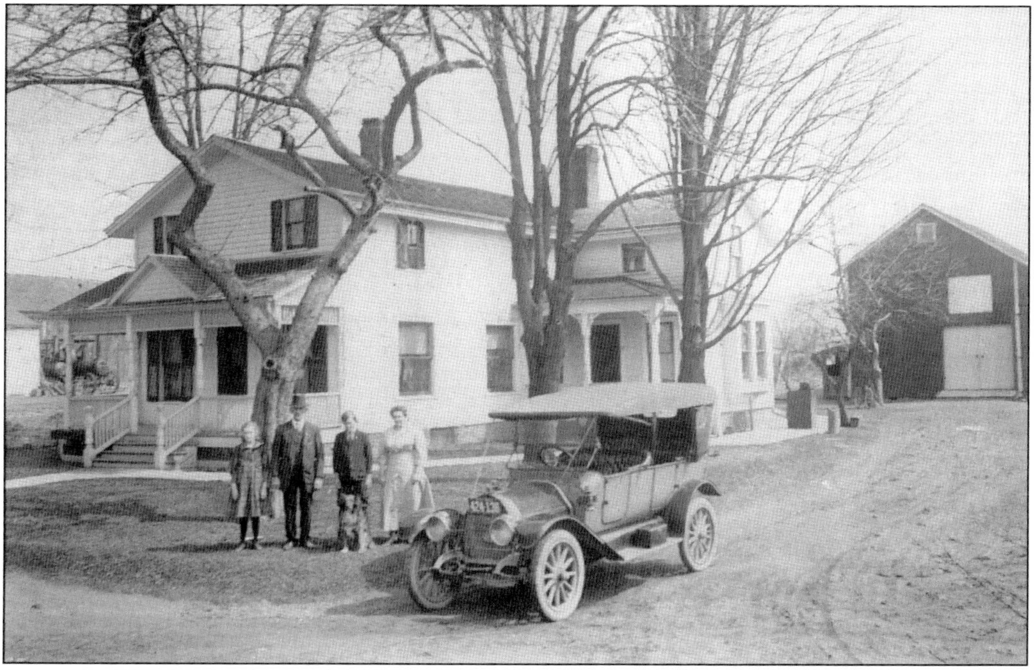

Dating to the mid-1800s, the house at 6028 East Henrietta Road was once home to Jacob and Adeline Galentine, a cooper recognized for his craftsmanship by the 1852 State Agricultural Society. The house was the childhood home of Vince Behnk, a well-known Rush resident and highway superintendent, and is where Vince and Bertha raised their family. The front porch was removed long ago. This is now the home of Vince's granddaughter Pam Bock Ebersold.

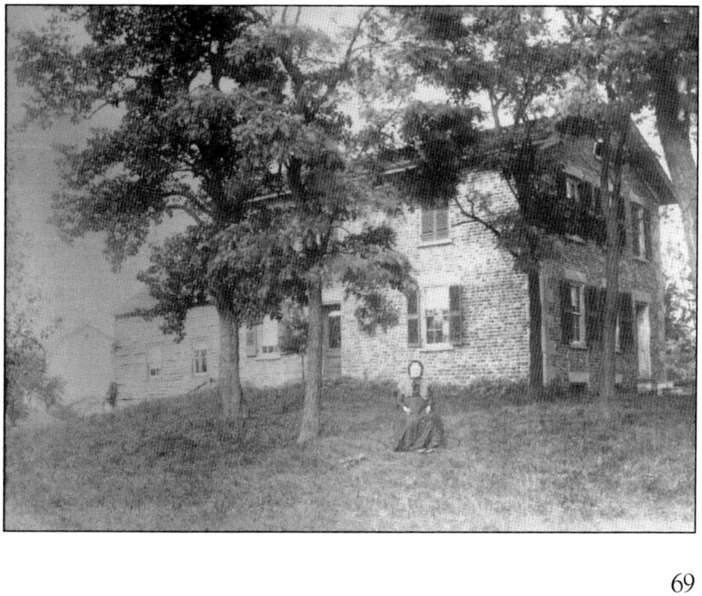

First the home of Nathan Rose, the cobblestone at 30 Lyons Road was next acquired by Joseph Ward. Joseph had arrived from England in 1845 and purchased the house in the mid-1860s. Joseph's son James inherited the home from his father and, in turn, passed the house to his daughter Nellie, wife of Charles Klick, in 1925. This photograph, taken around 1880, shows Mrs. Ward in the chair. Louise Bolger Harris is the current owner.

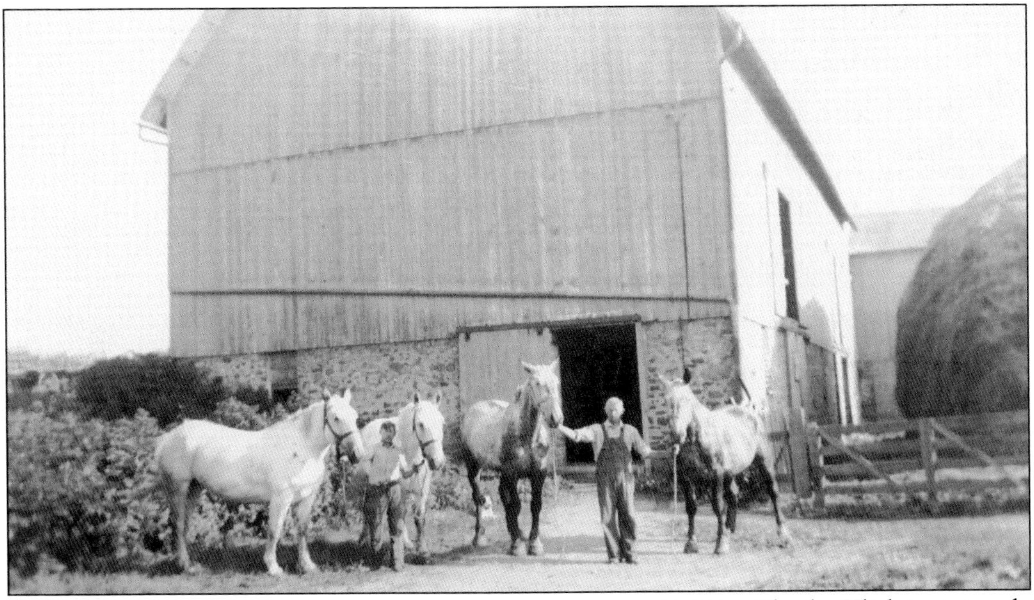

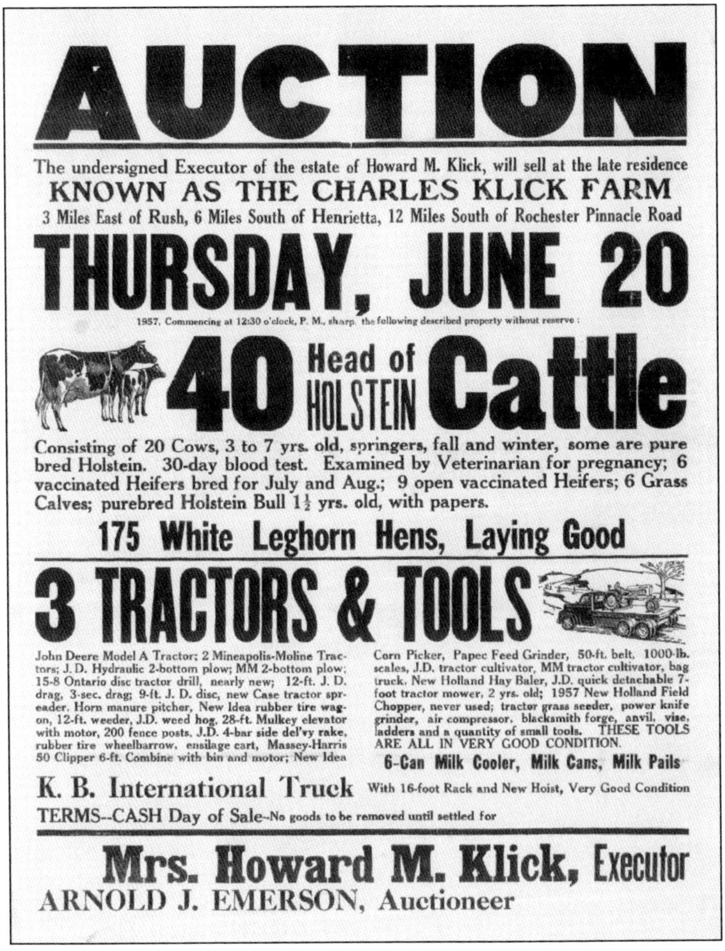

Charles Klick is pictured with his son Howard M. in this 1935-era photograph. Note the sizeable straw mound on the right side. Charles was married to Nellie Ward Klick, and his brother William was married to Nellie's sister Elsie. (Courtesy of Jim Klick.)

Howard M. Klick was operating the Charles Klick family farm on Pinnacle Road and raising a young family when he died at the age of 38. His widow, Genevieve, was left to raise six small children. She sold the farming operation via auction shortly after her husband's death. Their son Howard resides today at the Klick family homestead and continues to farm. (Courtesy of Jim Klick.)

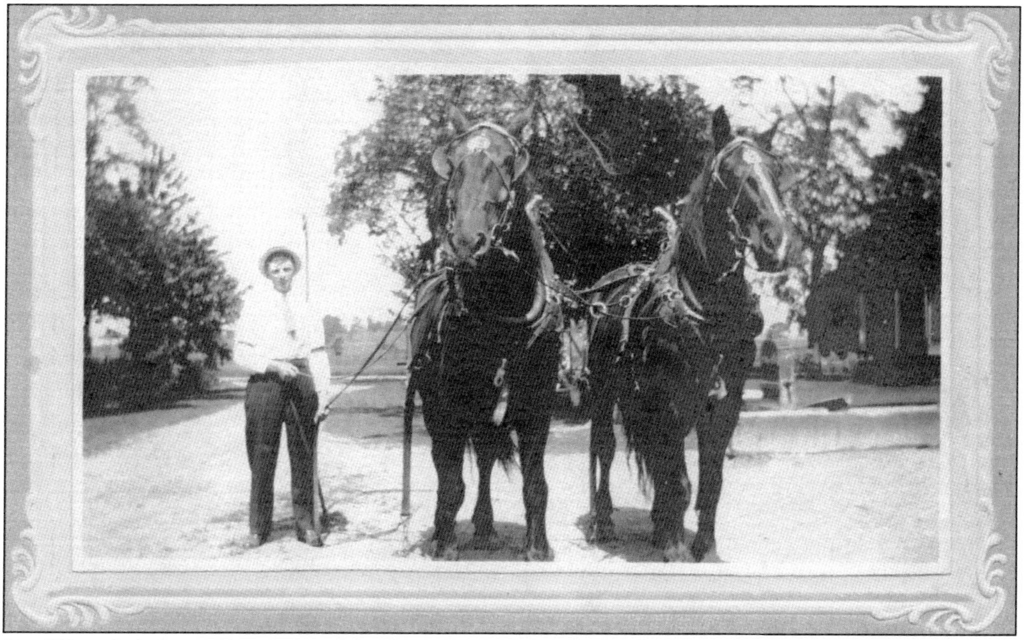

Emil David, father of former Rush highway superintendent John David and grandfather of current highway superintendent Mark David, is shown with his horse team around 1915. This is at the family farm on West Henrietta Road near the former bridge overpass and Lehigh Valley Railroad. (Courtesy of John David.)

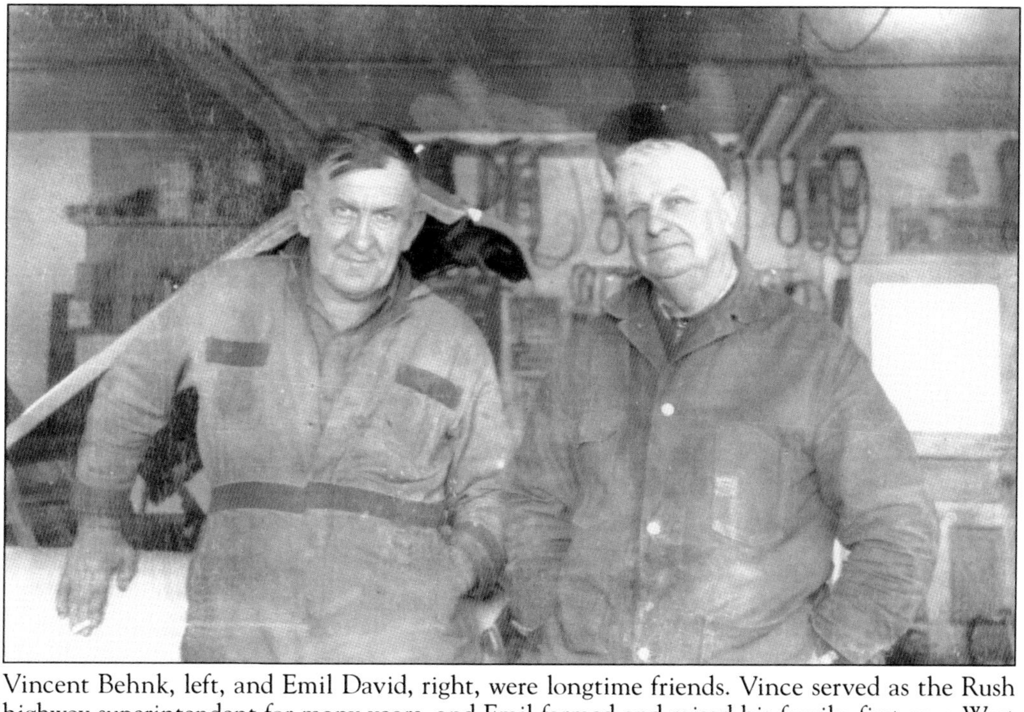

Vincent Behnk, left, and Emil David, right, were longtime friends. Vince served as the Rush highway superintendent for many years, and Emil farmed and raised his family, first on a West Henrietta Road farm and then at the present David farm on Rush West Rush Road. (Courtesy of John David.)

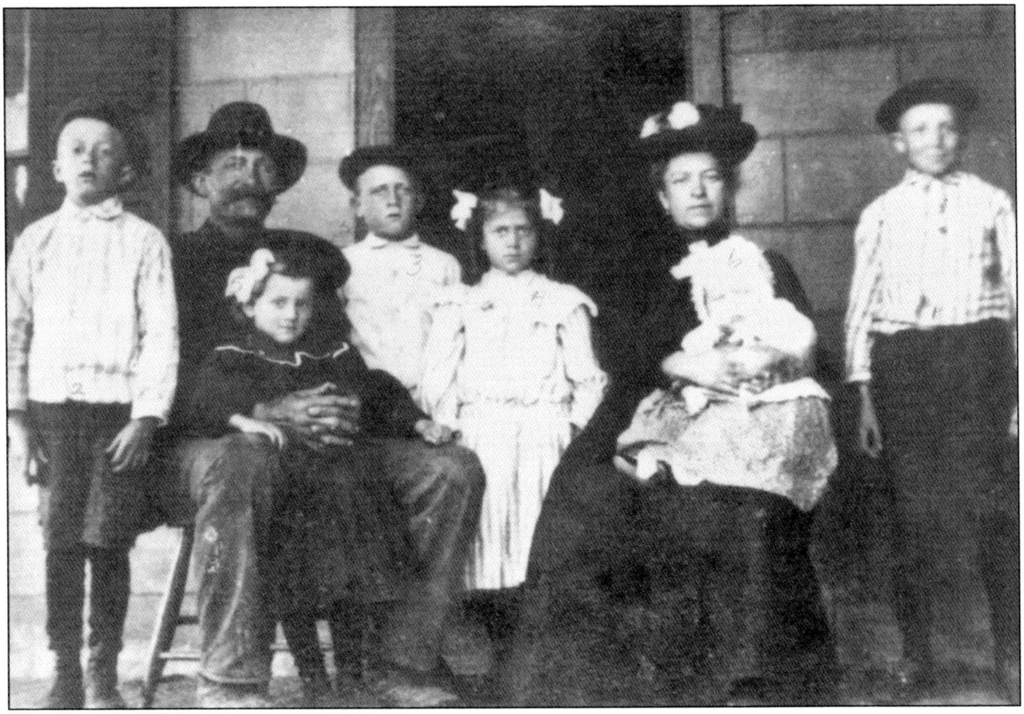

The Mack family is a well-known name in Rush. Margaret E. Meyer of Brighton married Balthasar Mack in 1896, and they raised a family of 13 children at their farm on Pinnacle Road. This photograph shows Balthasar and Margaret Mack with their six eldest children. They are, from left to right, John Mack, Balthasar (holding daughter Bertha), Carl, Louise, Margaret (holding Albert), and Frank Mack. (Courtesy of Gwen Mack.)

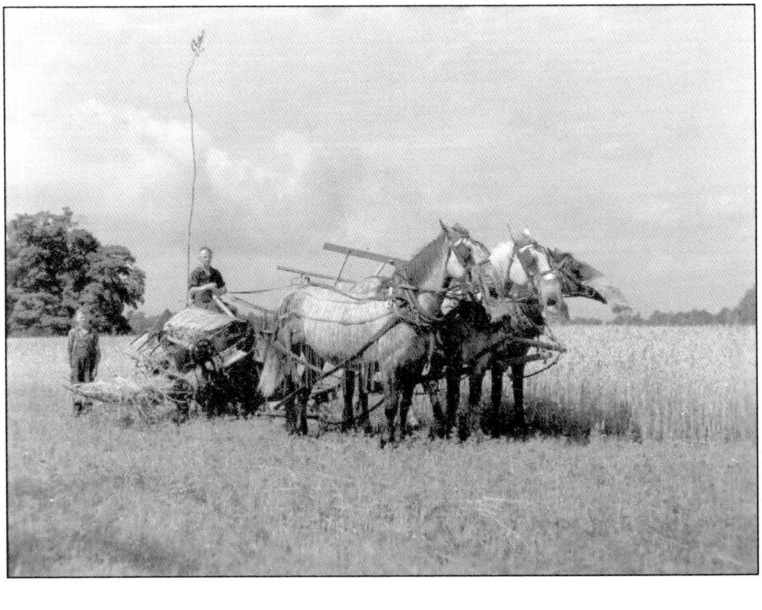

Father and son John Mack and John Mack Jr. are shown in this c. 1940 photograph at work in the fields of their West Henrietta Road farm. Note the long leather strips on the horse harness. These were commonly used to help keep the flies away as the leather strips would swish back and forth with every movement of the horse. (Courtesy of Gail Mack.)

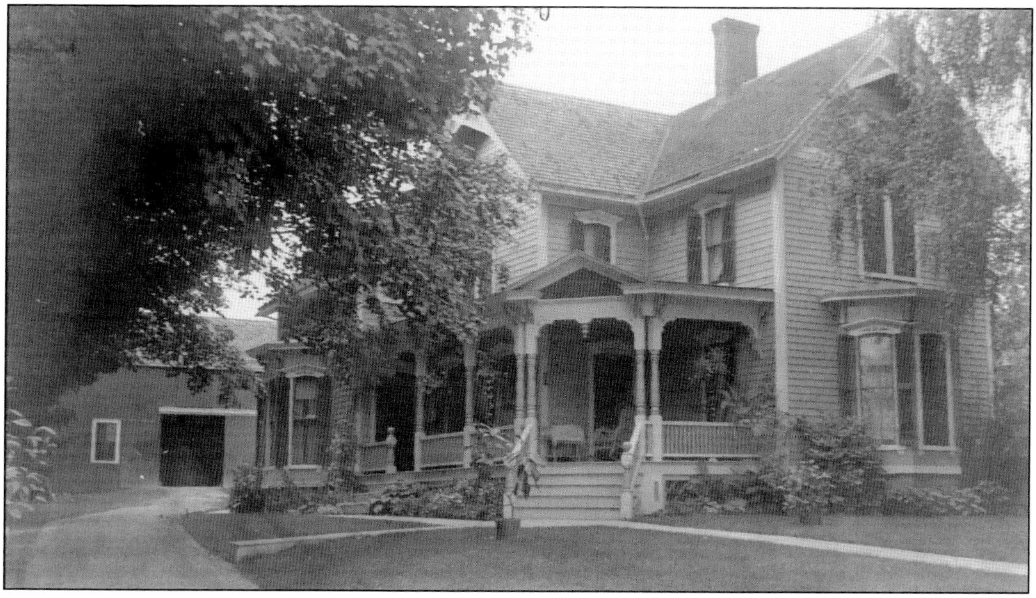

Located immediately west of St. Joseph's Church, this house was once the home of Charles and Mellie Sherman Strong. Mellie was the daughter of Fitz James and Lovina Martin Sherman. By 1913, it had become home to Marion and Daisie Decker. Features of the house, particularly the wraparound front porch, depict the Queen Anne style of architecture. (Courtesy of Eleanor Mason DeFreze.)

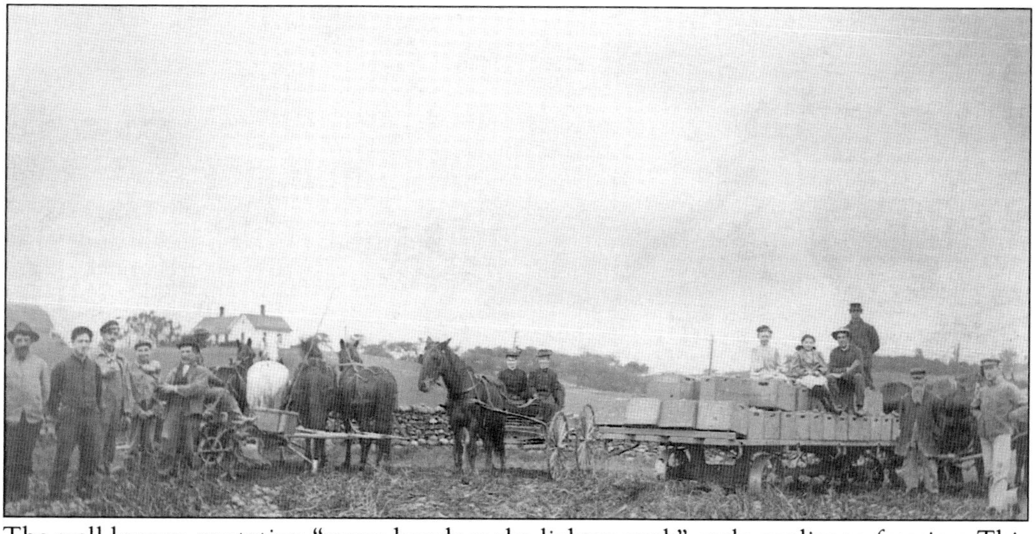

The well-known quotation "many hands make lighter work" aptly applies to farming. This photograph was taken at the T.E. Martin farm and shows the crew involved in harvesting potatoes. Potatoes were a large crop in Rush in the 1800s. An 1858 statistics report states 10,890 bushels of potatoes were harvested, and in 1892, a full 703 acres of potatoes were planted in Rush. In 1895, Rush was ranked among the front-runners as a "potato growing town." Potatoes were selling for 5¢ a bushel in 1896. (Courtesy of George M. Stahl.)

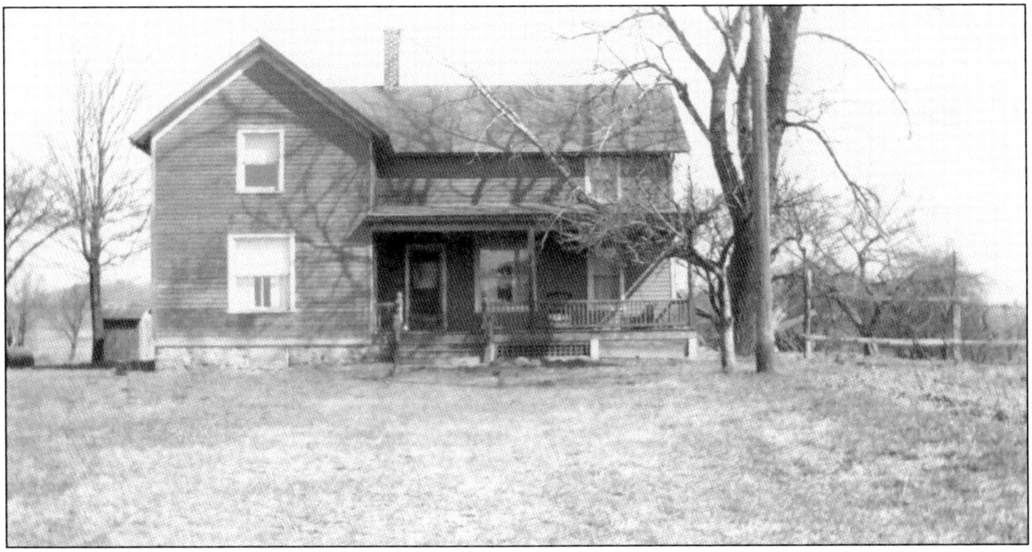

The address 226 Jeffords Road was the first farm Walt and Eleanor Kozimor owned in Rush. Eleanor's parents Waldo and Eleanor Miller lived there, too, and helped farm the 98-acre parcel. This photograph was taken in April 1946. (Courtesy of Walter Kozimor.)

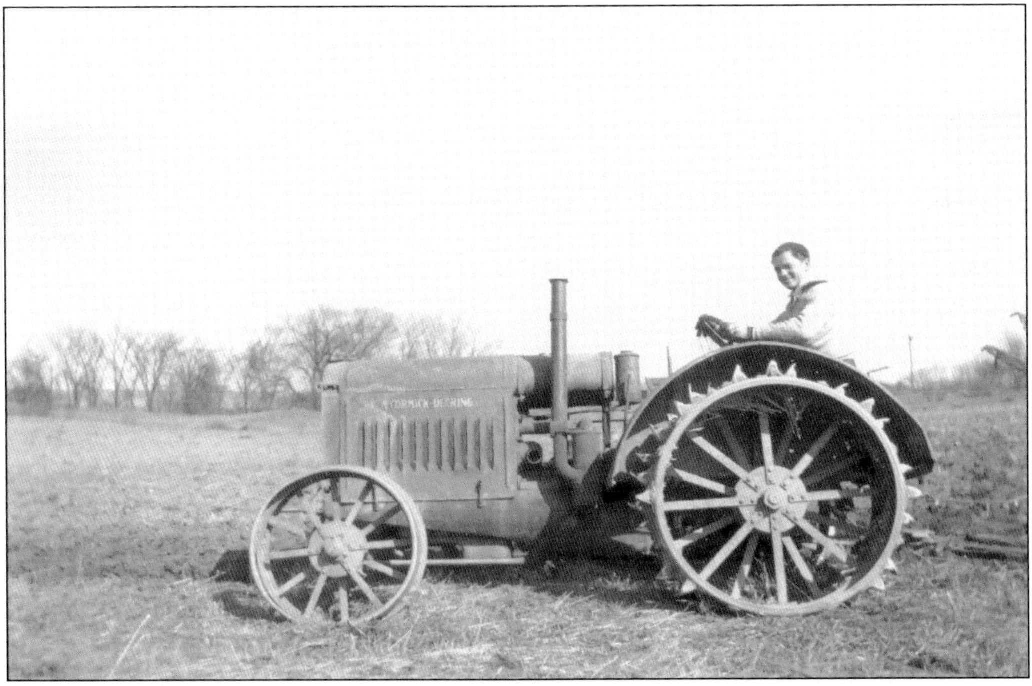

When one is speaking to longtime area farmers, the McCormick Deering 10-20 tractor seems to evoke many positive memories. First introduced by International Harvester in 1923, these popular tractors were manufactured until 1939. The 10-20 was initially priced at $785, had steel wheels, and ran on kerosene. Walt Kozimor is shown here in 1946 at his Jeffords Road farm, prior to moving to Phelps Road. (Courtesy of Walter Kozimor.)

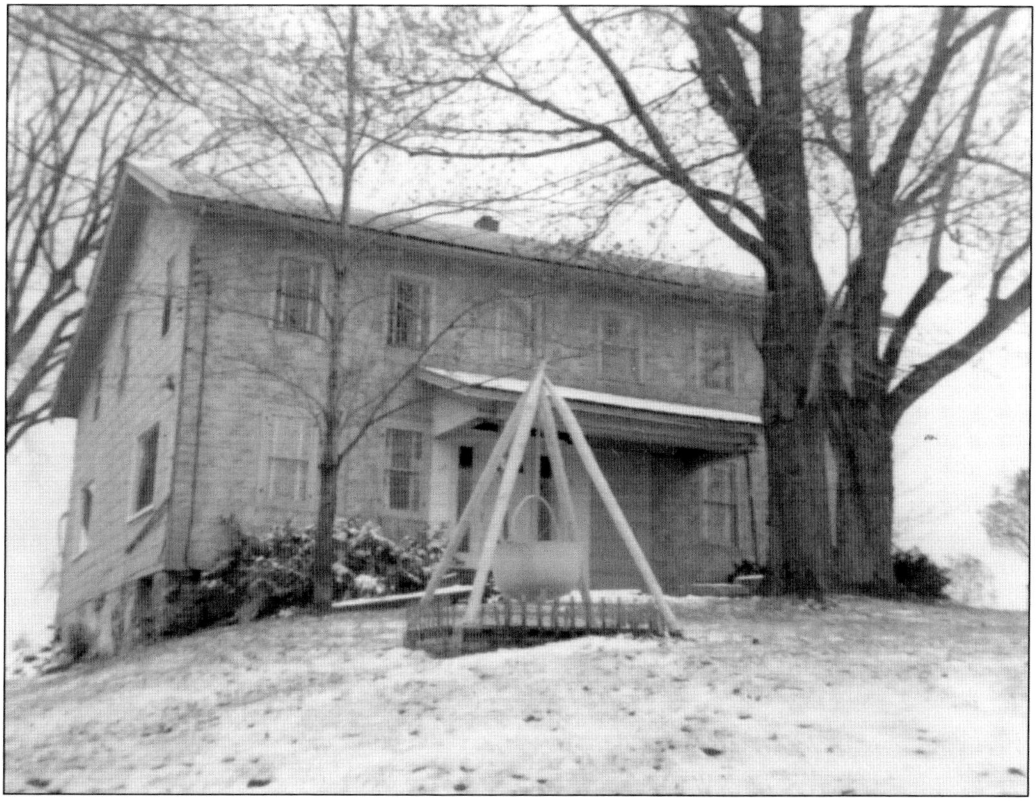

In 1810, Jeremiah Ruland purchased 50 acres from James Wadsworth and began building the house at 690 Phelps Road. Around the turn of the 20th century, there was a rathskellar in the basement of the house, complete with a honky-tonk piano, and meals were served on the terraced front lawn. Walter and Eleanor Kozimor purchased the home from Merle Bushman in 1955, and the road was called Wagner Road at that time. (Courtesy of Walter Kozimor.)

The cobblestone house at 791 Rush-Henrietta Townline Road had been the Gaffney homestead for more than 115 years when Mary R. Gaffney sold the home to David and Janet Glocker in 1984. The deed dates back to April 1846, when Elizabeth Henry and Jane and Elizabeth Bell transferred the property to Abner Bushman. The home changed hands several times during the 1860s prior to purchase by Michael and Ann Gaffney in 1869. (Courtesy of William Gaffney.)

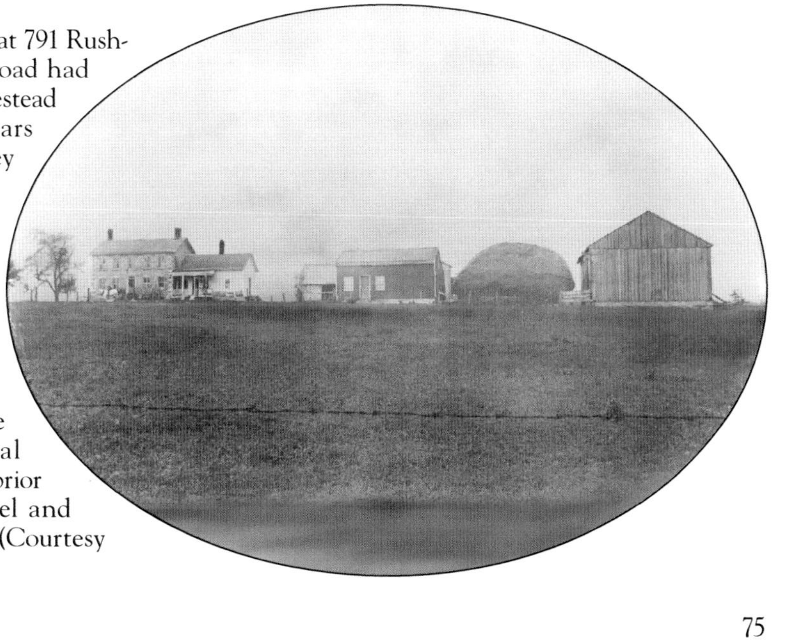

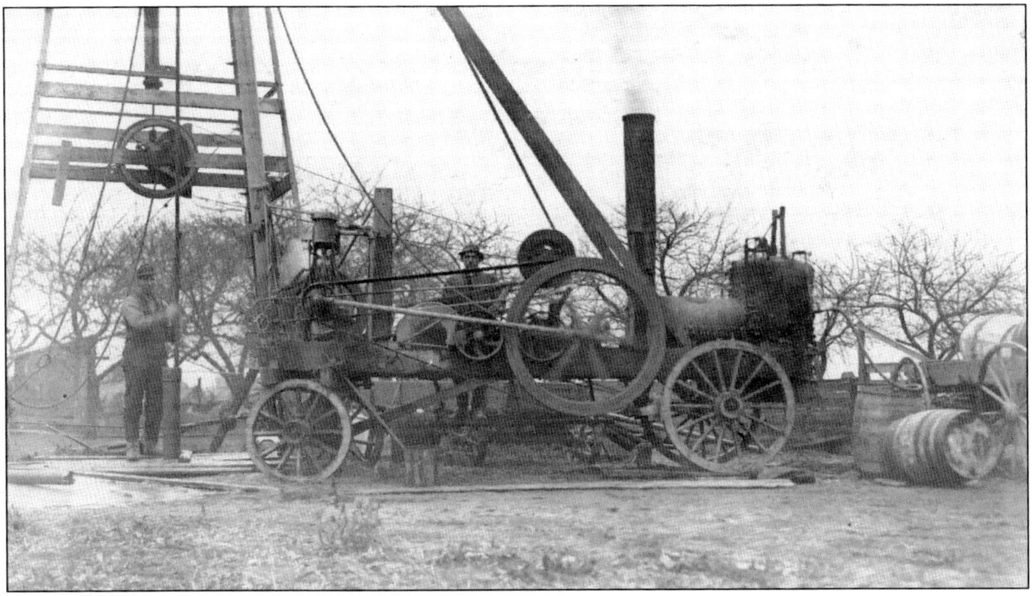

The Norris brothers at Cedarcrest Farm are using their steam tractor along with the windmill to obtain the necessary water from their well. Farmers would fill water barrels and then head to their fields to irrigate the crops. Windmills were very popular in rural America from 1880 through 1935, with over six million sold by the 20 largest manufacturers. This figure does not include those that were handmade. (Courtesy of Eleanor Mason DeFreze.)

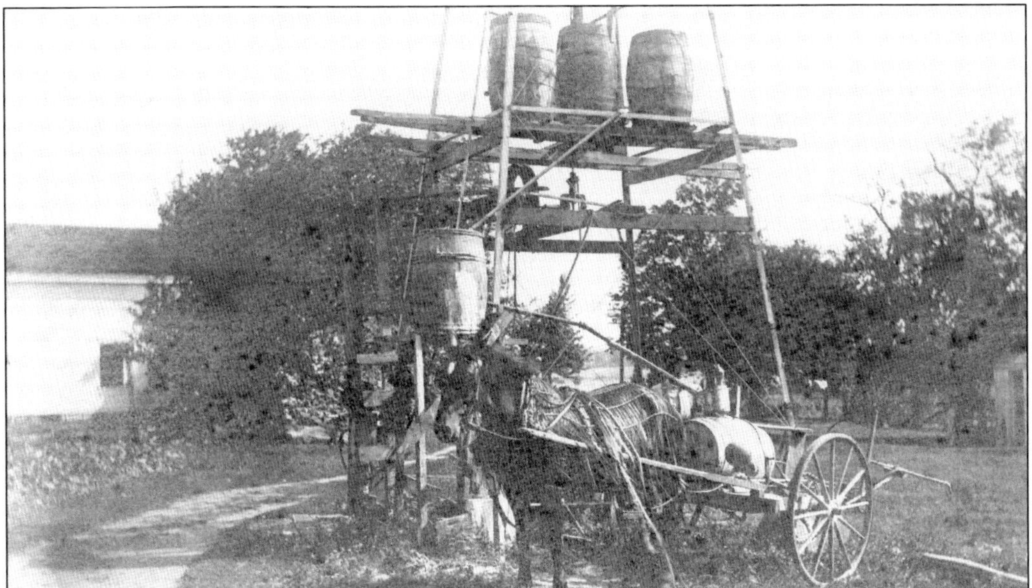

Barrels are in place for filling and storage on the windmill frame, and another barrel is already loaded on the wagon, ready to head to the fields at Cedarcrest Farm. The barrels placed on the windmill frame serve the same function as the water tower on stilts and water can be accessed from them via gravity feed. The windmill became less popular with the availability of rural electricity. (Courtesy of Eleanor Mason DeFreze.)

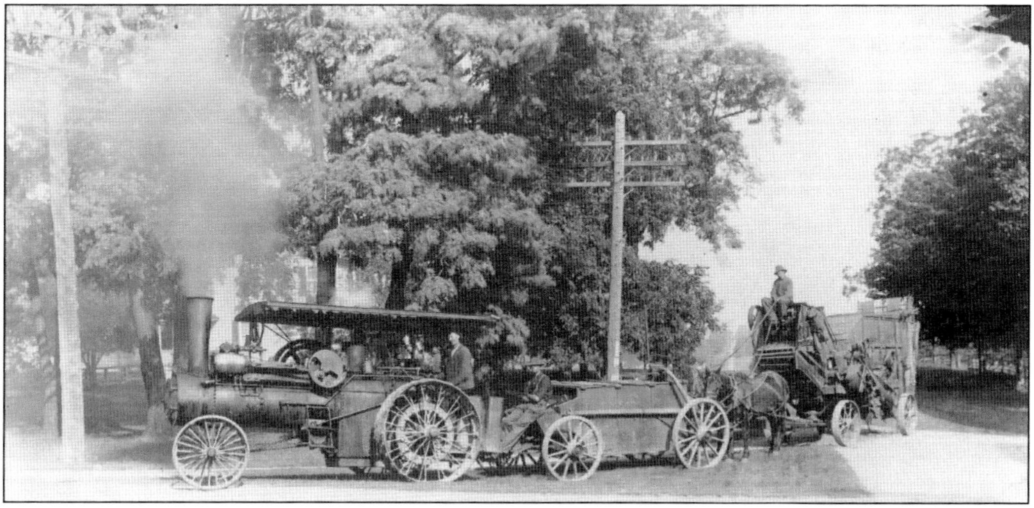

The first portable steam engines became available for agricultural use in the mid-1850s. Initially used to power the thresher, horses were still needed to transport the thresher from farm to farm, as in the image above. The self-propelled steam tractor came along in the 1870s, and by the 1890s, technology had improved the steam tractor sufficiently to allow it to handle the challenges of plowing the farm fields. Steam tractors were noisy—spewing smoke and cinders, often clanking, chugging, and rattling as they moved along at two to three miles per hour. Of course, horse and buggy travelers were not fond of sharing the roads with these machines, and they were often the cause of a bolting horse. Both photographs are of the Behnk family's threshing rigs. The image below, from around 1930–1932, is at the Millers' farm on Stonybrook Road. (Above, courtesy of Pam Bock Ebersold; below, courtesy of Jeanne Yawman.)

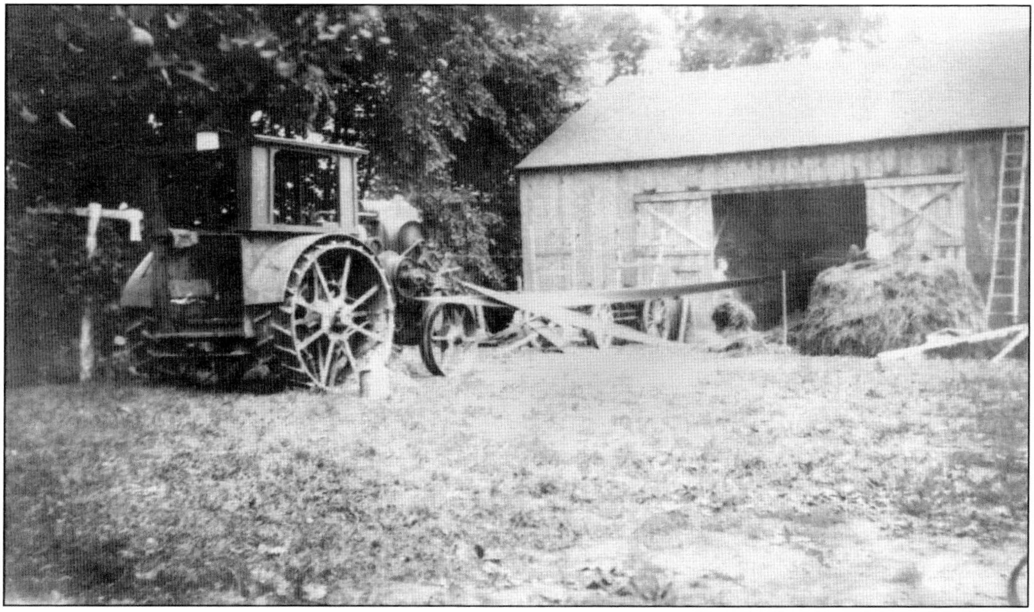

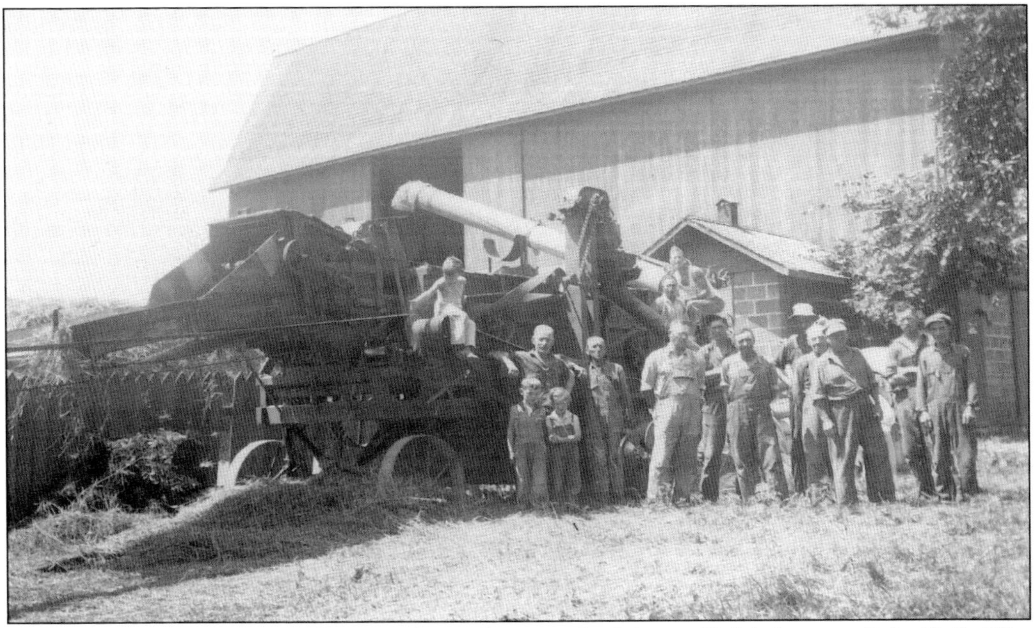

The Behnks' threshing machine is shown here at the Martin-Kuhls barn in July 1943. The thresher was a large rig that was hauled from farm to farm to harvest the grain crops. The arrival of the threshing machine signified hard work, and area farmers helped one another in the effort. It was also a community social event, which included a feast of home-cooked food made by the farmwives. (Courtesy of Robert Martin Kuhls.)

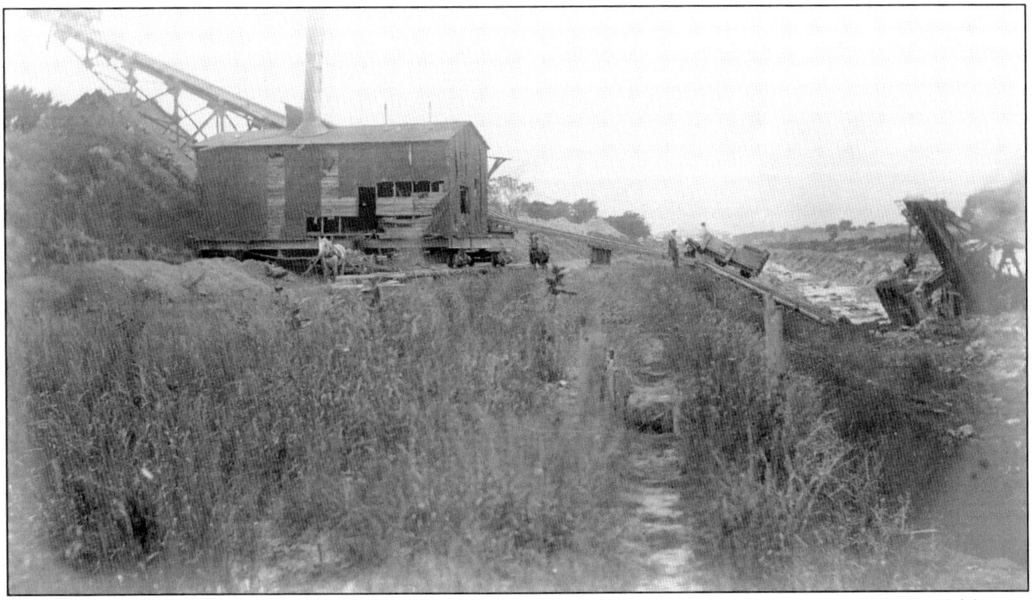

The viner was a part of the scenery in Rush and other rural communities. Farmers would bring their pea vines to the viner where a crew of men would be operating the machine. Steam engines were used to power the viner, and the vines were placed into a revolving drum. The drum would turn, causing the peas to hit against a board. That impact would shell the peas. The peas would be separated from the vines in the process. (Courtesy of Eleanor Mason DeFreze.)

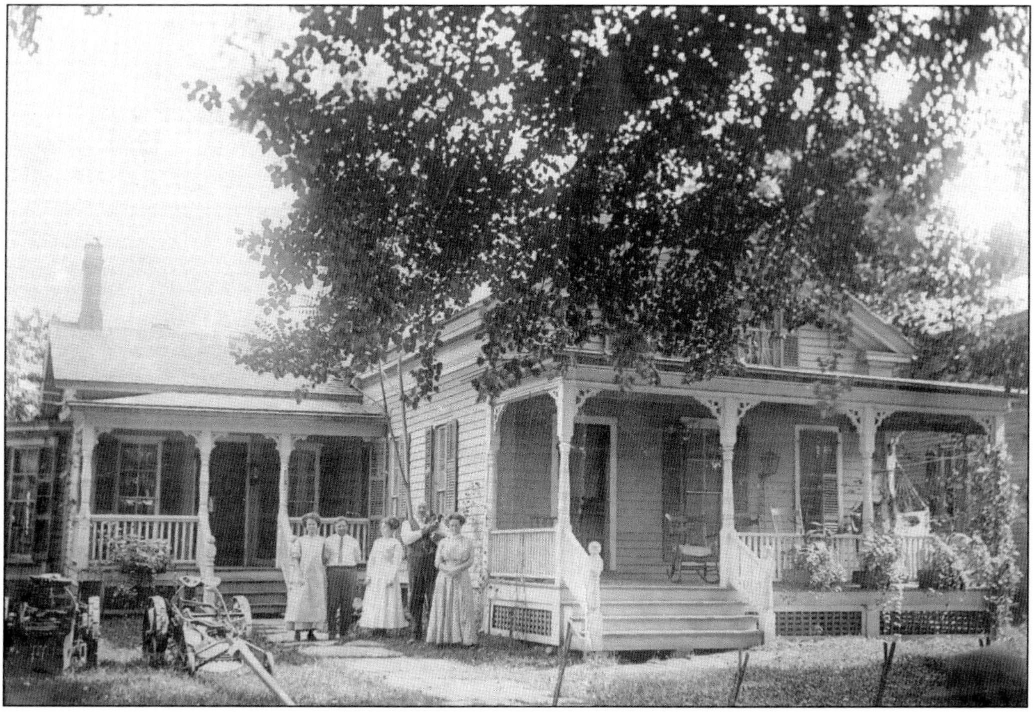

Located just south of the town hall, this home was that of the Longfellow family in the early 1900s. Jesse and Bertha Brooks are believed to be at the far left, an unidentified woman in the center, and Henry and Minnie Kinsey Longfellow at the far right. Henry operated a farm implement and produce business. Perhaps those are some of his wares on the lawn.

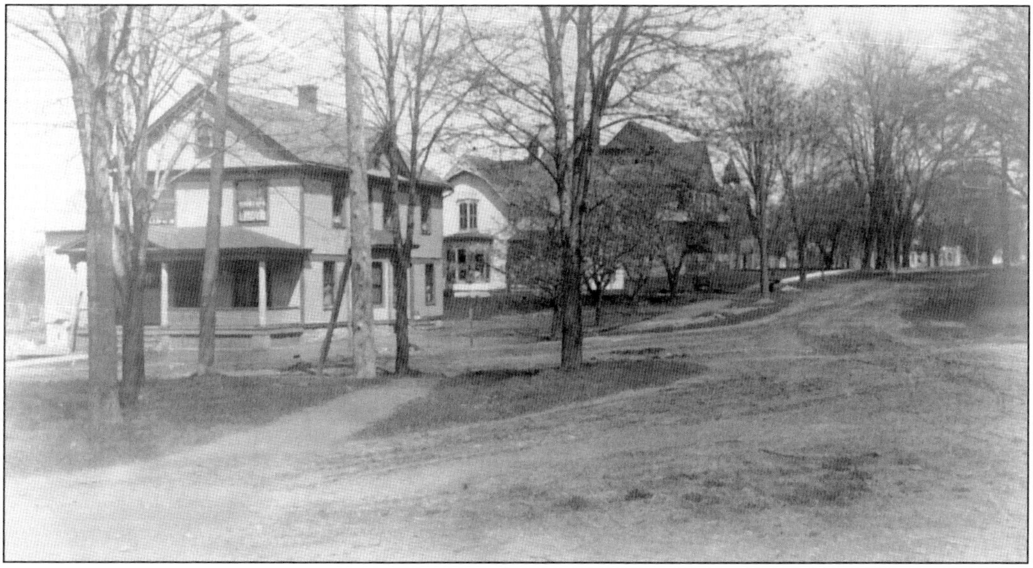

This Park Lane home was built in 1909 by general store owner Norman Sherman and his wife, Anna Dora Lange Sherman. The Sherman Store was on the north side of the creek, but in 1900, Norman moved his store to the Kinsey building and remained there until 1930 when he sold his stock to Harry Britton. Anna operated millinery and dressmaking departments in the early years of the store.

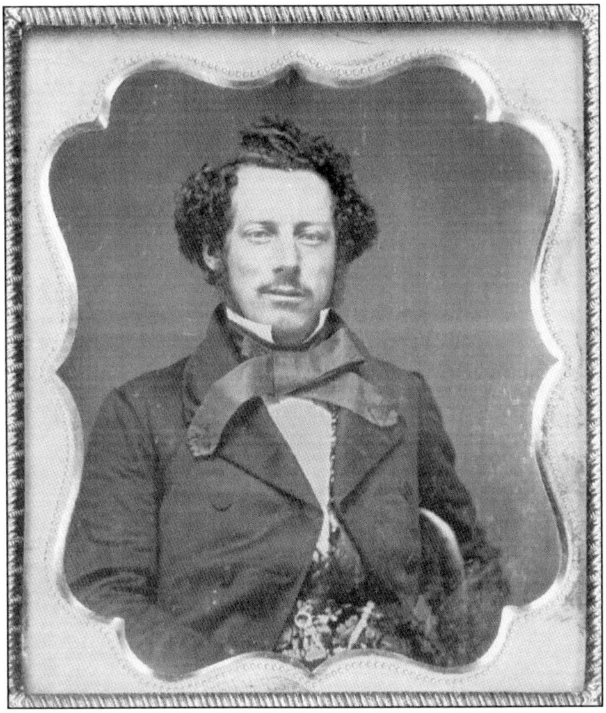

Dr. Socrates Smith moved to Rush in 1823 after graduating from the Vermont Medical School the year prior. In 1829, he married Matilda, daughter of Col. William Markham. Dr. Smith was an active community member, a leader in the temperance movement, and a founding member of the Rush Cemetery Association, belonged to the Rush Methodist Church, and served as a trustee of Genesee Wesleyan Seminary in Lima.

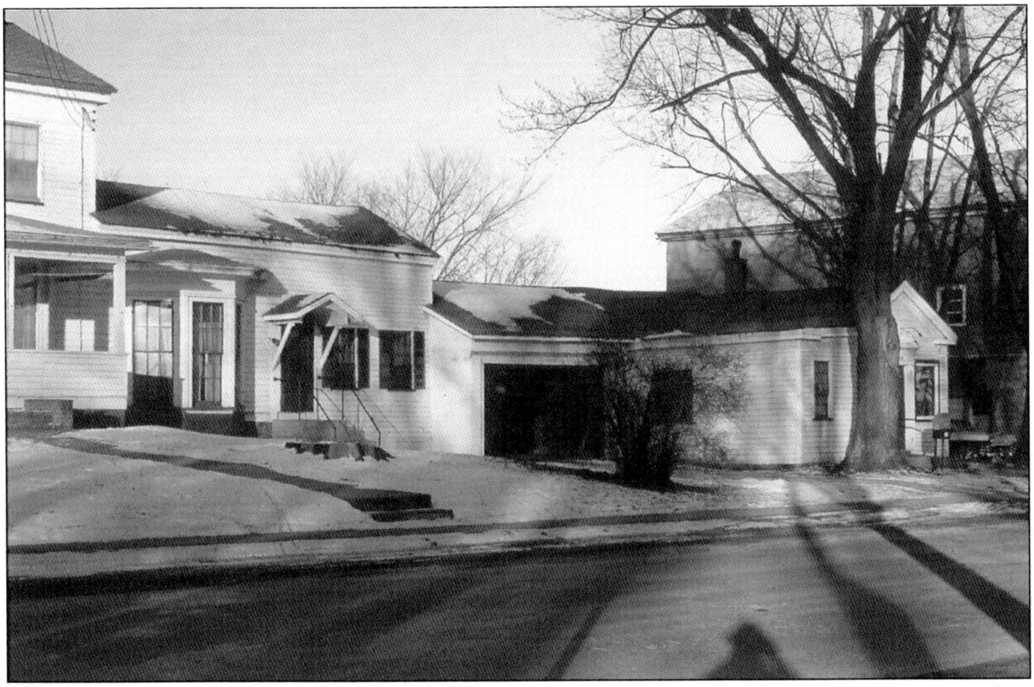

This house was originally the home of Dr. Socrates Smith. From Vermont, Dr. Smith arrived in Rush after medical school and remained here until his death in 1870. It later became the residence of Hallaway Sherman and his wife, Augusta Stull Sherman. Over the years, the small building on the right has served many purposes beyond the doctor's office, including library, post office, and lawn mower shop

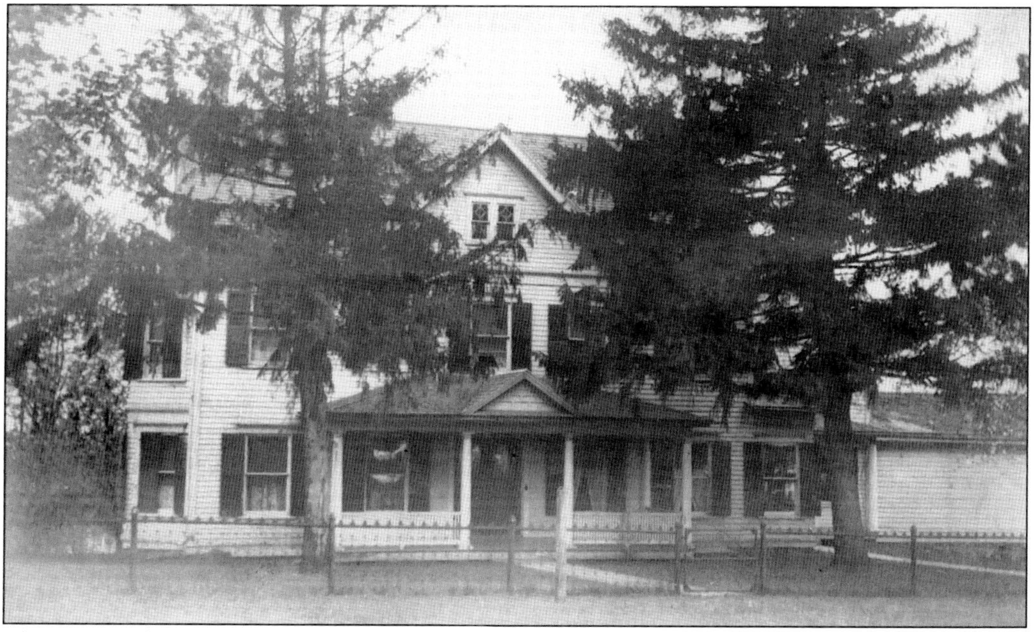

The crossroads of West Henrietta and Rush-Scottsville Roads has been known by a number of names over the years, but Mann's Corners is the name recognized by most. John Mann purchased the Stull homestead in the 1880s. Michael Shearing took ownership of the home and farm by 1900. Diamond's Limousine and Colby's Ice Cream, Bakery and BBQ are currently located on this same corner.

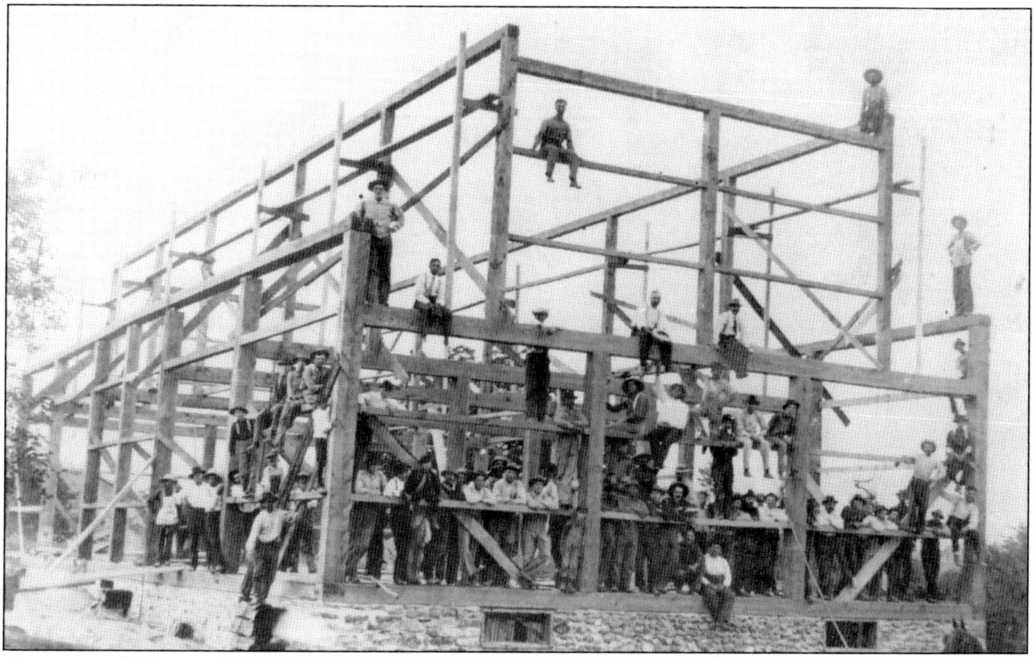

As was tradition at the time, Michael and Catherine Shearing called upon their friends, family, and neighbors to help build their new barn in 1907. The Shearing farm, named Robin's Rest, was a 120-acre property. Henry Krenzer purchased the farm in the late 1930s, and more than a hundred years later, the gambrel-roofed barn is still standing.

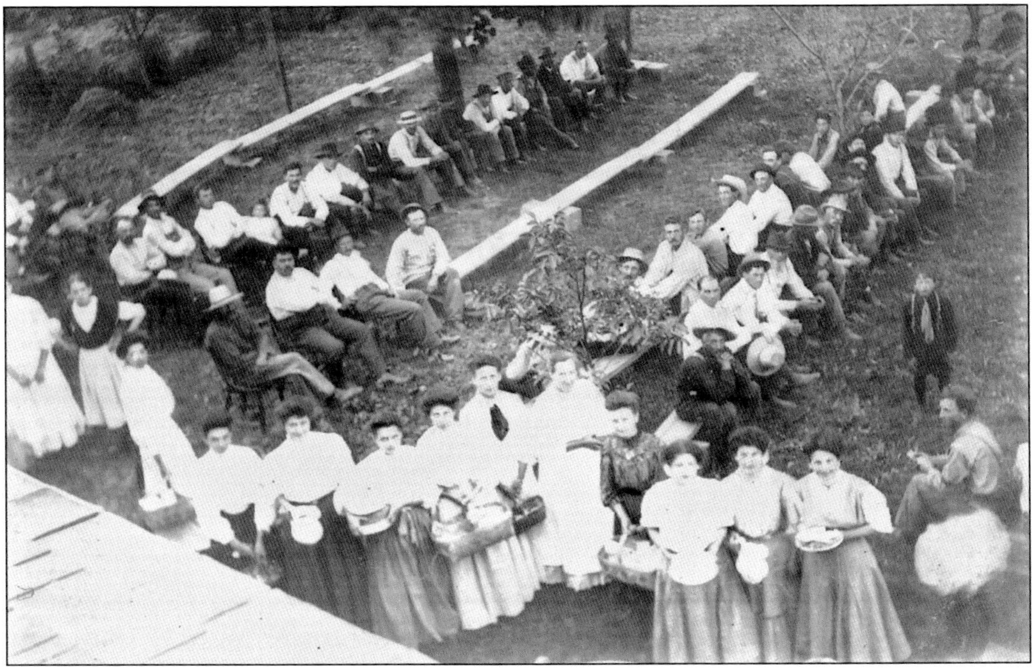

The difficult and dangerous work of building a barn likely worked up a good appetite at the Shearing barn raising. Here, all have gathered for a shared meal and a moment's rest with good food prepared by the women. Whether the occasion was a barn raising or a quilting bee, friends and neighbors came together in times of need and enjoyed one another's company, too.

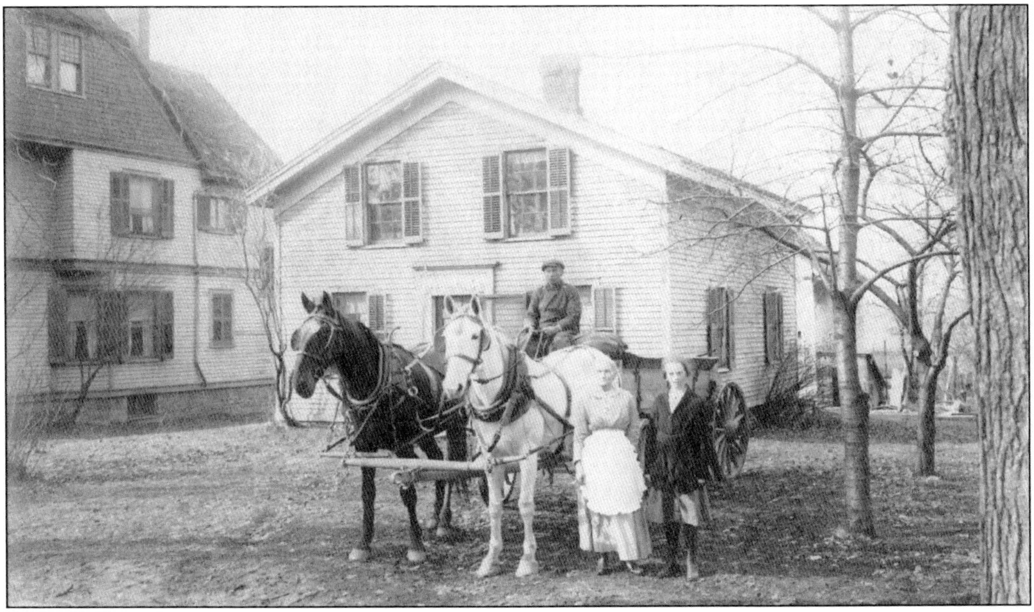

Horace and Alma Mack are pictured on their front lawn with their daughter Sarah Mack Page at 6132 Rush Lima Road. Horace used his team to pick up lumber and other goods from Rochester Junction and deliver it to the State Agricultural and Industrial School. Horace also worked for the Rush Highway Department during the summer months, and his grandson Robert Page worked for Rush Highway for 20 years, 1978–1998. (Courtesy of Robert M. Page.)

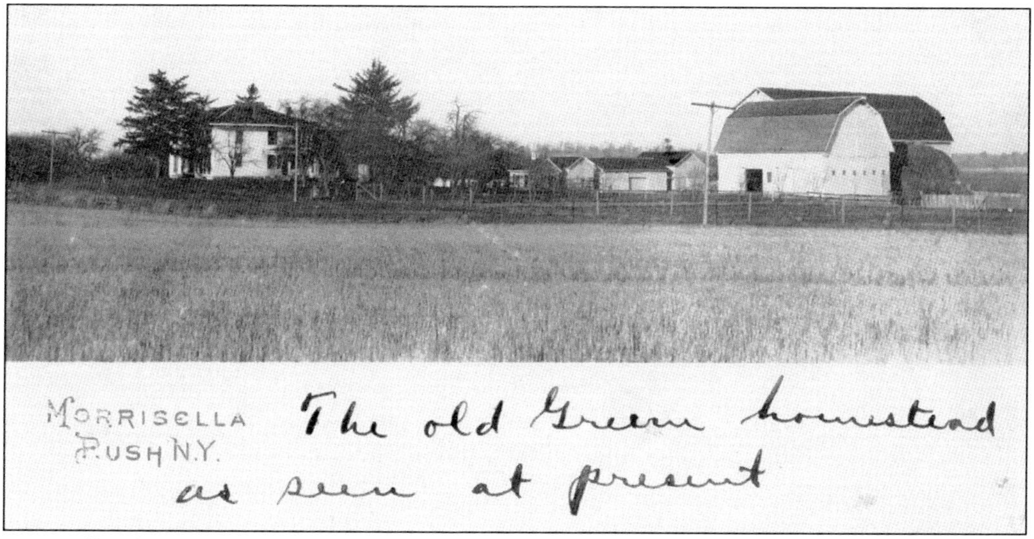

Morrisella, derived from the owners' names, was the name given the farm owned by Maurice C. "Morris" and Ellen Greene Darrohn. The farm had been Ellen's childhood home and she and Morris bought out the heirs. The house dates to the early 1800s. Ellen's father, Nathan Greene, purchased it in 1833 from Beneziah Billings. 902 Rush-West Rush has been the David family farm since 1915. (Courtesy of John David.)

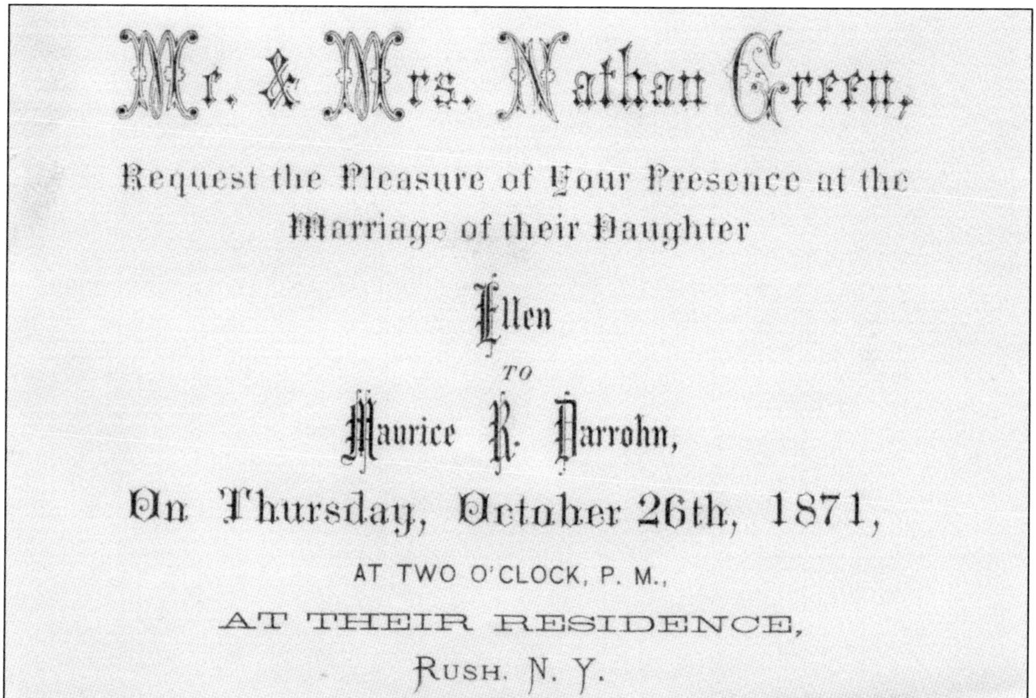

Mr. & Mrs. Nathan Green,

Request the Pleasure of Your Presence at the
Marriage of their Daughter

Ellen

TO

Maurice R. Darrohn,

On Thursday, October 26th, 1871,

AT TWO O'CLOCK, P. M.,

AT THEIR RESIDENCE,

RUSH. N. Y.

Morris was the son of Samuel and Harriet Simpson Darrohn. Samuel was the miller in East Rush. Morris and Ellen met after Morris returned from serving with Company C of the 108th New York Volunteers in the Civil War. Both Morris and Ellen were attending the singing school in North Rush. They married in 1871, on the 25th wedding anniversary of Ellen's parents, and raised a family of seven children. (Courtesy Elaine Darrohn Tennity.)

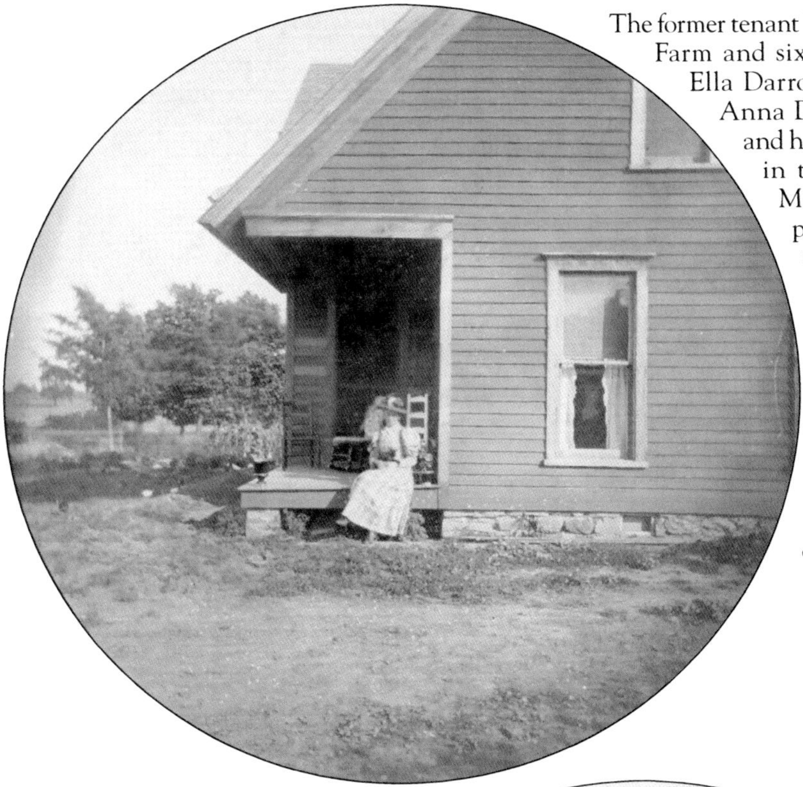

The former tenant house on the Hallock Farm and six acres were sold to Ella Darrohn Hallock's sister Anna Darrohn Millspaugh and her husband, William, in the mid-1890s. The Millspaughs had previously lived in Geneva, but the sisters wanted to live closer to one another. Anna and William remodeled the house, built a barn, and named their new home Mulberry Place. Anna is shown here on the porch.

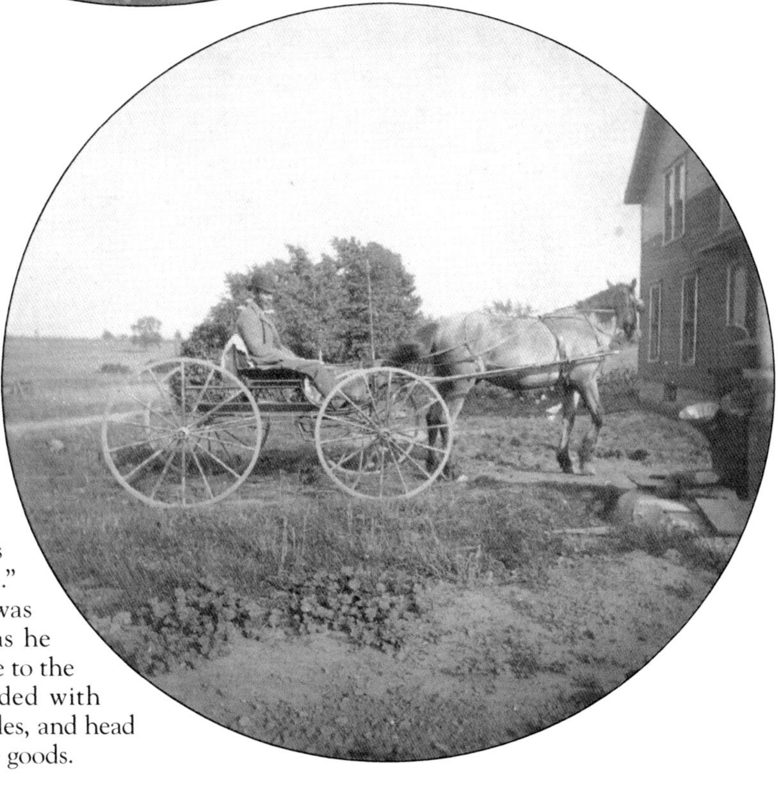

William Millspaugh is pictured here with his horse Neptune, known as the "slow, roan horse." In Bessie Hallock's book, *Here on this Hilltop*, she refers to this same horse as the "laziest horse alive." William, apparently, was a very patient man, as he would harness Neptune to the democrat wagon, loaded with Anna's jellies and pickles, and head to Rochester to sell the goods.

In 1846, William and Phebe Hallock moved to Rush with their three adult sons—James and twins John and William. James soon married Catherine White and they had a son named William Townsend in 1857. He married Ella Darrohn and they had one daughter, Bessie Hallock. Ella was the sister of Morris Darrohn. Bessie was the first historian for Rush, serving from 1944 to 1969. Family members are shown around 1895 in front of the Hallock home, after an extensive 1870 renovation.

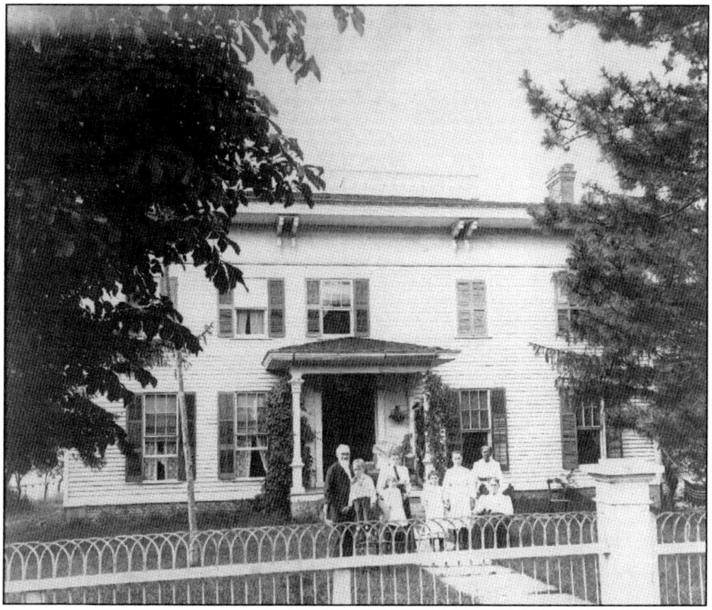

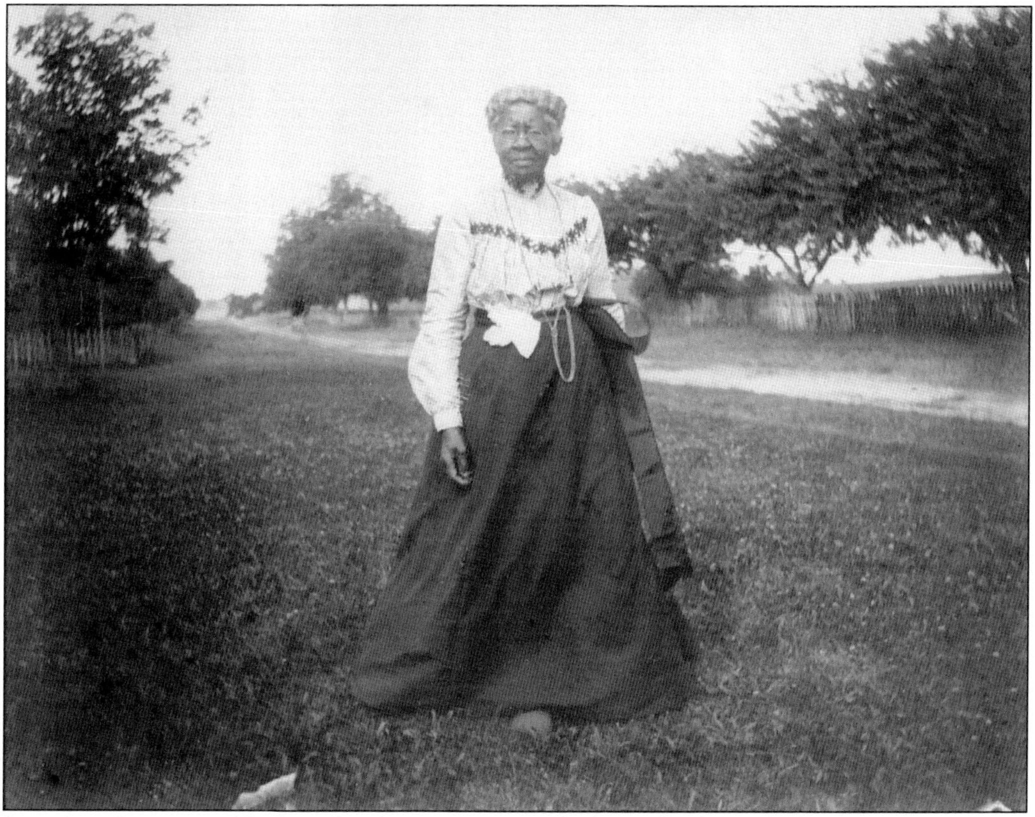

Jane Ann Pierce was 18 when she chose to move with the Hallock family from Ulster County in 1846. Jane cared for the family but was also treated as a member of the family. Other than leaving to help another young family in Rochester for one year, she remained with the Hallocks until her death in 1904. She is buried with the Hallock family in the Friends' Cemetery in Mendon.

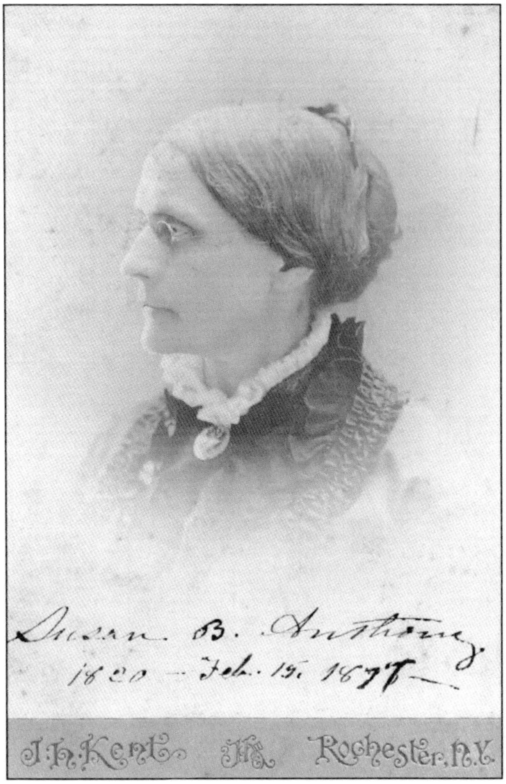

Susan B. Anthony, Frederick Douglass, and Sojourner Truth were all said to have been friends of the Hallock family. The Hallocks were Quakers, and William Hallock and Douglass were known to have discussions with differing views. During one of Douglass's visits, he shared the speech he planned to deliver the following evening in Lima. After the conversation, Douglass reconsidered and adopted the Quaker nonviolent view in his speech. (Courtesy of Ralph Keyes.)

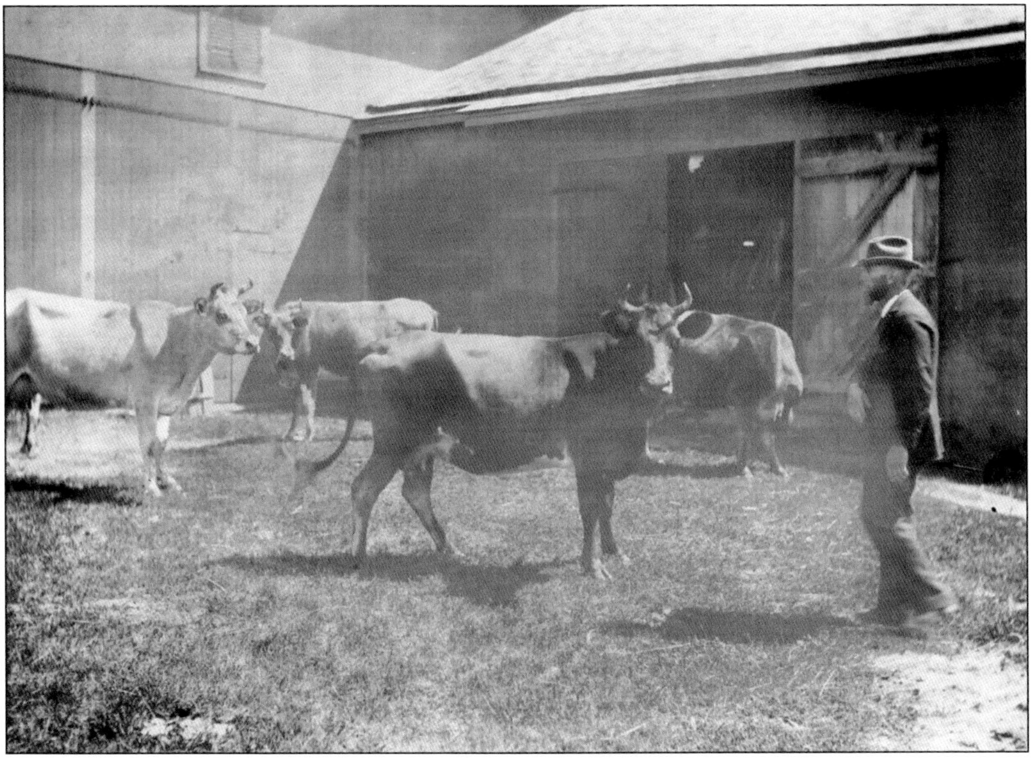

At one time, the Hallock farm consisted of 500 acres and included the brick house on Keyes Road. The junction of Scofield, Keyes, and Rush-Lima Roads was known as Hallock Corners, and the farm was named Cherry Hill Stock Farm. The Hallocks raised pigs, Jerseys, and fruit trees (especially cherry and apple), and had a cider mill. In later years, they also raised flowers. Shown here is William Townsend with his registered Jerseys in the upper barnyard around 1900.

Twin William Hallock married Louisa Root and the couple moved to Keyes Road. Their daughter Phebe Ann married Wayland Addison Keyes in 1891. The wedding was a gala event held at the Hallock house and catered by Rochester chefs. The brick house had been closed upon the death of Phebe's mother and reopened once again to become home for Phebe and her new husband. The residence is currently owned by Ralph Keyes.

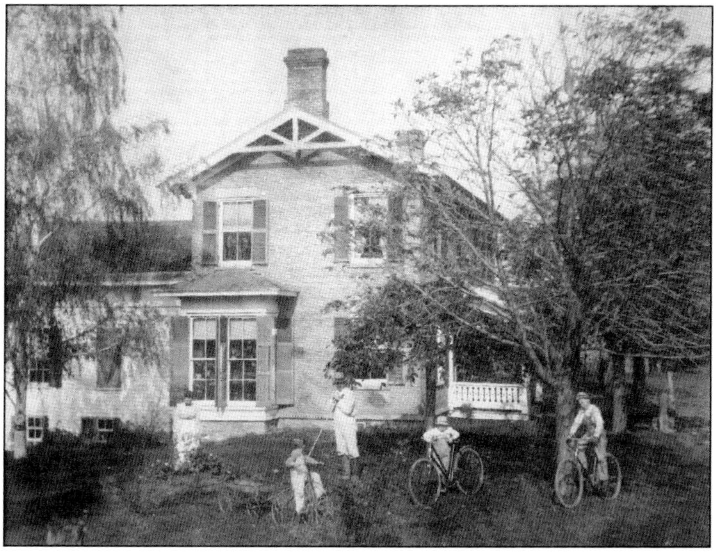

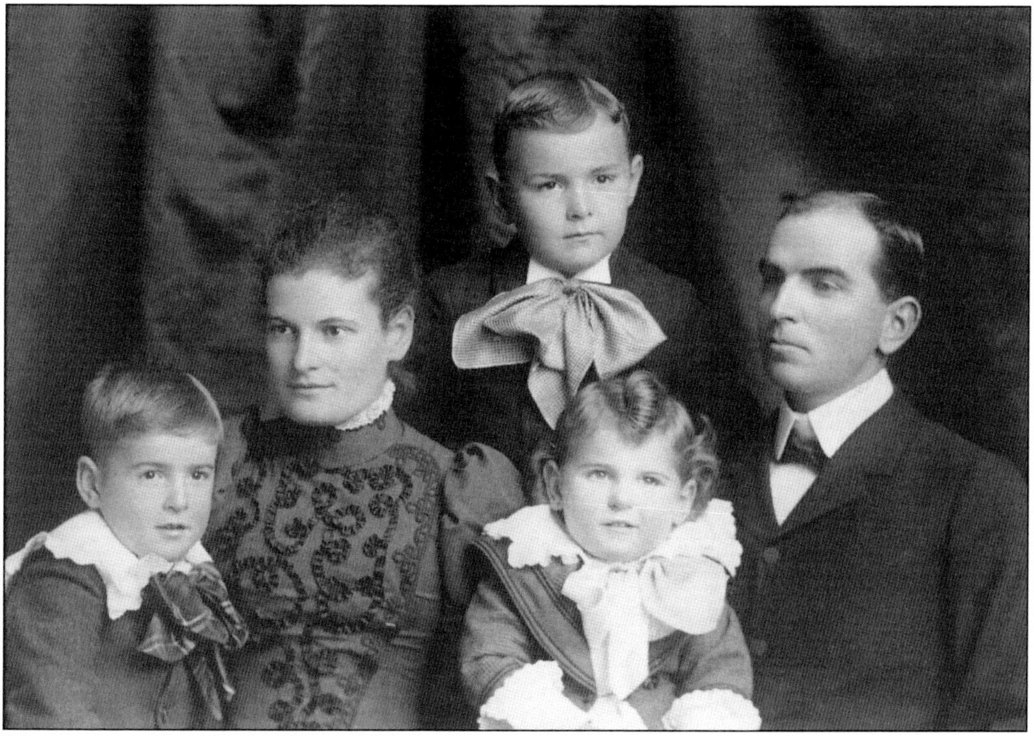

This portrait (c. 1896–1900) is of Wayland and Phebe Keyes with their three young sons. From left to right are Bertram, Phebe Ann, Harold, Dean, and Wayland. Their c. 1814 brick house was once the home of Baptist minister Deacon Lawrence, and the area was known as Abraham's Plains, after Abraham Wright. The 1810 census shows 52 African Americans living in this area, and it is thought perhaps some of them crafted and laid the bricks for the home.

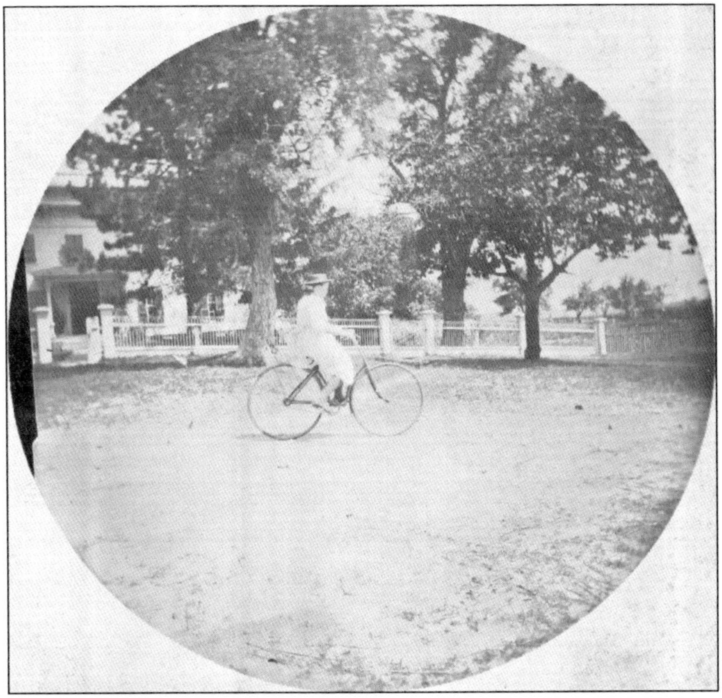

Bessie Hallock seems to have been part of the bicycle fad of the 1890s. The craze reached across all classes and one-third of bicyclists were women. Susan B. Anthony said, "I think it has done more to emancipate women than anything else in the world. It gives women a feeling of freedom and self-reliance." Due to increasing number of bicyclists, special paths were constructed between East Henrietta, Rush, and Honeoye Falls. (Courtesy of Ralph Keyes.)

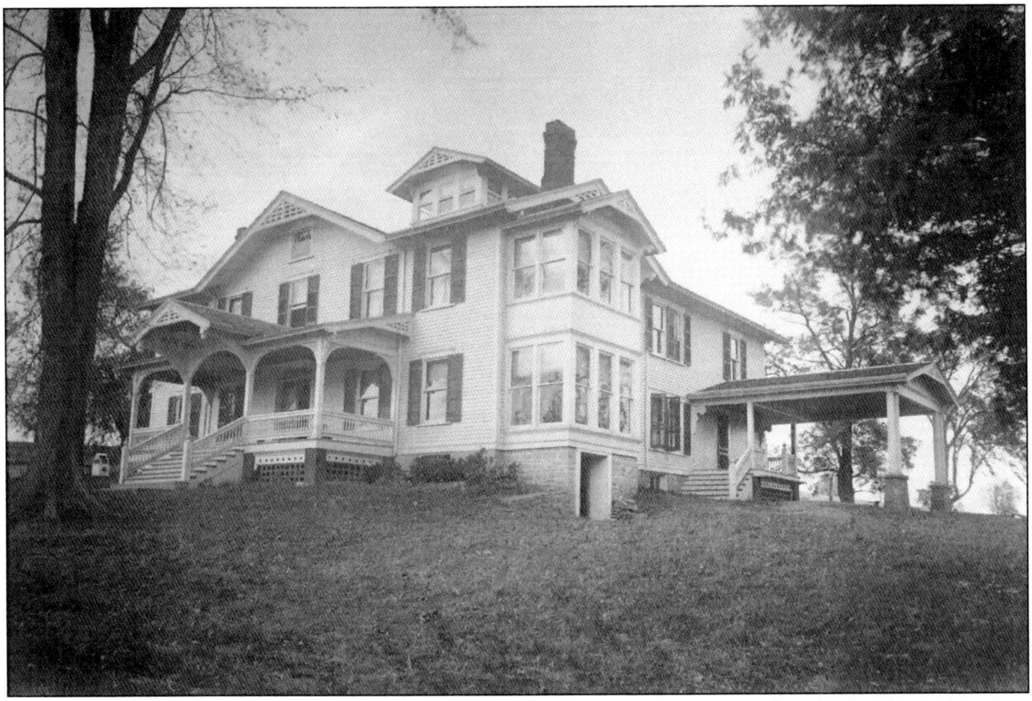

Revolutionary War soldier Nathan Jeffords Sr. came to Rush in 1805. He first built a log cabin, but in time replaced the cabin with a much larger frame house. The home at 1658 Rush-Scottsville Road was sold to Albert W. Keyes in the late 1890s and underwent an extensive renovation. The house suffered a fire in 1929 and was rebuilt without the gable, dormer, and a portion of the second story.

Six

Early Education

As evidenced by the existence of a Rush schoolhouse as early as 1804, it is clear that education was important to the families settling in this area. Although attendance was not mandatory, by 1835, Rush had established 12 school districts. The district lines shifted in the upcoming years. Statistics for 1858 report 10 school districts with a total of 646 students. In 1894, there were 463 school-aged children in Rush. Ten teachers were employed, and their total salaries amounted to $2,801.40.

Over the years, some district schoolhouses were closed and torn down. Others were converted to private homes. The Rush and Henrietta schools centralized, effective July 1, 1947. Prior to centralization, some of the districts consolidated and sent their students to School No. 10, the current site of the Rush post office. School District No. 1, North Rush, was the last school to send its students to the new Rush-Henrietta School. School District No. 1 finally closed its doors in 1951.

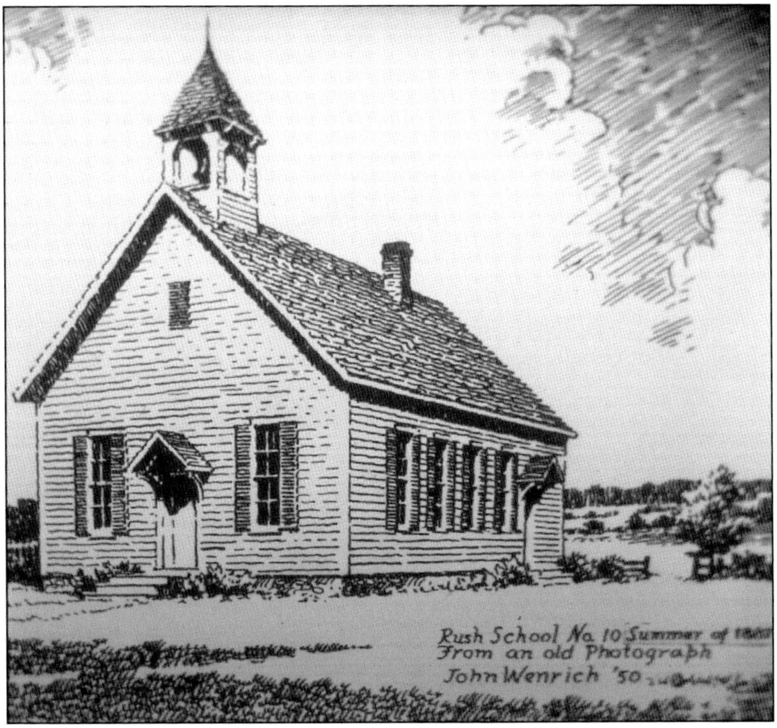

John Wenrich sketched this picture of School No. 10 from a photograph taken in the summer of 1887. The two-room frame schoolhouse was built in 1884 by carpenters James Congdon and Leonard Goff, replacing the earlier 1840s cobblestone building. The 1884 schoolhouse burned in 1916 and was replaced by a larger, brick building the following year. School No. 10 is currently the Rush post office.

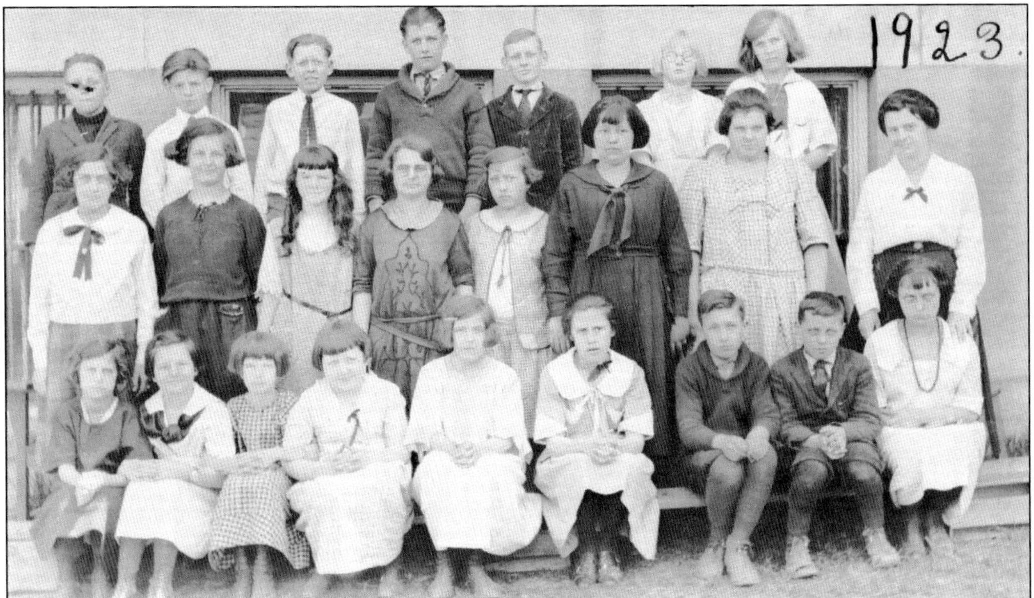

Pictured in 1923 are the fifth-grade students in Miss Upton's class at School No. 10. From left to right are (first row) Elizabeth Harris, Mellie Sherman, Laura Harris, Catherine Brooks, Gladys Dell, Marguerite Cunningham, Roy Welderly, Stanley Bailey, and Jennie Bailey; (second row) Mildred Schoen, Eleanor Kinsey, Margaret Olson, Rayma Keyes, Margaret Welderly, Orma Thomas, Ida Martin, and Miss Upton; (third row) Staton Bailey, Joe Cunningham, Donnell Wood, Joe Slattery, Martin Spallman, Wanda Witlock, and Mary Loss.

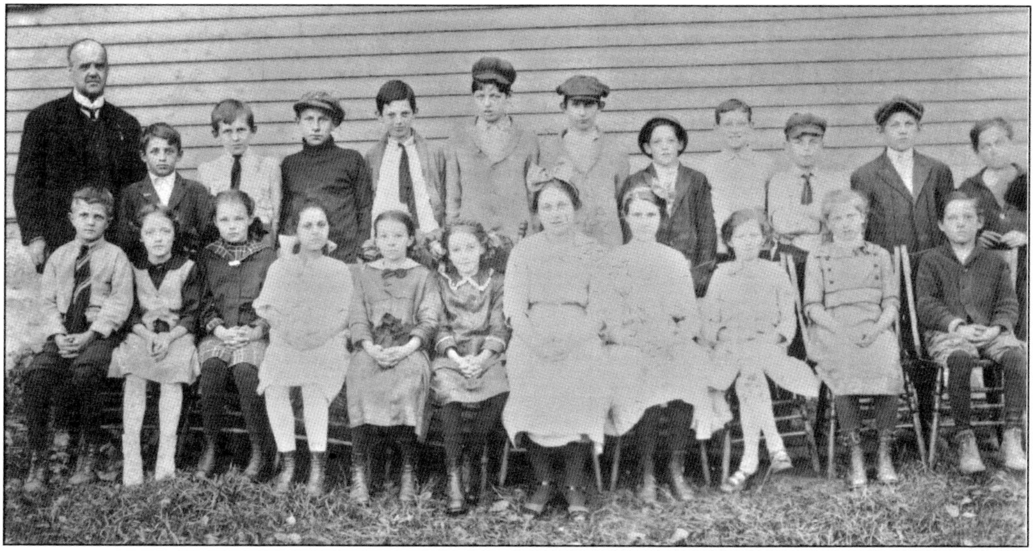

S.T. Jennings was the teacher in the "Big Room" at School No. 10, also referred to as the Rush Graded School. Pictured here, from left to right, are (first row) Harry Kinsey, Elsie Fishell, Dorothy White, Cornelia Price, Virginia Wood, Esther Diver, Mabel Long, Frances Bower, Sarah Mack, Augusta Lawrenz, and unidentified; (second row) Jennings, Raymond Bock, Vincent Behnk, Herb Behnk, Jessy Hopkins, Schyler White, Johnny Straub, James Riley, unidentified, Graydon Lonthair, and the last two are unidentified. (Courtesy of William Gaffney.)

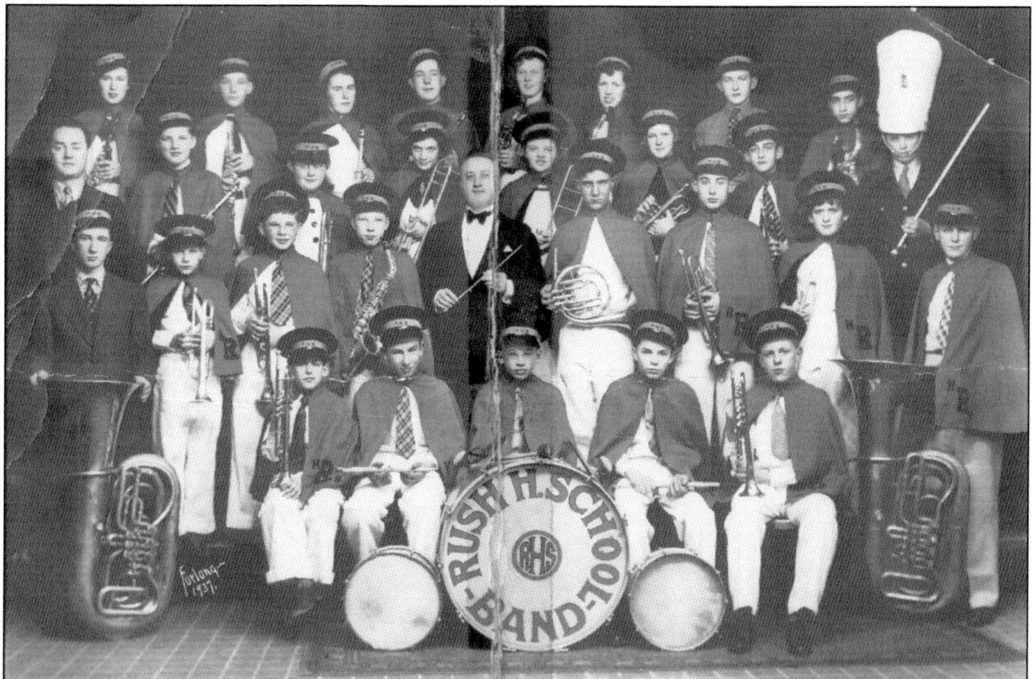

The 1937 Rush High School Band is shown in full uniform. Nelson Doescher was the band instructor, and George Yackel was the school principal. Since rebuilding and opening again in 1919, School No. 10 was officially named the Union Free School District. Many, however, still referred to it as School No. 10.

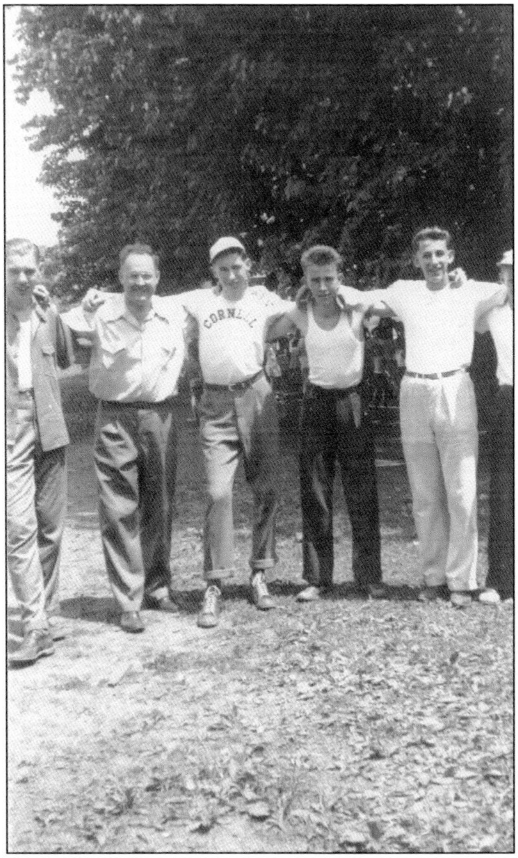

This c. 1941 photograph is of a group of Rush High School students with principal George C. Yackel. From left to right are Joe Swartz, Yackel, Jim Gaffney, Ken Martin, Lynn Behnk, and Art Klick (partially shown). (Courtesy of Jeanne Yawman.)

The third building on the site, School No. 10's brick structure, opened in 1917. An annex was built in 1927 to ease crowded conditions. During a school afternoon in 1948, fire broke out and the students had to evacuate quickly—everyone exited without injury. The 1938 statistics show that the school had 11 teachers, 180 students, and 12 rooms. In 1952, School No. 10 was closed and students attended the new Central School.

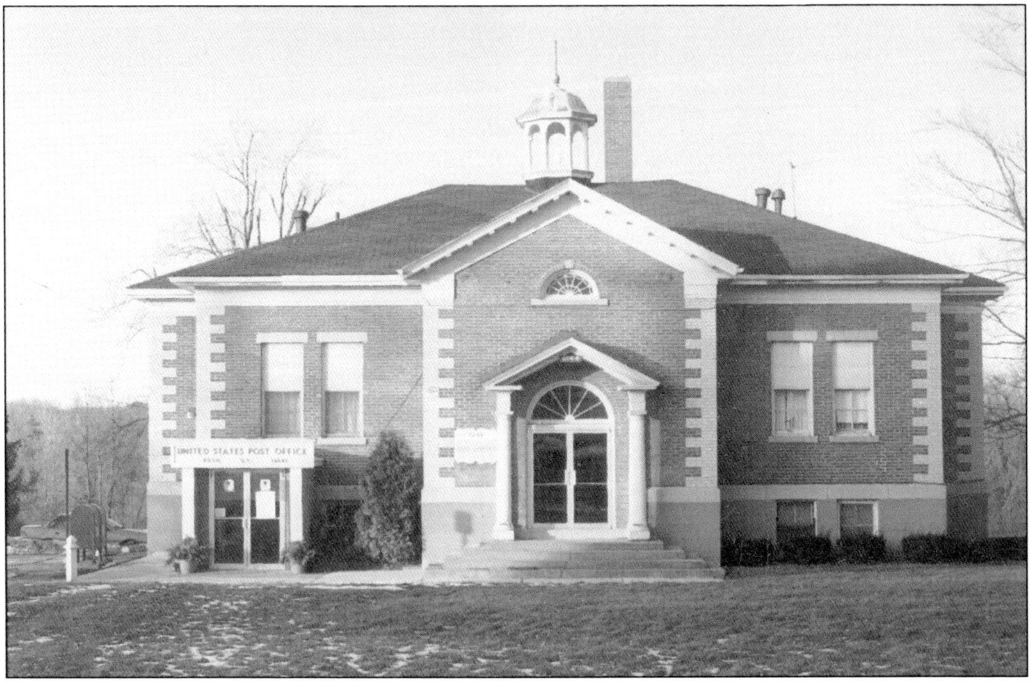

Students attending the Mann's Corners school, known as School No. 4, in this c. 1911 photograph are, from left to right, (first row) Hyman Goldstein, unidentified, Cornelia Price, Dorothy Fielder, Sarah Goldstein, Alice Klink, and Howard Keifer; (second row) Harry David, Ed David, teacher, unidentified, and Dewey Schearing. (Courtesy of John David.)

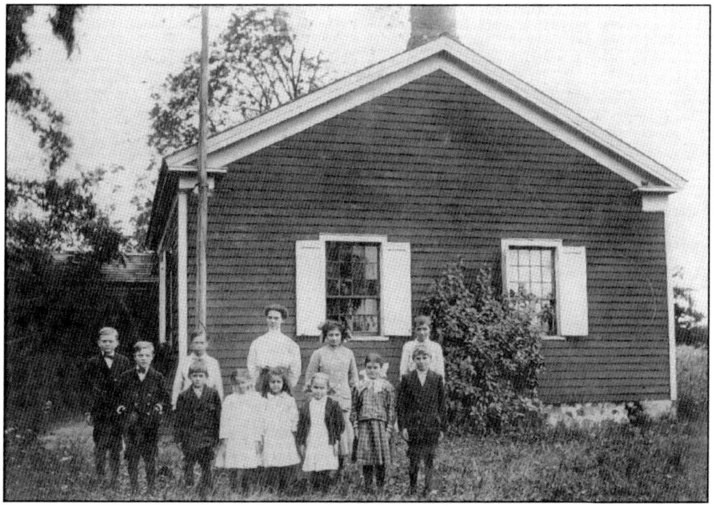

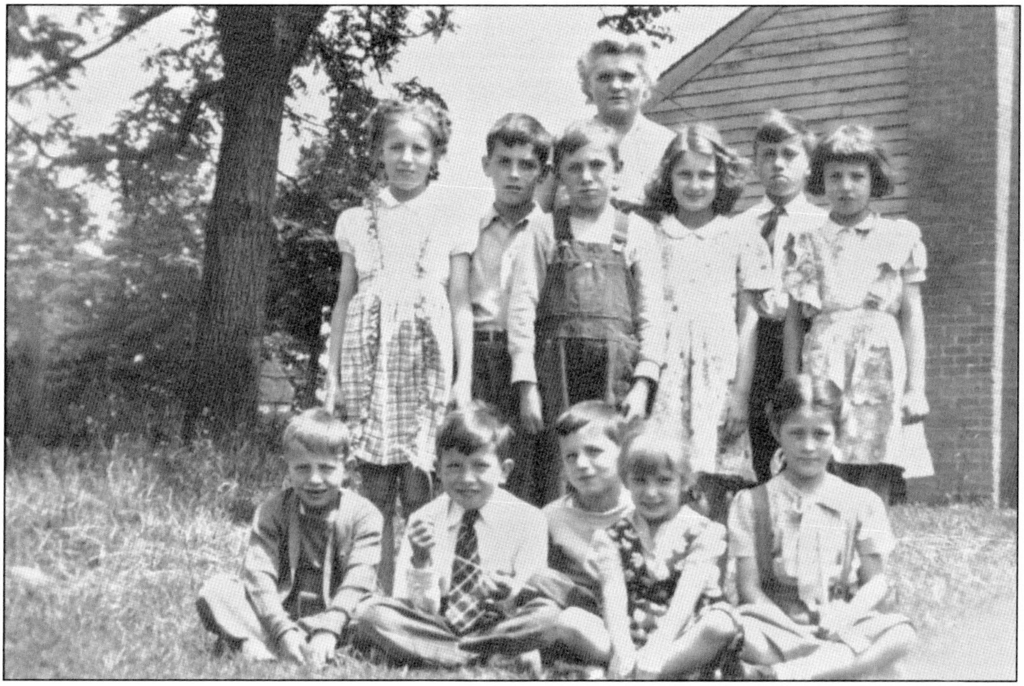

In 1946, Mrs. L.B. Hetzer was the teacher at the Mann's Corners schoolhouse. A neighbor, Emma Green, came once a week and provided music instruction. Ellsworth Wasson, of Wasson's Lunch Counter, was the photographer of this class picture. Each student received a copy by mail over the summer. Pictured, from left to right, are (first row) Richard Mason, Don Gruschow, Gerald Lonthair, Joyce Smith, and Barbara Sawdey; (second row) Joan Mason, Fred Spooner, Russell Lonthair, Dorothy Krenzer, Norman Gruschow, and Eleanor Mason; (in back) Mrs. Hetzer. (Courtesy of Eleanor Mason DeFreze.)

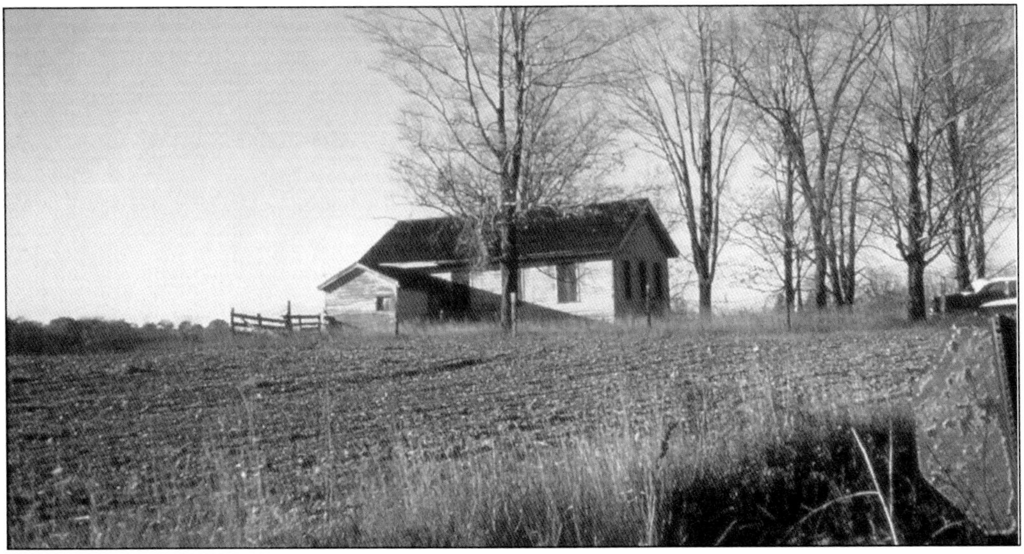

The North Rush School was Rush District School No. 1 and records indicate the first school building was a log structure built in 1822. In 1830, a stone schoolhouse was built on the south side of Rush-Scottsville Road, west of East River Road. In 1850, Henry B. Hart provided land for the schoolhouse pictured here, across from the church on East River Road.

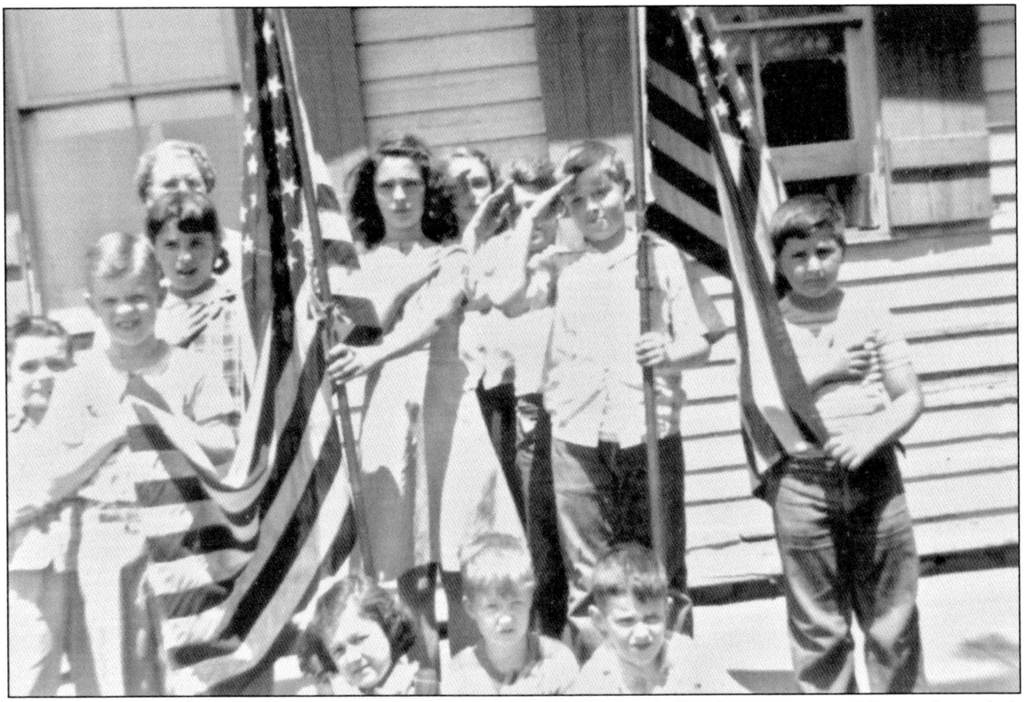

May Papka was the teacher in the final years of School No. 1. Students pictured here, from left to right, are (first row) Sharon Slocum, Paul Little, and Scott Stebbins; (second row) Johnny Checker, John Wheeler, Pat Checker, Mrs. Papka, Mary Ellen Checker, unidentified, Al Moulton, Curt Quince, and Sam Caffelone. This picture was taken in about 1950. School No. 1 closed in 1951, the last of the district schools to send its students to the Rush-Henrietta Central School. (Courtesy of Pat Dart Page.)

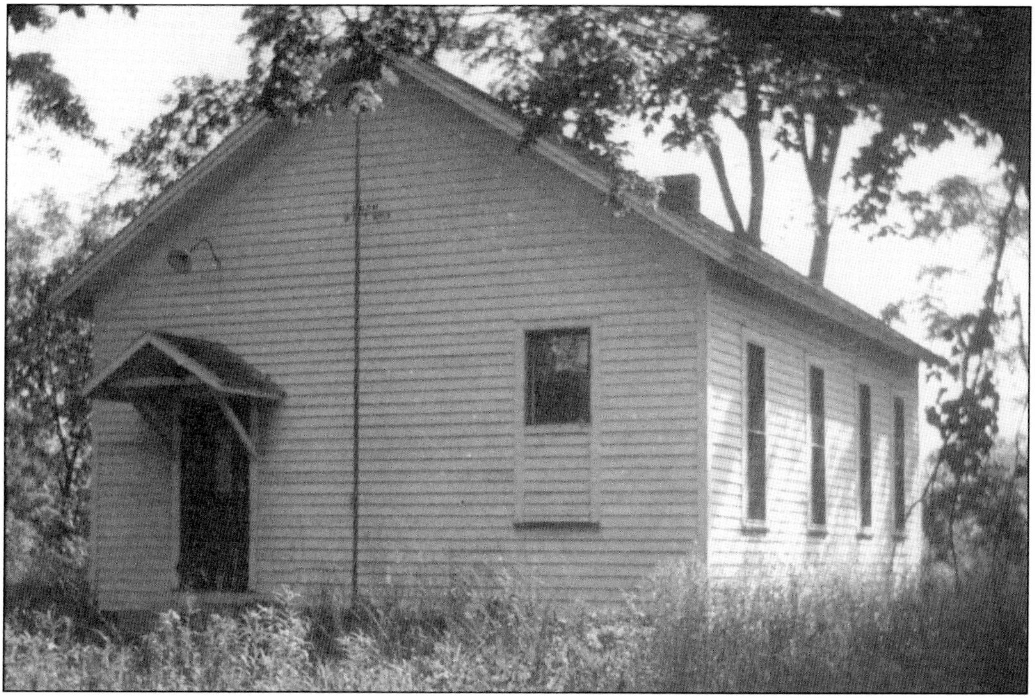

Constructed in 1864, the building at 575 Five Points Road was originally Rush District School No. 9. The land for the schoolhouse was deeded from the Galentine family for the purpose of a school building site. Prior to centralization with Henrietta, some of the Rush District schools began to consolidate. School No. 9 made an agreement with School No. 10 for transportation and instruction in 1945, and the little schoolhouse was closed. It was sold by public auction in 1947 and converted to a private home.

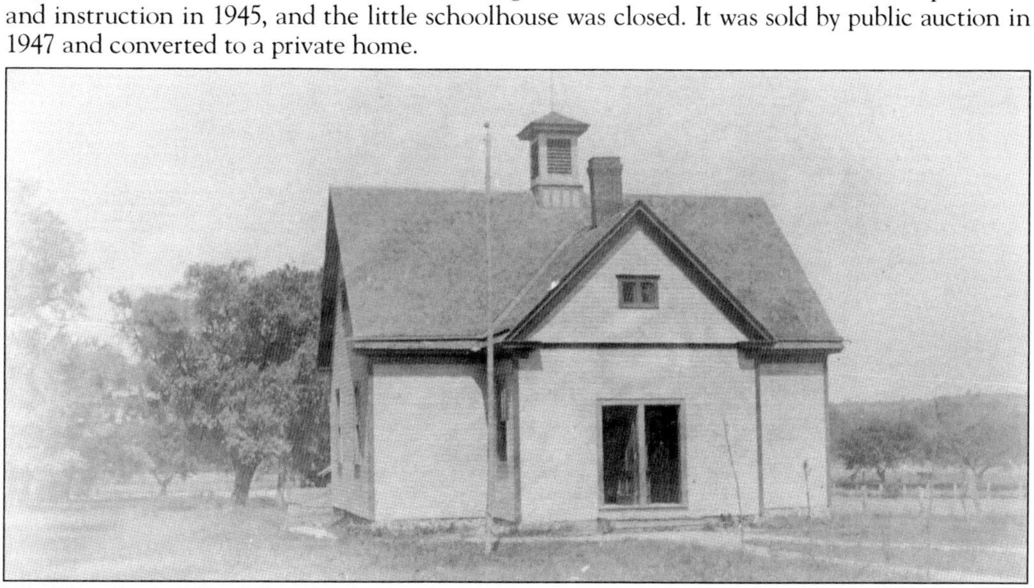

The West Rush School dates back to 1812. In 1849, an acre of land was purchased as the location for a new schoolhouse. A new building was constructed on the same site in 1897. In the 1940s, centralization was being discussed, and the decision of whether to join with Avon or Rush-Henrietta was under consideration. In 1946, West Rush School No. 7 joined the Rush-Henrietta Central District. (Courtesy of Eleanor Mason DeFreze.)

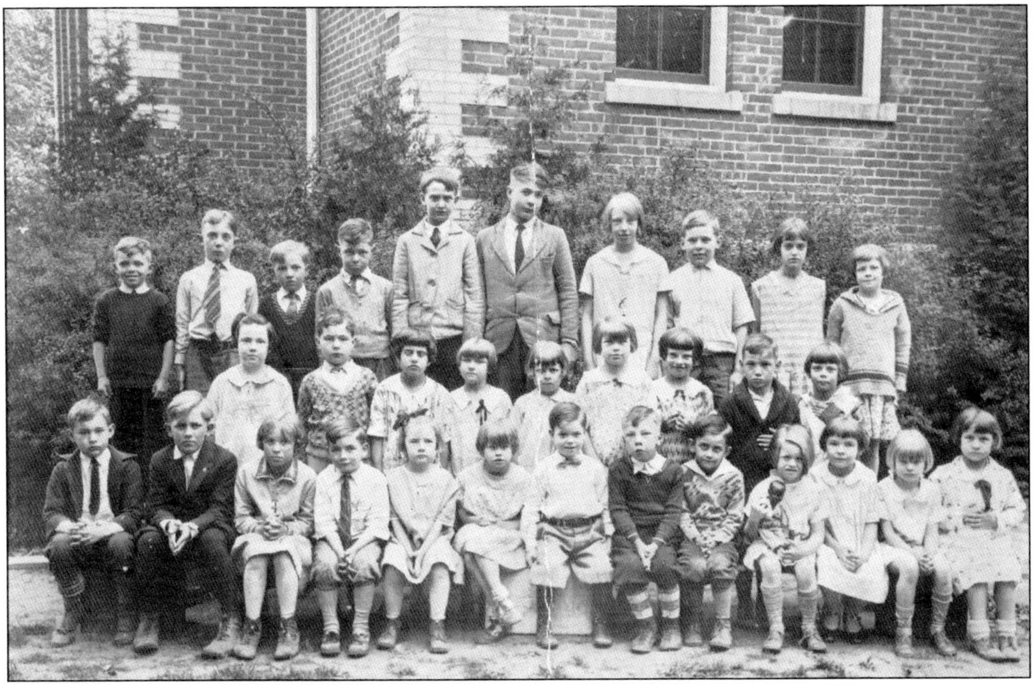

This is Mrs. Harry Hart's second-grade class at School No. 10. The year is 1930.

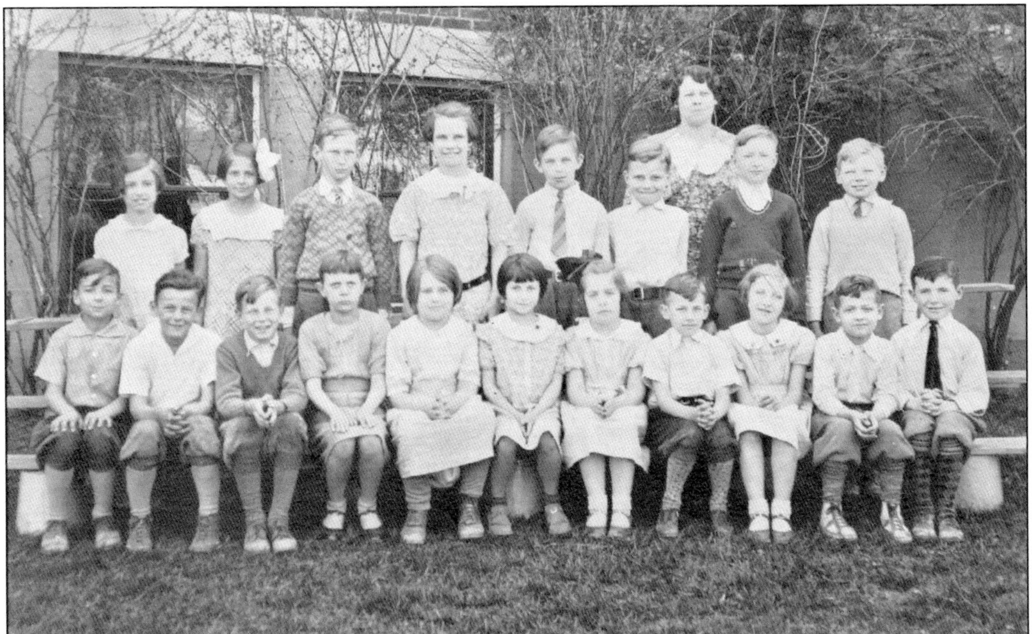

Mrs. Moulton is shown here in the early 1930s with her third and fourth graders at School No. 10. Lined up, from left to right, are (first row) Earl Yawman, Richard Bock, Teddy Faugh, Betty Lonthair, Emily Keyes, Norma Miller, Lois Fishell, Lynne Behnk, Caroline Finley, Billy Fyle, and Jimmie Gaffney; (second row) Jeanne Yawman, Mary Rose Fuoco, Harold Shultz, Ruth Sherman, Harold Fergusen, Gordon Christintine, Leslie Stowl, and Milton Desens. (Courtesy of Jeanne Yawman.)

Seven

Churches

The first religious society in town was the Associated Baptist Society of Rush. Members began their meetings in 1804 and formally organized the society in 1830. The Evangelical Lutheran Reformed Church of Rush and the First Methodist Episcopal Church of Rush were formed in 1830 and 1831, respectively.

Several different churches and societies have existed in the community's past. Some thrived and grew larger, some merged and formed new churches, and others dissolved altogether. Regardless of the religious belief, it is the role that religion and church have played in the lives of the community members that is important. Religion was an integral part of daily life, and the church was an important part of the social fabric of the community.

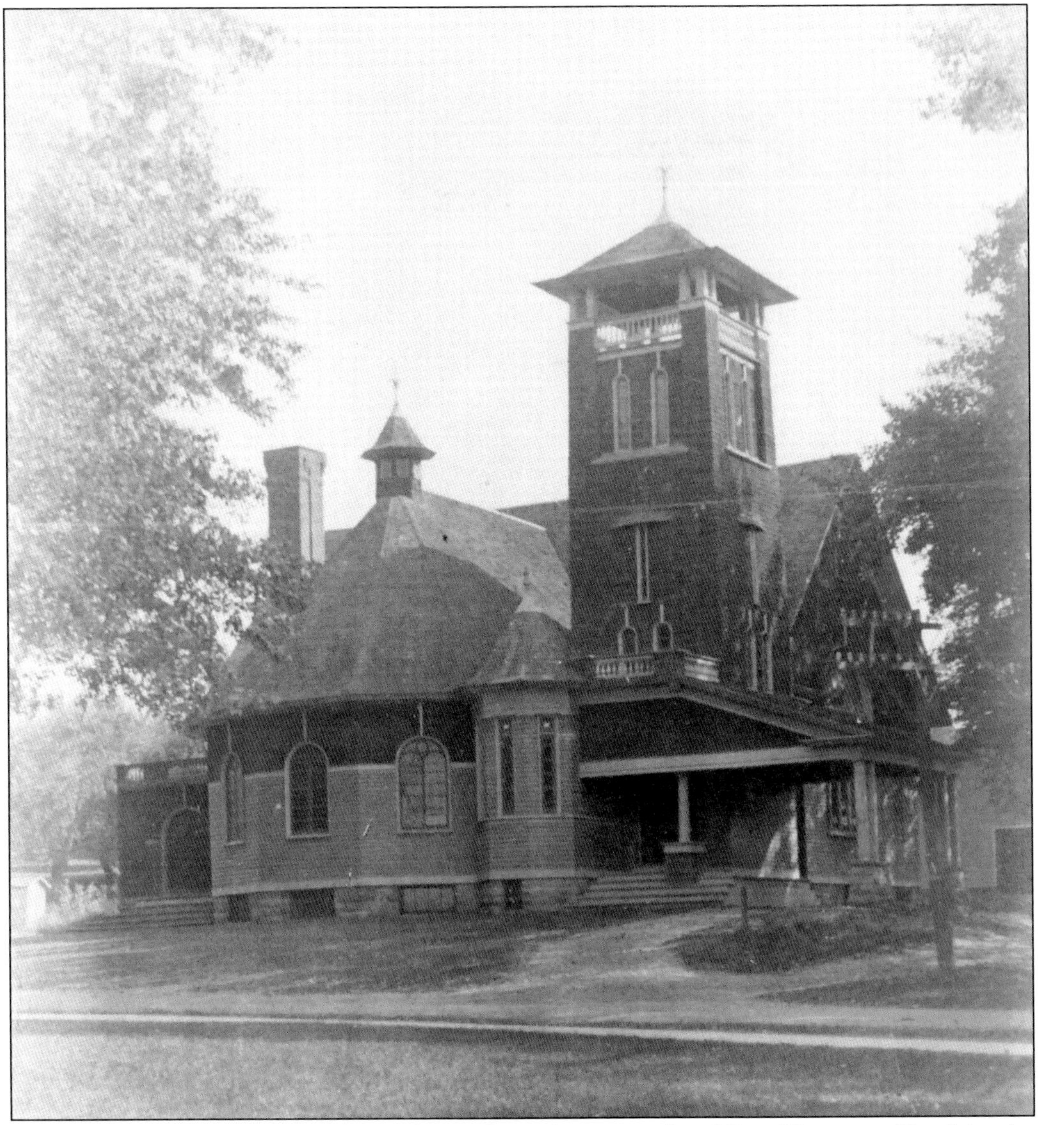

In 1844, the Methodist church was located on the west side of East Henrietta Road in the hamlet. It was rebuilt after an 1850 fire, but the "Big Fire" of 1892 consumed multiple buildings, and the church was rebuilt at 6131 Rush Lima Road (photograph taken around 1909). In 1995, the Methodist church relocated to its present home just east of the old church. Shiloh Church of God in Christ is the current owner of the old Methodist church.

After the fire of 1850, the Methodist parsonage was relocated to an existing house just west of School No. 10. A new parsonage was built in 1889 on the west half of the parsonage lot. An old stone meetinghouse at Mann's Corners was torn down about this same time and some of those stones were used in the foundation of the new parsonage.

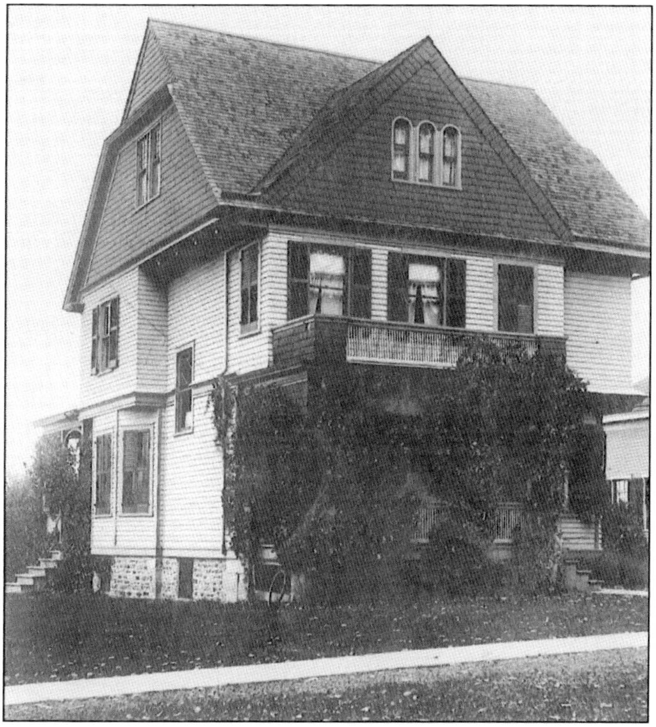

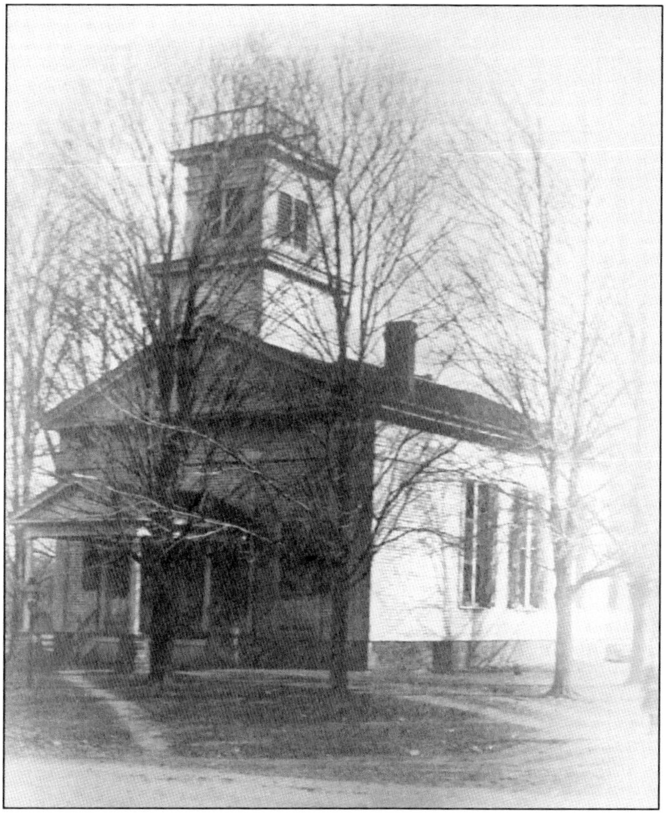

In 1834, the First Christian Society of the Town of Rush was formed, and in 1835, a church was built at the fork in the road at North Rush. Known as the North Rush Church, it faced south and had a porch covering the two front entrance doors. A new church was built in 1873, and this church was moved to an adjoining farm and turned into a barn. (Courtesy of Eleanor Mason DeFreze.)

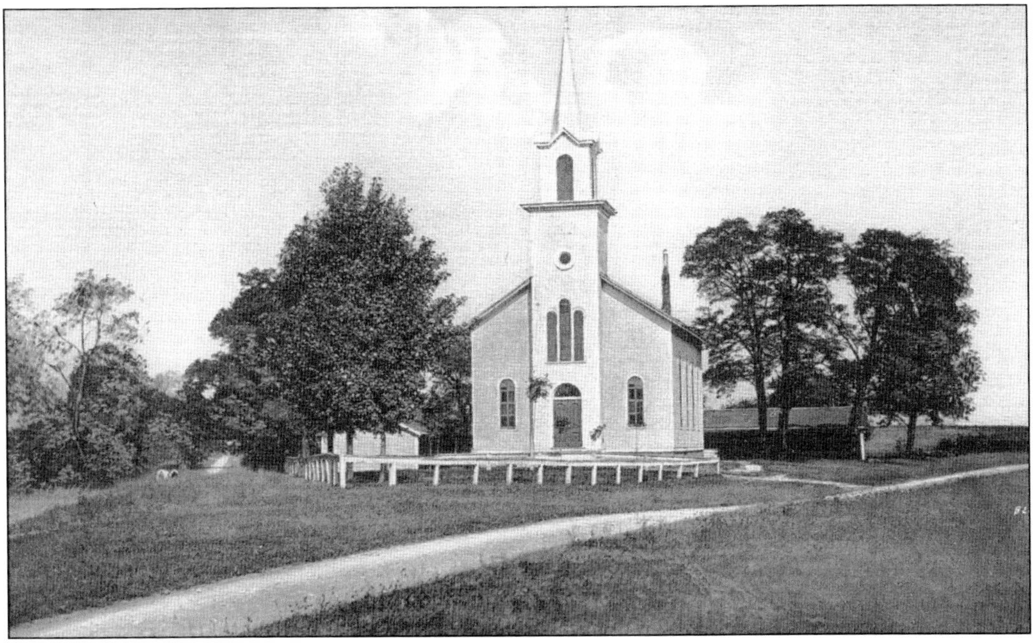

The new church at North Rush was dedicated in January 1874. The carriage and storage sheds behind the church were built in 1843, with the second shed added approximately 30 years later. The society purchased a bell from a church in Dundee in 1902, and in 1934, the church celebrated its centennial. The building was lost to fire in 1958 and reconstructed of brick. Today, the building is the Wheatland Community Church. (Courtesy of Eleanor Mason DeFreze.)

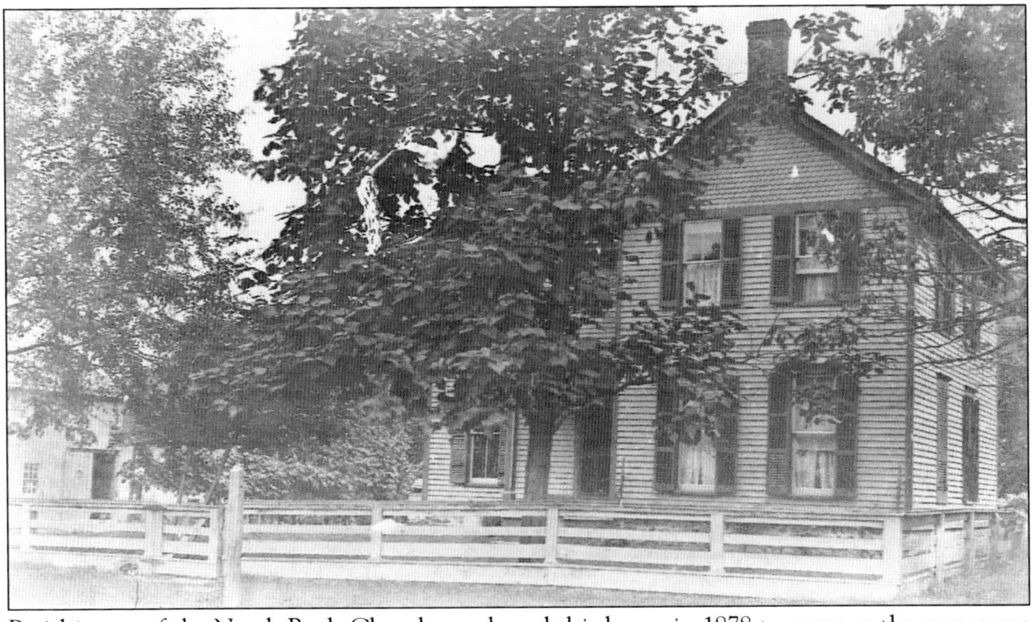

Parishioners of the North Rush Church purchased this home in 1878 to serve as the parsonage for their church. The home had previously belonged to a former pastor, Rev. William A. Sibley. The house is located at 6879 East River Road and is currently owned by Rob Lewkowicz.

In 1934, the North Rush Church observed its 100th anniversary. It was noted at that time that four families had been associated with the church from its beginning. They were the Hart, Ely, Martin, and Bushman families. This 1941 photograph is of pastor Gordon Gilkey and his wife, Mary. (Courtesy of Eleanor Mason DeFreze.)

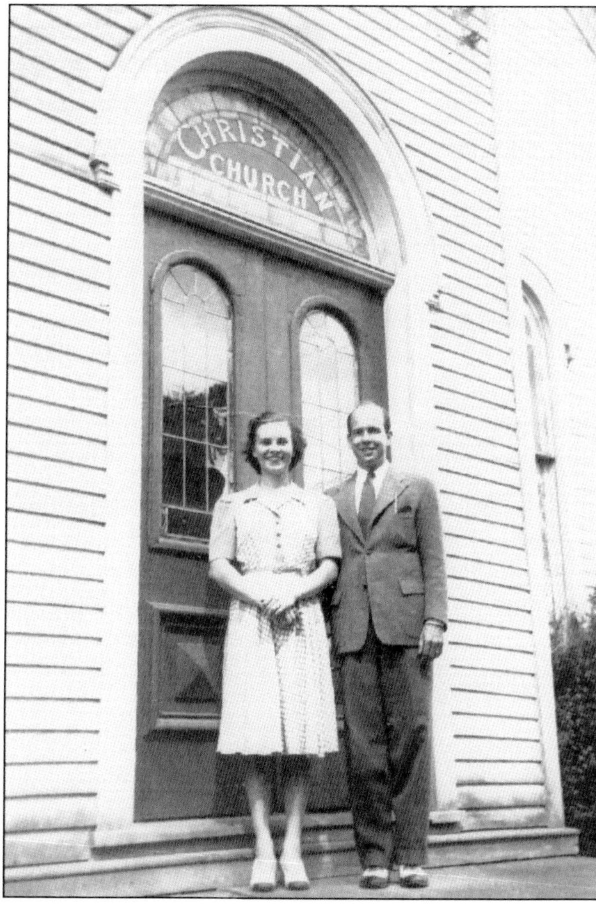

Plans were made in 1863 to build a Catholic church in Rush. At the time, there were approximately 18 Catholic families in town. It was during the Civil War, so funds were tight, and labor was also difficult to find. Nonetheless, the church was completed by November 1864, and Bishop Timon traveled from Buffalo for the dedication. The photograph was taken around 1900.

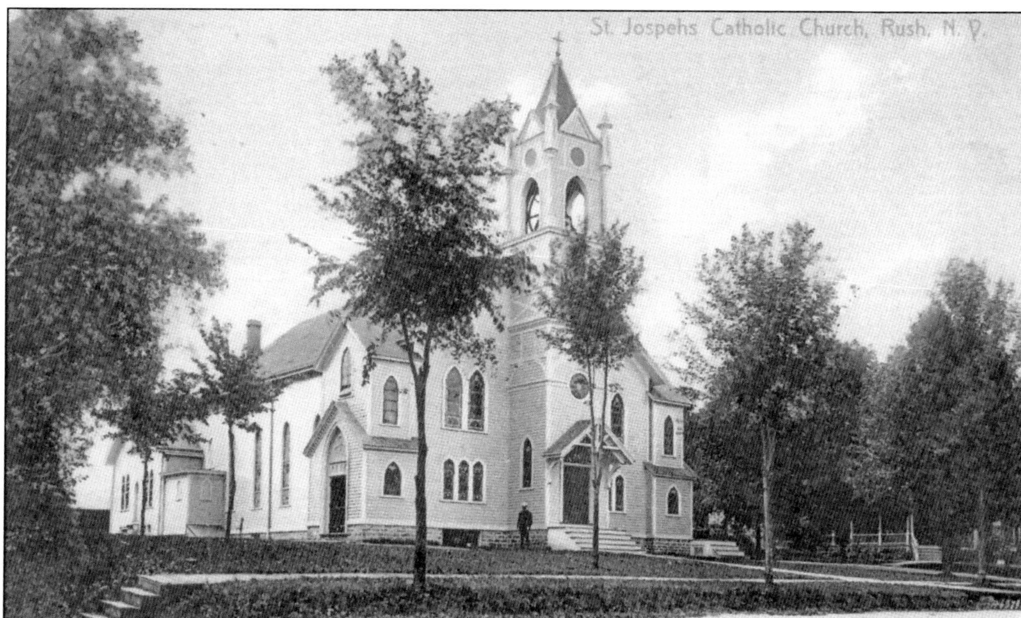

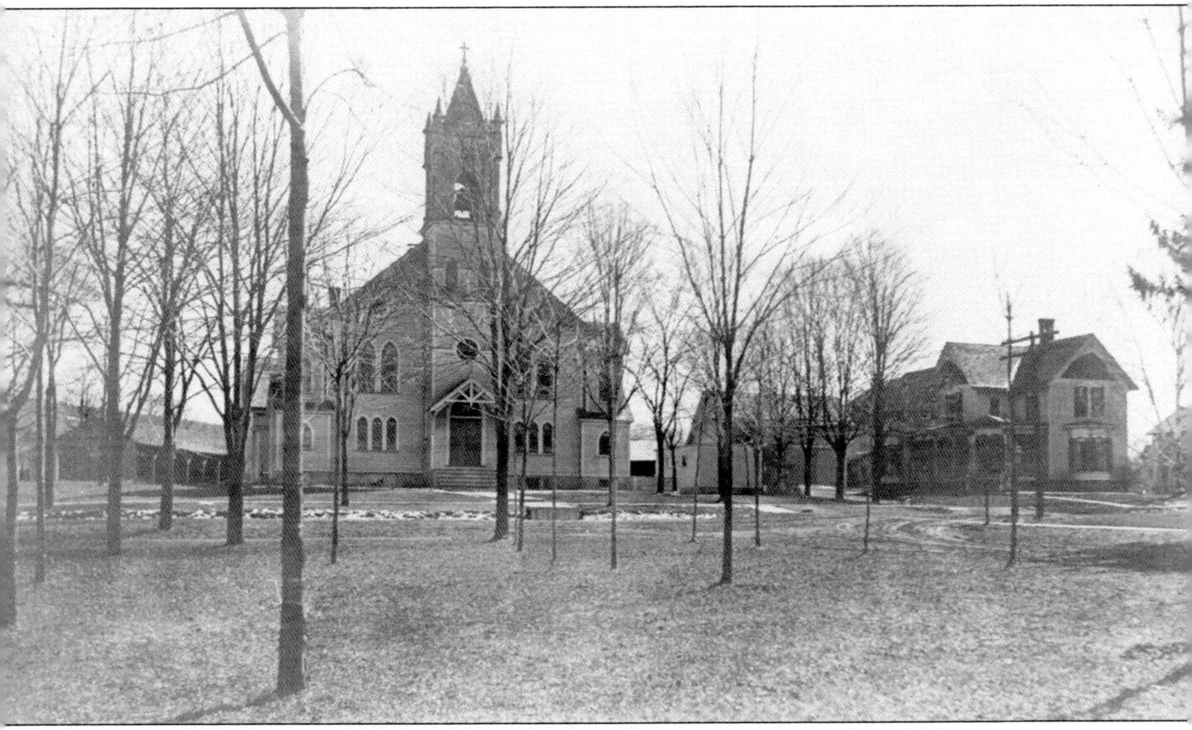

This view of St. Joseph's Church was taken from the Commons around 1900. The original church was damaged from heavy winds and rebuilt in 1884. The carriage barn can be seen to the left of the church. The first sheds were built in 1891 and replaced after damage from heavy snow in 1900. (Courtesy of Eleanor Mason DeFreze.)

Eight

Roads and Transportation

Only the trails of the Seneca existed when the earliest settlers arrived in the area. In 1792, a road was started from the Pennsylvania border northward, eventually making its way to Canandaigua and then Avon. This road became State Routes 5 and 20. In time, the trails and pathways widened and became roads. Pathmasters were assigned to care for sections of roads and to keep them passable. The year 1806 brought the first stagecoach route from Geneseo to Rochester, passing directly through Rush. By 1838, there was a daily stagecoach leaving Honeoye Falls at 8:00 a.m. and arriving in Rochester three hours later, with a daily afternoon return trip.

The first Lehigh Valley train passed through Rush in 1892, bringing further change. Transporting produce, livestock, and other goods became more convenient. A trip to Rochester was no longer an exhaustive ordeal. By 1893, the days of the stagecoach were coming to an end. The advent of the automobile brought even further change and independence to daily life.

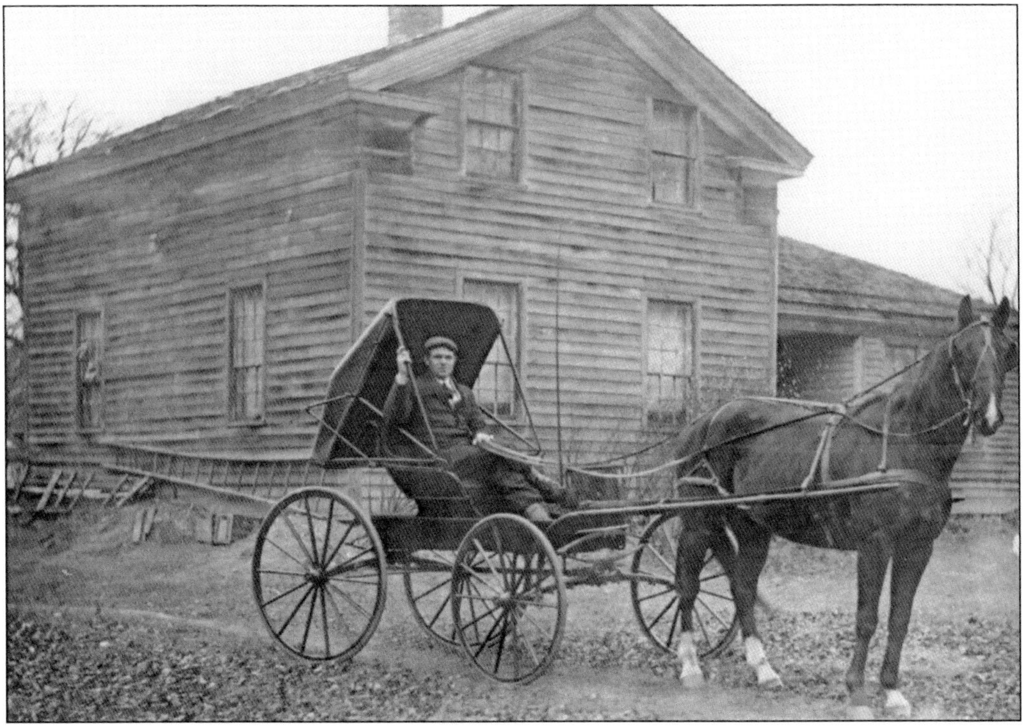

The horse and carriage was the usual form of transportation in the 1800s. The person in this photograph is believed to be Edwin Galentine. He and his wife, Maria Price Galentine, owned 414 Honeoye Falls Five Points Road in the late 1800s before moving to Rochester. Mr. and Mrs. Little were longtime residents, and the house was purchased by Joe and Jana Delibert in 2008. (Courtesy of Joe and Jana Delibert.)

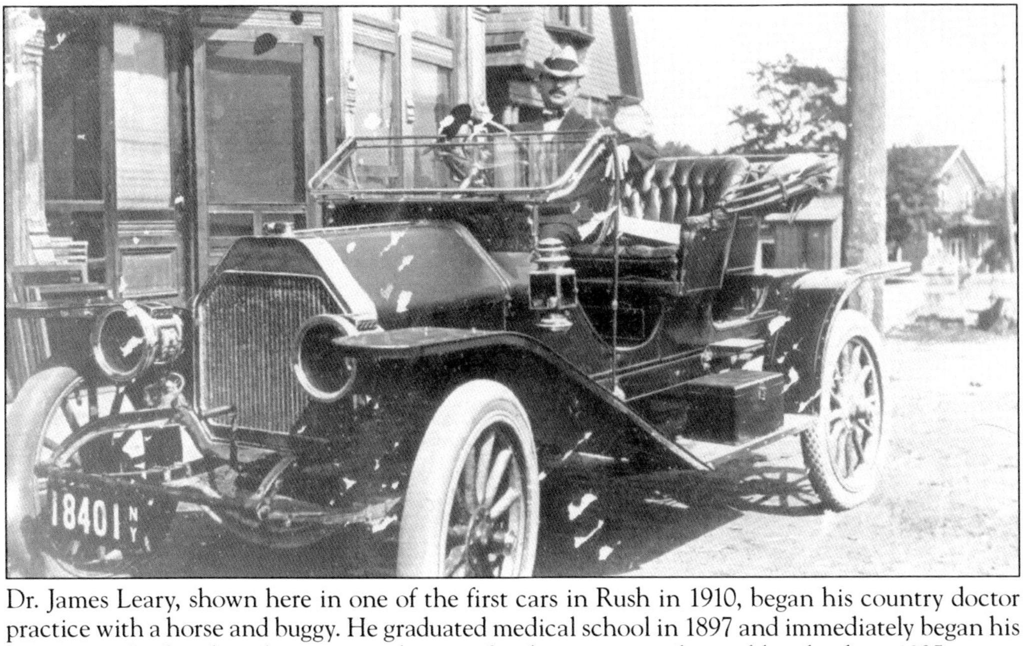

Dr. James Leary, shown here in one of the first cars in Rush in 1910, began his country doctor practice with a horse and buggy. He graduated medical school in 1897 and immediately began his practice in Rush, where he continued caring for the townspeople until his death in 1935.

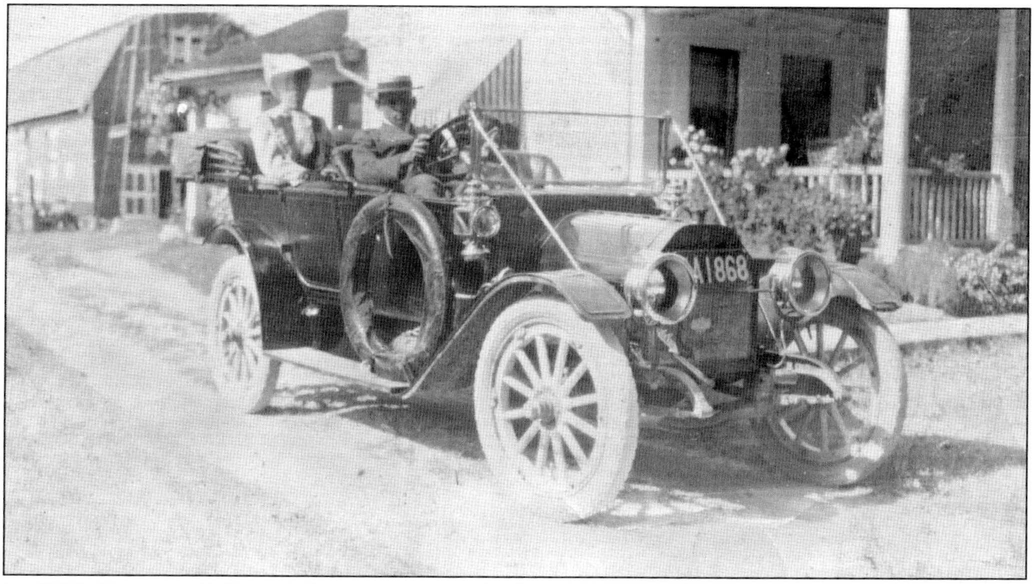

In 1908, Honeoye Falls and the near vicinity had a count of 14 automobiles. By 1914, Rush alone had 19. Traffic must have been increasing, because in 1913, it became a misdemeanor to travel faster than 10 miles per hour through the village of Rush. The penalty was a heavy fine and an indefinite term in the "lock-up." Shown here in 1918 are Mr. and Mrs. Lloyd Norris. (Courtesy of Eleanor Mason DeFreze.)

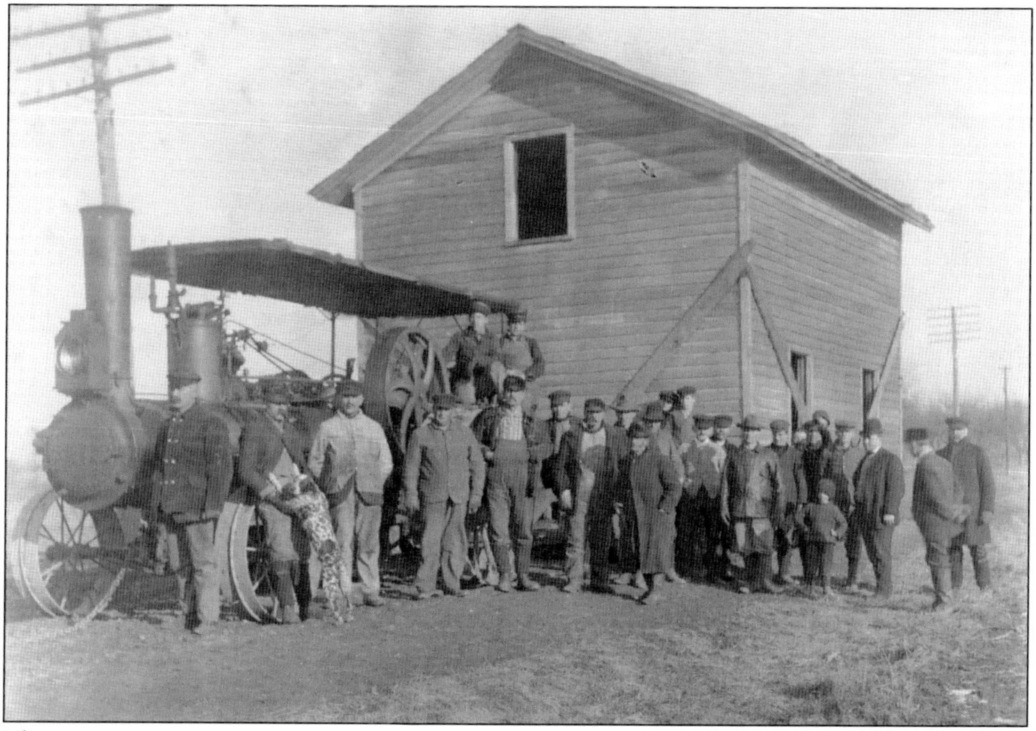

This steam tractor was put to work moving the home of Walter and Ella Years more than a mile, from 500 feet west of Pinnacle Road to its new location at 1839 Rush-Scottsville Road. This move took place around 1900.

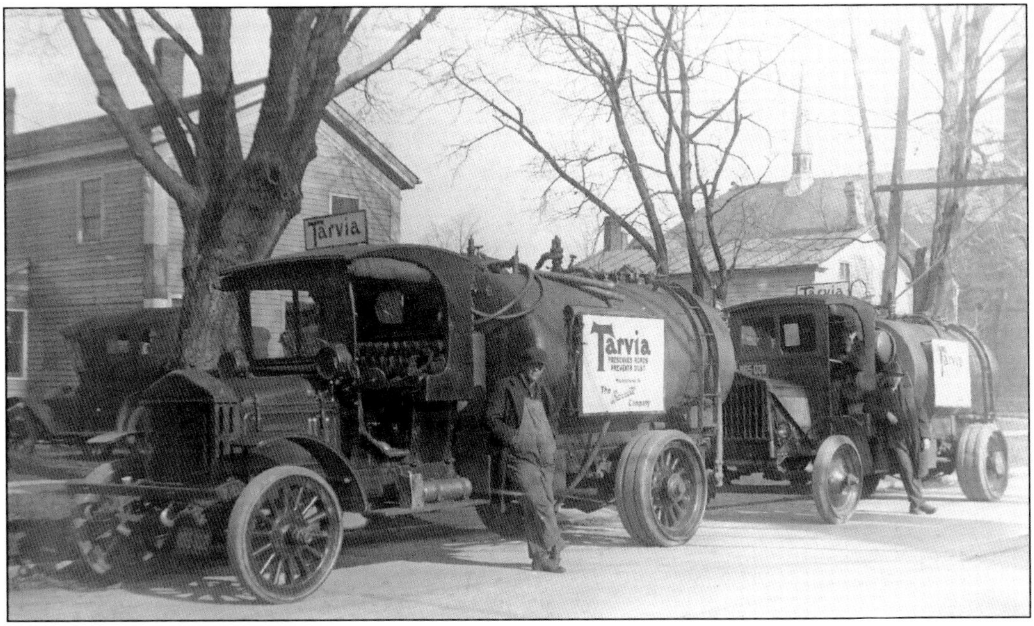

Prior to paved roads, the town was divided into 31 districts, with each having its own pathmaster. Those living within the district were responsible for maintaining that section of road. Excerpts from the *Honeoye Falls Times* record that, in 1885, "bad roads are the main topic of conversation," and in 1890, "pathmasters will have ample opportunity to display their genius in road-making. The roads are in horrible condition in some sections of our town [Rush]". The paper also reports that in 1906 "the roads in the south part of the town are like the boy's education—a little neglected." A June 1915 *Honeoye Falls Times* article reports that Cleveland & Sons Co. of Brockport submitted the lowest bid at $33,561 for the Rush-Henrietta improved road, a distance of 4.54 miles. Shown here are early Rush highway crews. In the photograph above, from left to right, Bruce Jefferds, Myron Faugh, and John Lozier are visible. The photograph below shows the Rush-West Rush Road being improved with the use of the town scraper and the county steam roller. (Above, courtesy of Bob Bock; below, courtesy of George K. Lusk family.)

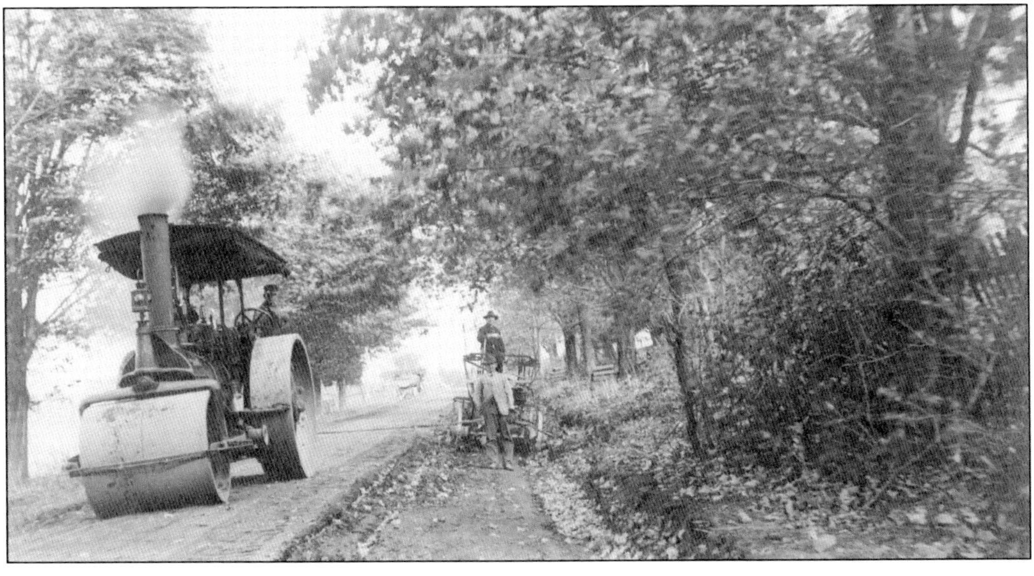

Shown here is one of the early Rush highway department trucks at the Rush Gravel pit, owned by the Schillinger family, on Kavanaugh Road. In the photograph are, from left to right, Butch Covert, Harold Pheta, Marty Barhart, Roy Hart, and Butch Straub.

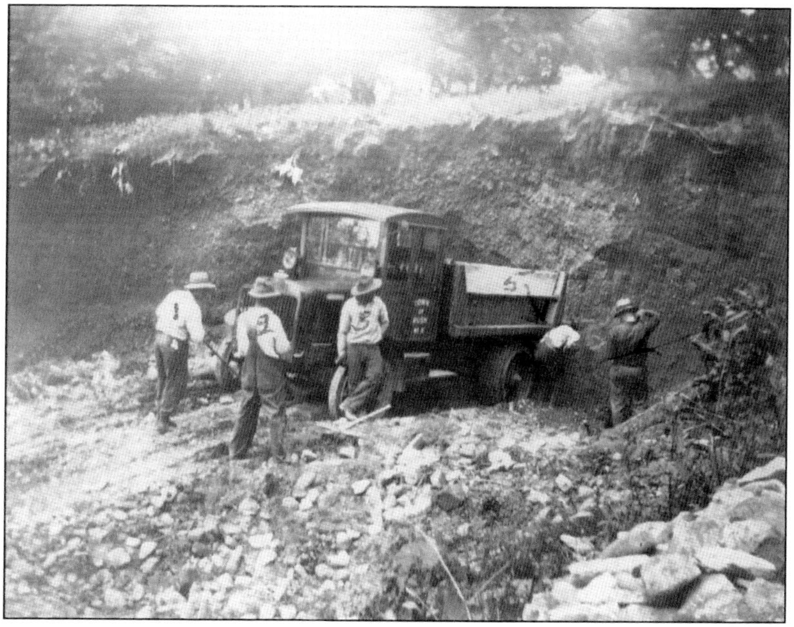

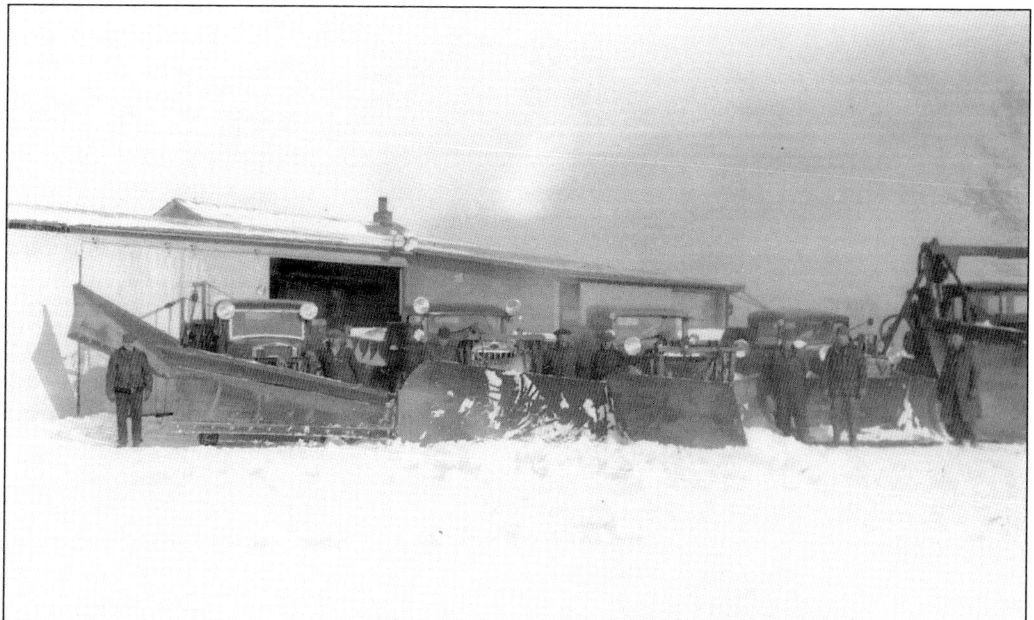

Taken at the town garage in 1944, this photograph shows both the equipment and crew of the Rush Highway Department. The trucks are identified as, from left to right, a truck with cab and wing used for pushing snow to the right; a dump truck with a side plow; a tractor with a cab and bucket or V-plow; a plow truck; and a 1928 Best Caterpillar, fondly referred to by the locals as "Big Bertha." Bertha had a continuous, or tank tread, track that provided good traction in soft surfaces, especially in snow. In addition to its keeping Rush's roads cleared, neighboring towns would request the services of Big Bertha in times of heavy snowstorms.

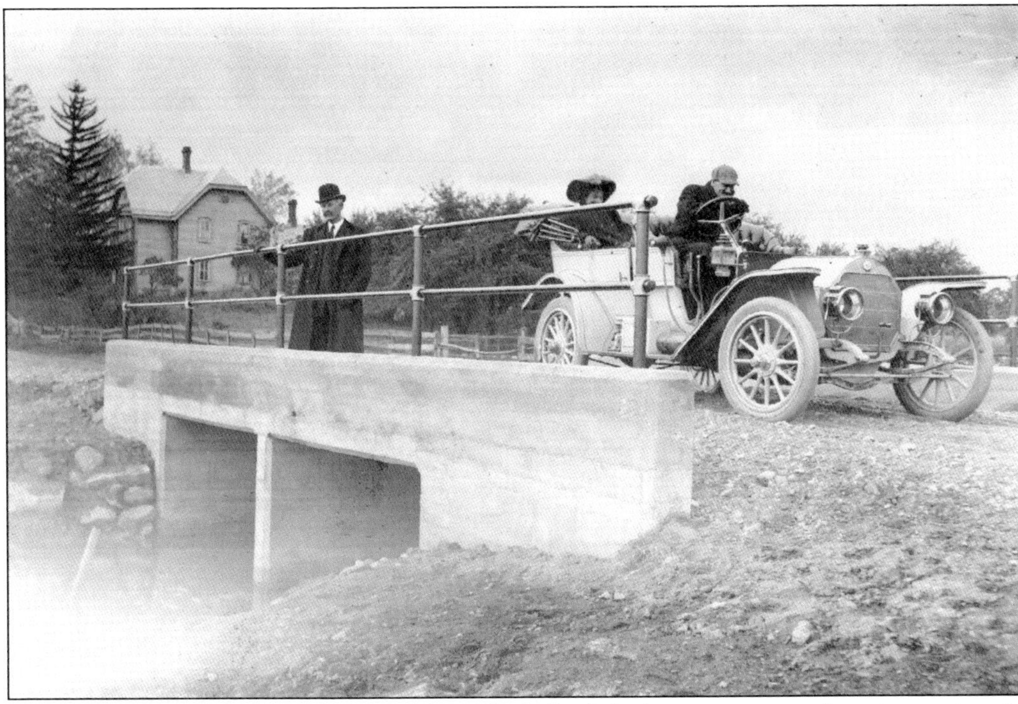

This October 1909 photograph shows John Behnk, Rush highway superintendent, inspecting the bridge he and his crew built on the Honeoye Falls Road. (Courtesy of George K. Lusk family.)

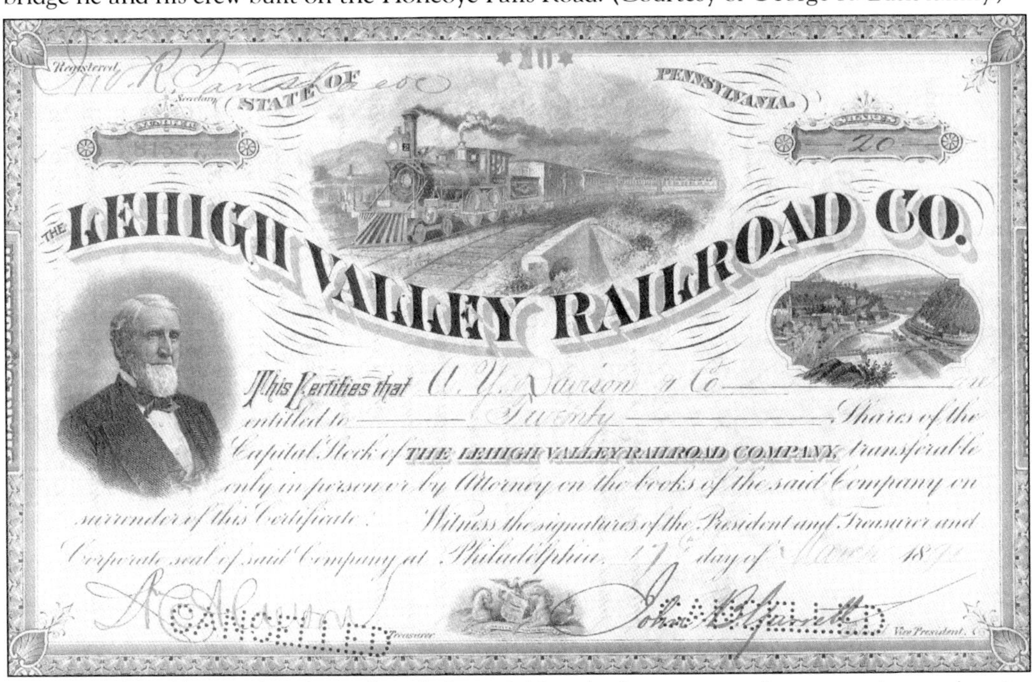

The Lehigh Valley Railroad was founded in 1846 with the mission of transporting anthracite coal from the coalfields of Pennsylvania to New York and New Jersey destinations. The railroad expanded to include passenger service and saw tremendous growth in both its freight and passenger service in the late 1800s and early 1900s. (Courtesy of George M. Stahl.)

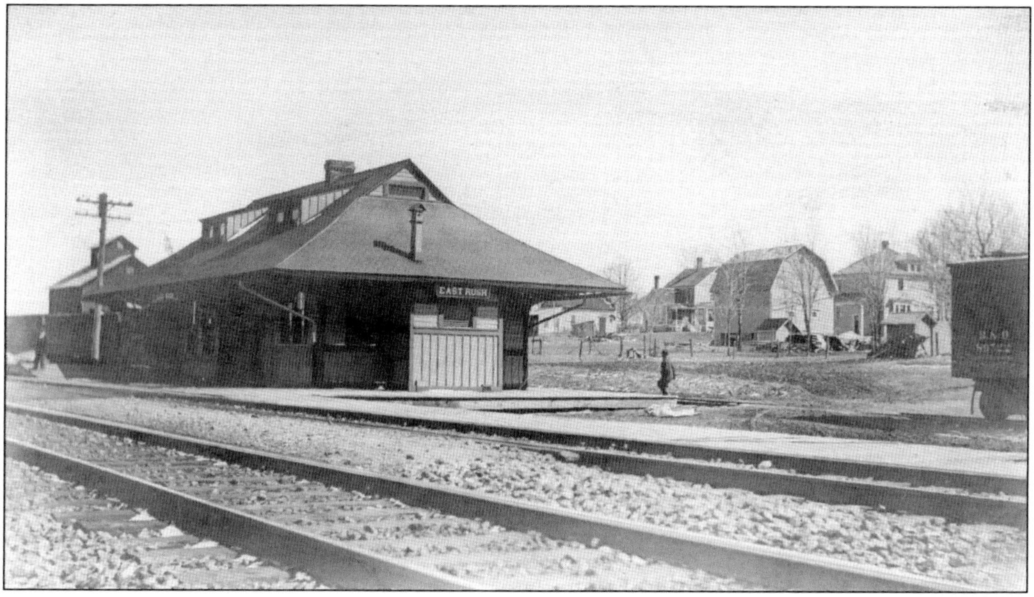

Talk of the railroad coming through the center of Rush began about 1886, bringing with it great hope and excitement to the townspeople. Railroad work began in May 1890 with 50 teams of horses and men arriving from Buffalo. The building of the railroad made a big impact on the town, creating a demand for housing and a need for additional paid work. Rush carpenter William Roudenbush was hired to build the East Rush depot and work began in April 1892. The Lehigh Valley Railroad made its maiden run through Rush in early September 1892. The following spring brought the announcement of passenger service being added to the Rush station. Nine flyers and express trains would be making daily stops in East Rush—how the world was about to change. (Below, courtesy of Eleanor Mason DeFreze.)

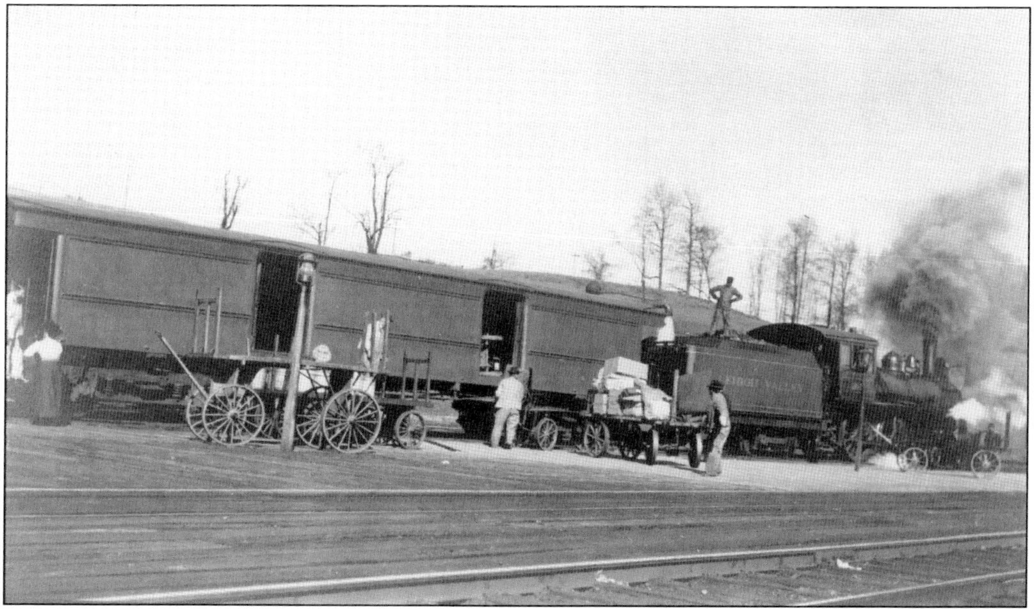

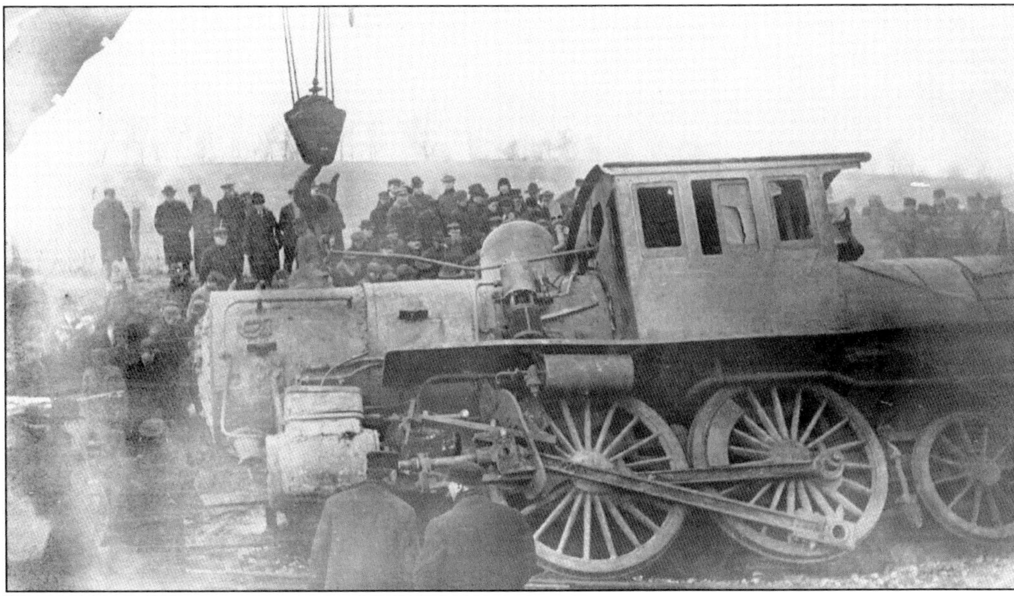

Only days after the initial run, tragedy struck. A train derailment at the East Rush station resulted in 14 cars sliding into the creek and the untimely death of the engineer, Charles Wilson. Many area papers, including the *Silver Creek Gazette*, reported that a coroner's jury ruled the accident was "due to negligence of the railroad company for not having the embankments in proper order."

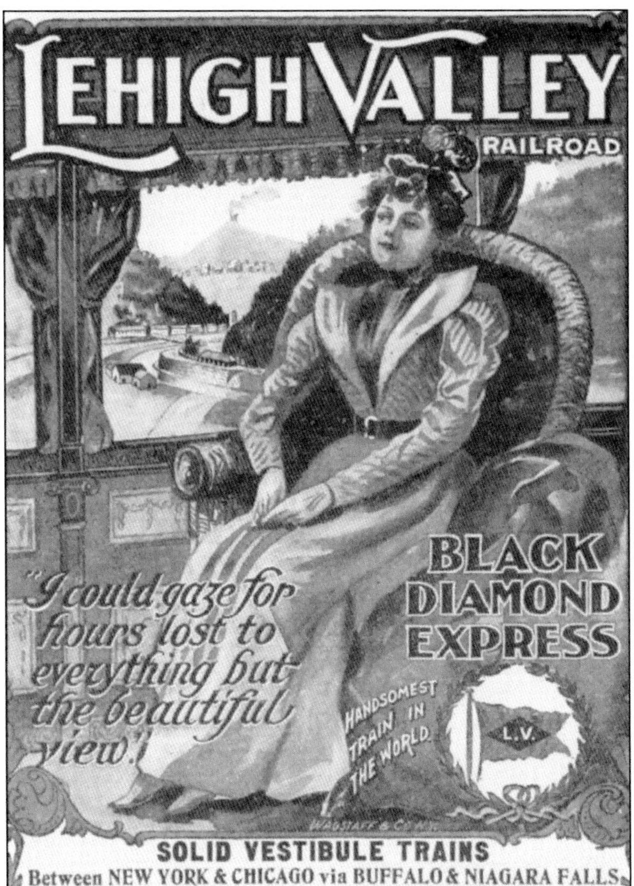

The premier passenger train was the Black Diamond Express. The Black Diamond was advertised as a train of luxury with plush velvet seating, chefs on board, and smoking rooms. It passed through Rush daily, but boarding took place at Rochester Junction. (Courtesy of George M. Stahl.)

Nine

People, Organizations, and Events

This chapter attempts to capture some of the activities and events that have taken place in Rush over the years. Numerous organizations and clubs have been formed, some still in existence, to meet the needs and interests of the times. The community has benefited from the drive and hard work of the organizations that strove to create a better town and provide a good place to live and raise a family. From the parades, carnivals, and other social events, it seems there was a lot of fun, too.

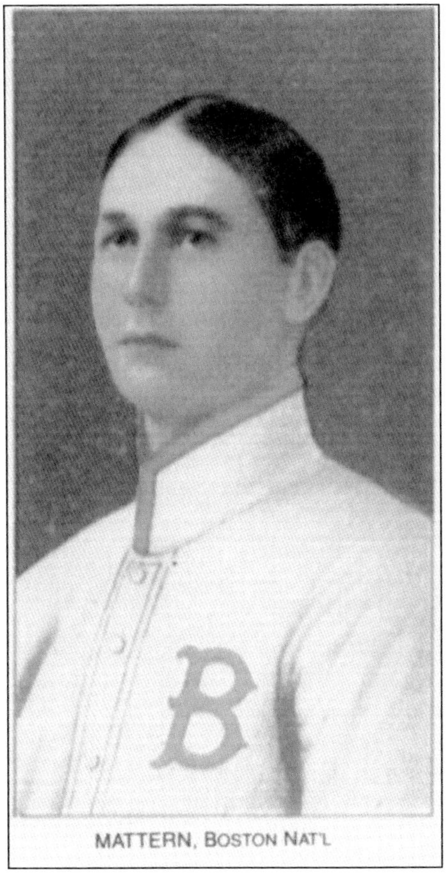

Al Mattern, a native of West Rush, made his Major League Baseball debut pitching for the Boston Doves on September 16, 1908. Throughout his professional career, 1908–1912, he played for the Boston Doves and Braves. Upon his return to West Rush, he opened an auto dealership.

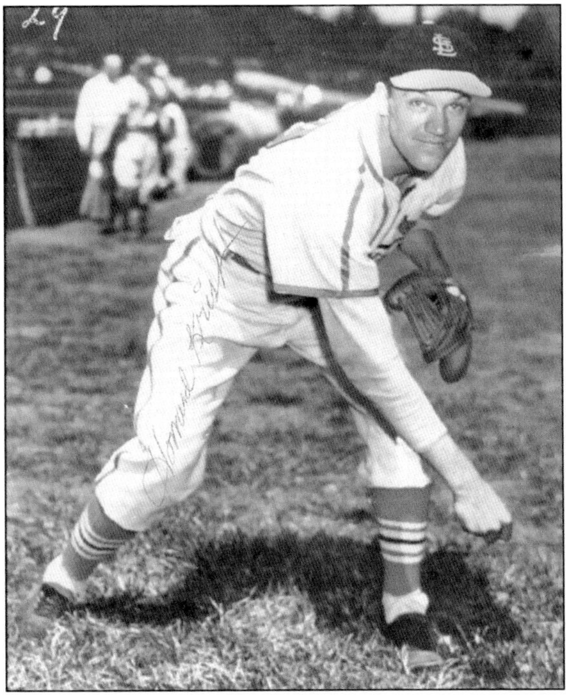

Howard Krist was a talented athlete who played baseball and basketball during his Rush High School days. Winning 12 consecutive games his senior year of high school led to a minor-league baseball contract upon graduation in 1934. Howie "Spud" Krist pitched for the Rochester Red Wings and St. Louis Cardinals the majority of his career, playing in two World Series. (Courtesy of John Krist.)

The Ingleside Club was formed in 1907 as a literary club to promote the intellectual advancement of its members. The name Ingleside was chosen because the club met in women's homes and the word means the "area immediately surrounding the fireplace or hearth." The club met monthly with scheduled topics and still exists today.

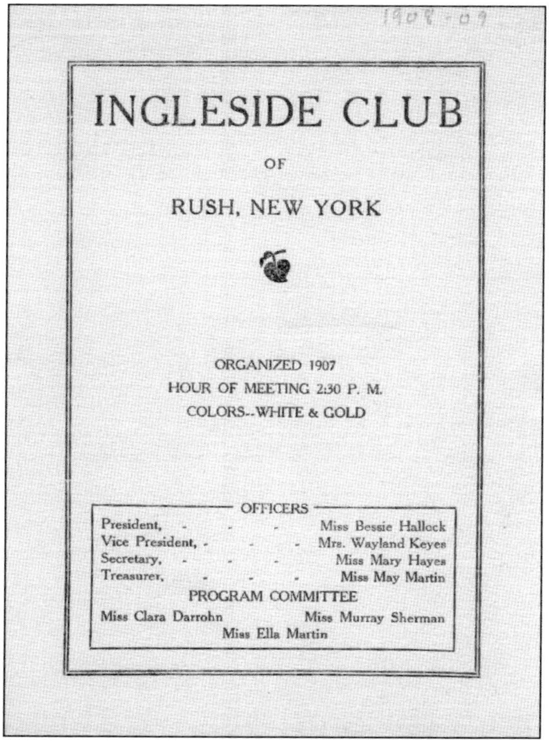

1908-09

INGLESIDE CLUB

OF

RUSH, NEW YORK

ORGANIZED 1907

HOUR OF MEETING 2:30 P. M.

COLORS--WHITE & GOLD

OFFICERS

President, - - -	Miss Bessie Hallock
Vice President, - - -	Mrs. Wayland Keyes
Secretary, - - -	Miss Mary Hayes
Treasurer, - - - -	Miss May Martin

PROGRAM COMMITTEE

Miss Clara Darrohn — Miss Murray Sherman — Miss Ella Martin

In March 1938, members of the Ingleside Club met to discuss plans for the formation of a Rush Historical Society. Pictured, from left to right, are Zaida Mattern, Mary "Mattie" Hayes, Etta Diver, and Minnie Greene. Hayes became the president of the Rush Historical Society. (Courtesy of *Honeoye Falls Times.*)

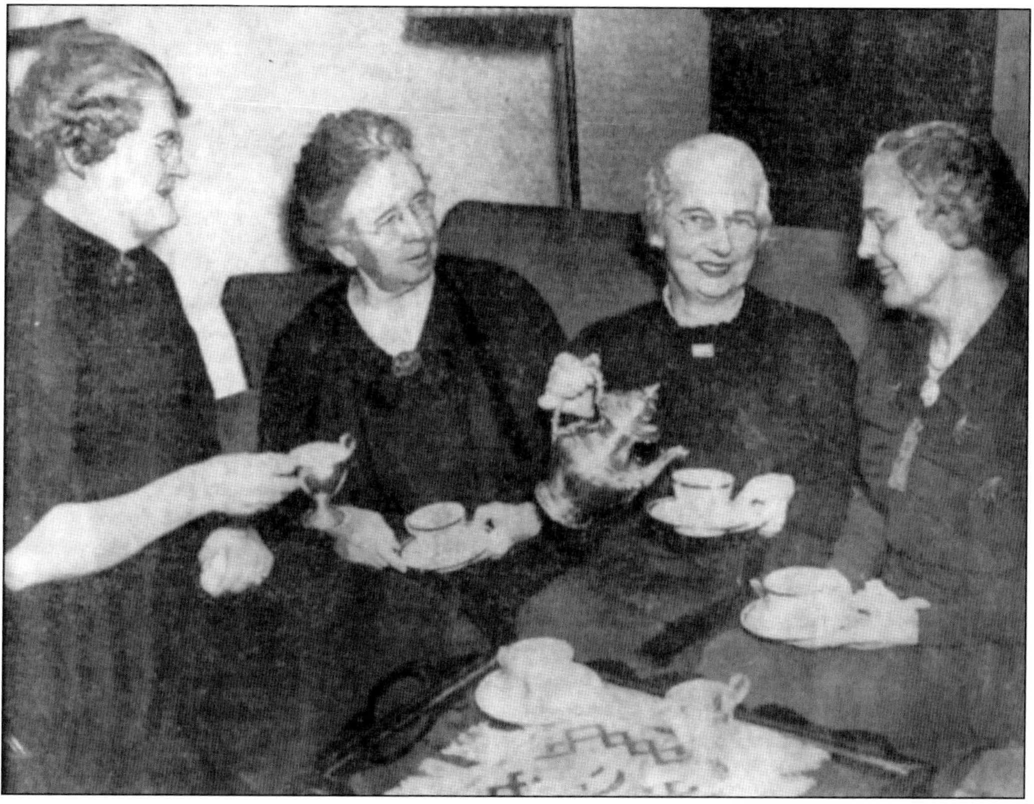

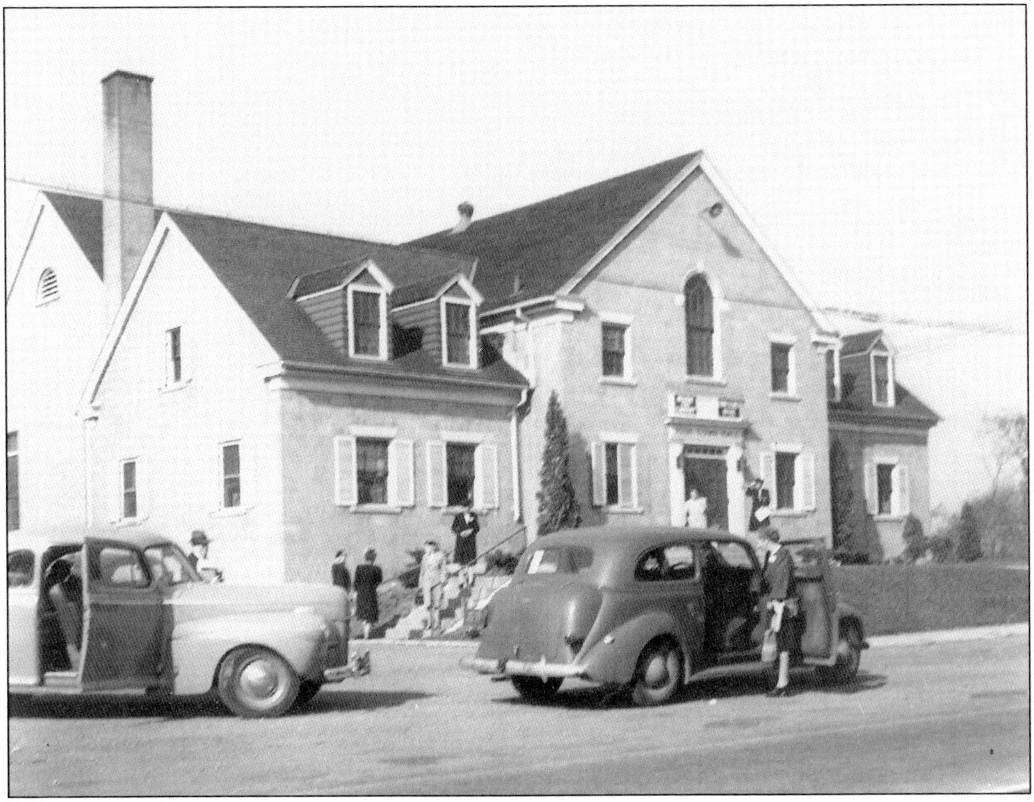

In October 1947, Rush historian Bessie Hallock, along with fellow Rush Historical Society members, led a "Historical Pilgrimage" throughout Rush for historical society members and other town historians. A turkey dinner was prepared and served at noon by the local churchwomen for the more than 50 participants. The day concluded with a visit to Elm Place, the Markham family home on East River Road, currently owned by Karen Hopkins.

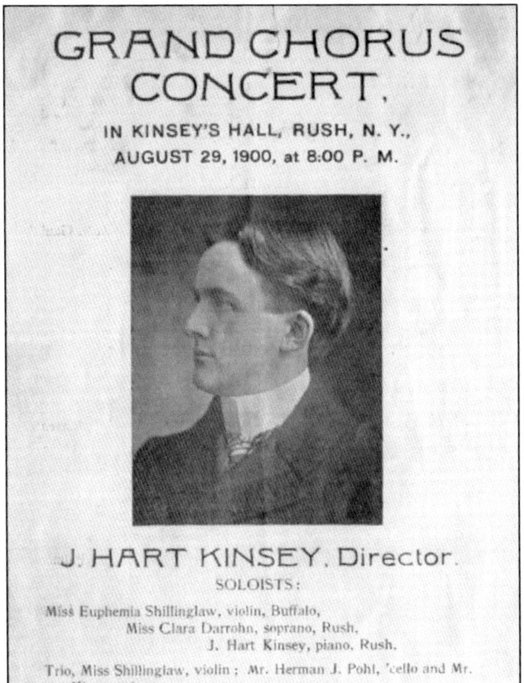

GRAND CHORUS CONCERT.

IN KINSEY'S HALL, RUSH, N. Y., AUGUST 29, 1900, at 8:00 P. M.

J. HART KINSEY, Director.

SOLOISTS:

Miss Euphemia Shillinglaw, violin, Buffalo,
Miss Clara Darrohn, soprano, Rush,
J. Hart Kinsey, piano, Rush.

Trio, Miss Shillinglaw, violin; Mr. Herman J. Pohl, 'cello and Mr. Kinsey, piano.

Although a small rural community, Rush was rich in cultural activities. Kinsey Hall served as a venue for a number of talks, lectures, concerts, and dramatic plays. A Grand Chorus Concert took place on August 29, 1900, where J. Hart Kinsey was both the director and piano soloist, and Clara Darrohn performed as a singer.

The Rush Improvement Association was formed with the goal of acquiring the former mill site to create a park on both sides of Honeoye Creek. Town events were held to raise funds to purchase the land, and the former mill owners donated a portion as well. The Veterans Memorial Park was dedicated May 31, 1964, "to all those who had served Rush in time of war."

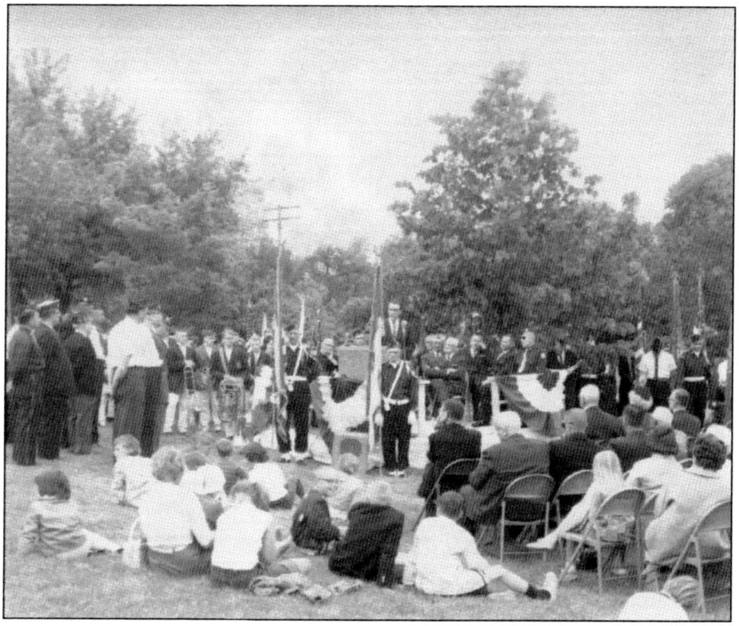

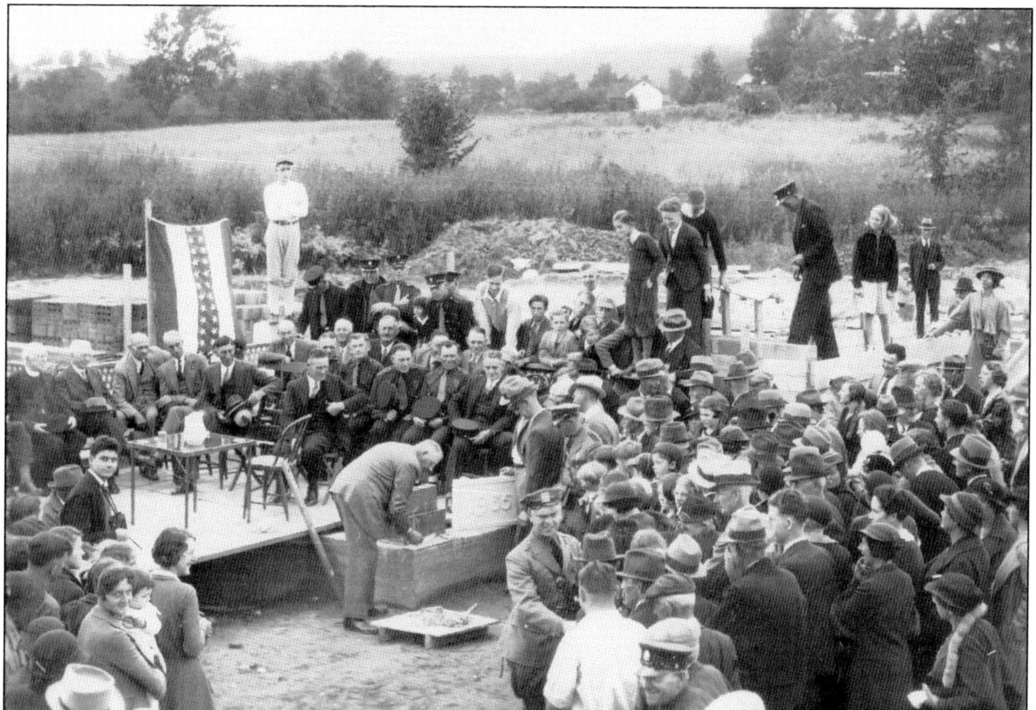

Town residents voted 160 to 40 in favor of building a town hall in 1934. Town supervisor Eugene Barker, with ceremonial trowel in hand, is shown here laying the cornerstone at the September 28, 1935, ceremony. Constructed by the Works Progress Administration, the town hall served the needs of the community with its town offices, fire department, library, dining room, auditorium, and gymnasium. The building underwent an extensive renovation in 2003–2004.

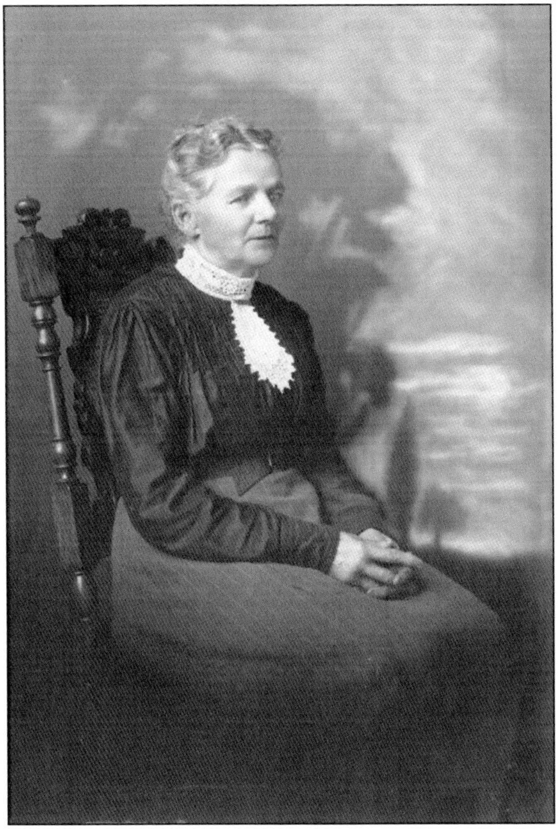

Barbara Schinster Smith, "Barbarry" to the children, was a beloved icon of the Rush community. As a young woman, she worked and cared for the family of Morris Darrohn. Her husband John Smith served in the Civil War with the 140th New York Volunteer Infantry under the command of Col. Patrick O'Rourke. Together, they cared for many of the veterans' graves in Pine Hill Cemetery. Mrs. Smith died at age 83 in January 1934. (Courtesy of Elaine Darrohn Tennity.)

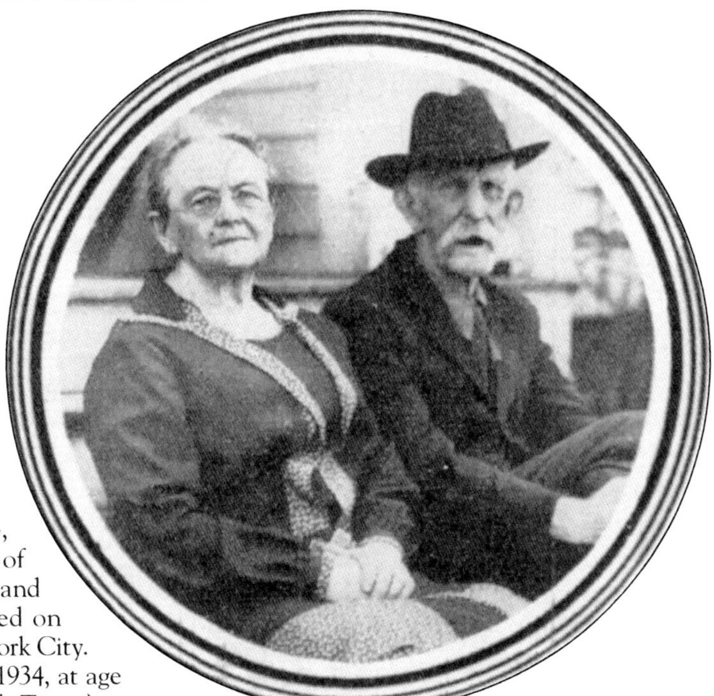

Charles D. Lozier was both the last surviving Civil War veteran in Rush and also the last surviving member of the Lewis Gates Post, Grand Army of the Republic in Honeoye Falls. Born in New York City, in February 1843, he served with Company F of the New York Engineers. He and his wife, Mary, were married on December 24, 1872, in New York City. Charles died on January 24, 1934, at age 90. (Courtesy of *Honeoye Falls Times*.)

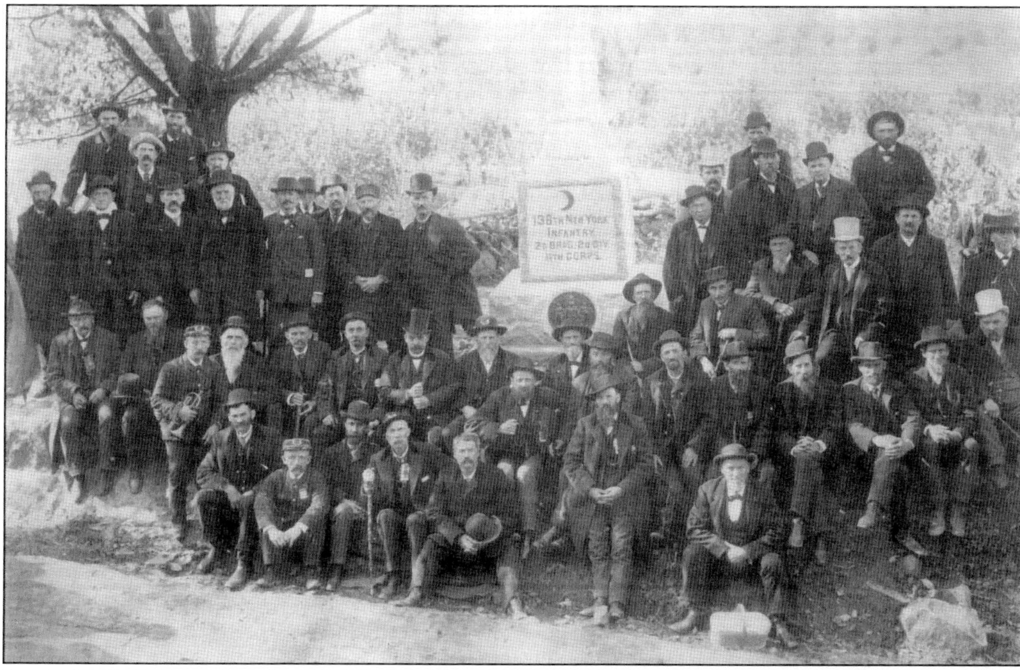

Jacob Stull Galentine enlisted with the NY 136th Volunteers at age 28. He was born and grew up in Rush, the son of John and Isabella Stull Galentine. Jacob lived his adult years in Lima, where he served as town justice, assessor, and Lima supervisor. This 1888 photograph was taken at the NY 136th monument dedication at the Gettysburg Battlefield. Jacob is in the back row, immediately to the left of the monument. (Courtesy of John DuBois.)

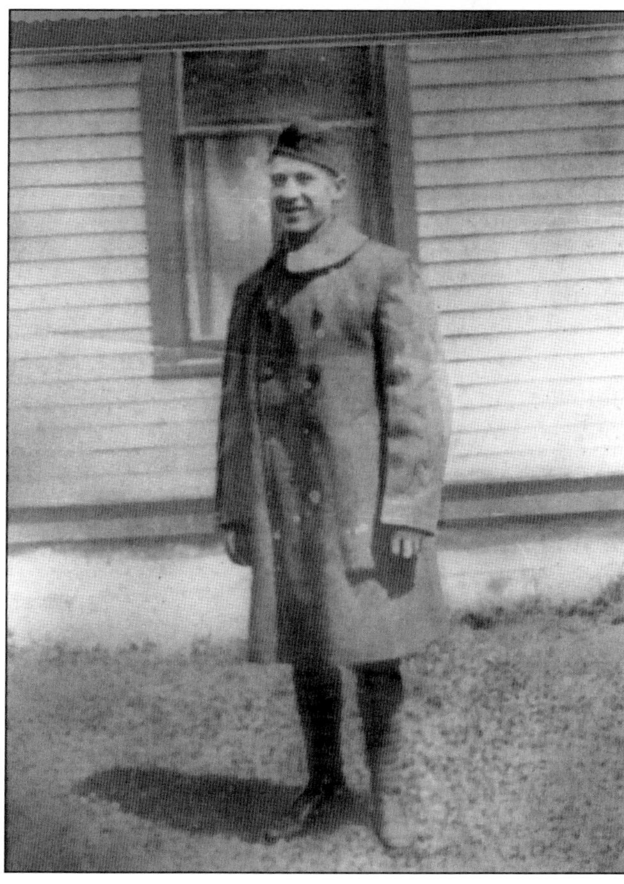

In September 1943, World War I veteran Lee Wiles called a meeting to form an American Legion post. The Stevens-Connor Post No. 1330 was organized in 1945 and named in honor of two fallen Rush men who served in World War II—John H. Stevens and John F. Connor. In 1947, the post purchased School No. 2 on Pinnacle Road. Wiles, shown in this c. 1914 photograph, was the first post commander. (Courtesy of Norman Miller.)

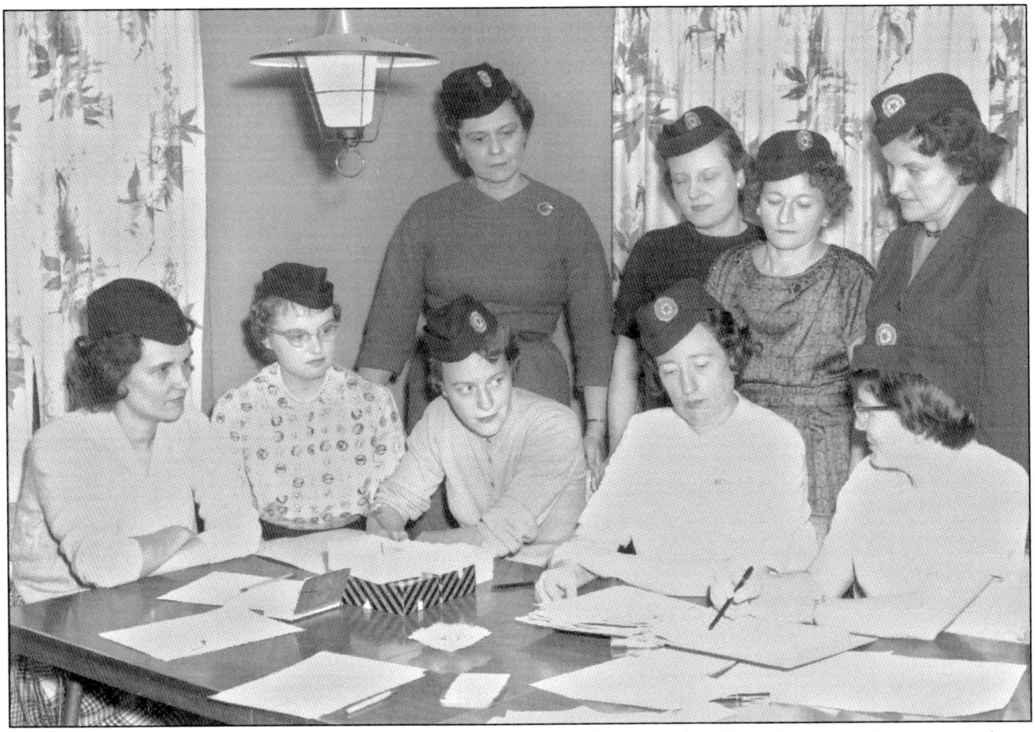

In earlier years, the Legion post sponsored a variety of events. In this photograph are members of the Legion Post Auxiliary, planning the annual smorgasbord dinner. They are, from left to right, (first row) Rita Morrell, Ruth Bock, unidentified, Nell Geisler, and Louise Miller; (second row) Ruth Marlow, Ruth Moran, Vicki Faugh, and Cleo Eisenberg. The Legion Post building has recently become one of Monroe County's park lodges. (Courtesy of Norman Miller.)

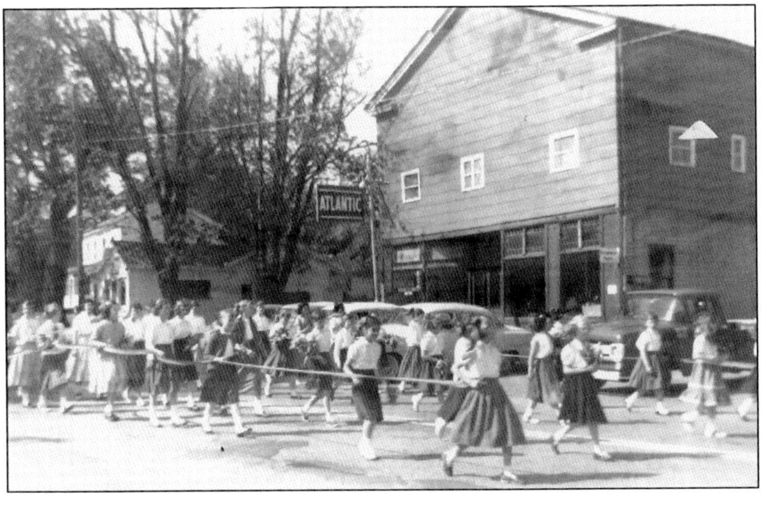

The annual Memorial Day parade, seen here around 1959, is passing in front of Lonthair's Barbershop. (Courtesy of Dorothy "Pud" Lambert.)

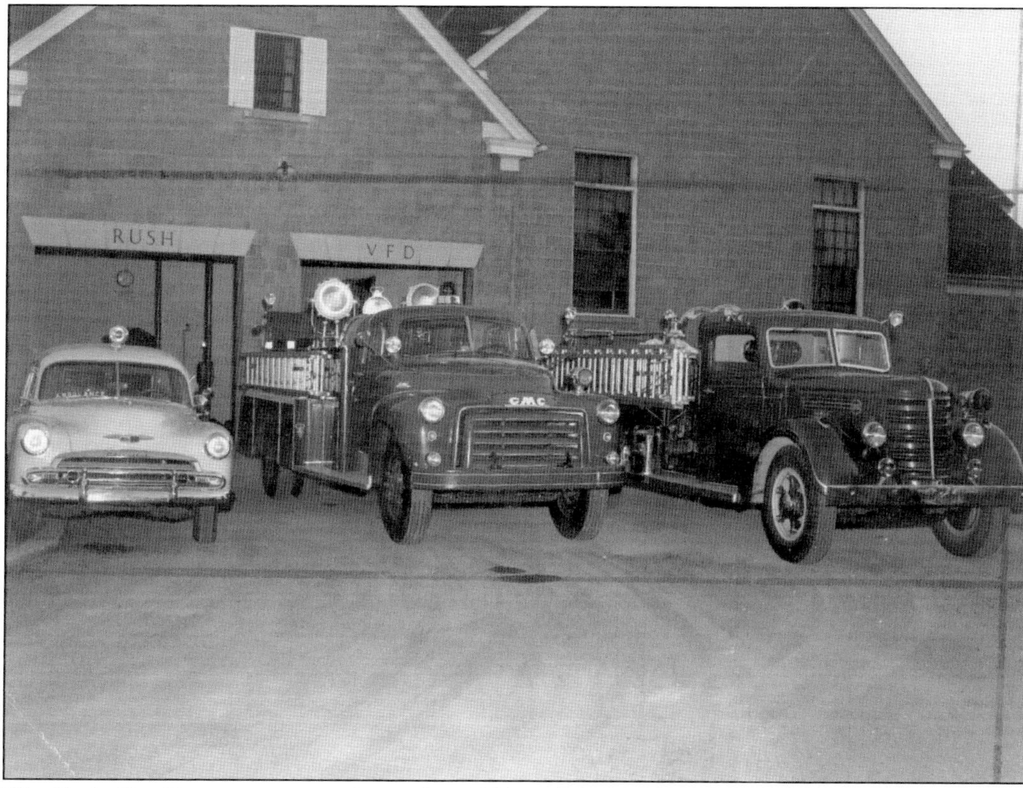

The Rush Fire Department was formed in 1920 with Marion Decker and John Wiles named as president and vice president. The department housed its first vehicle, a Model T chemical truck, in John Behnk's barn. The fire department was located within the town hall from 1936 to 1971 when it moved to its present location.

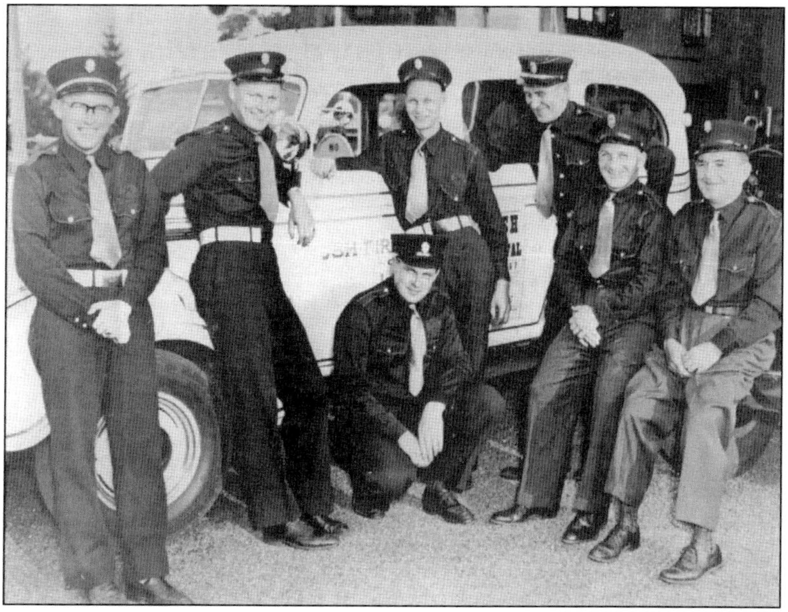

The Rush Ambulance service was initiated in 1939. In this 1948 photograph are, from left to right, (standing) Leo Collins, James Fletcher, Les Faugh, and Vince Behnk; (kneeling) John Tracy; (seated) William Finley and Irving McAvoy. (Courtesy of Bertha and Vincent Woolaver family.)

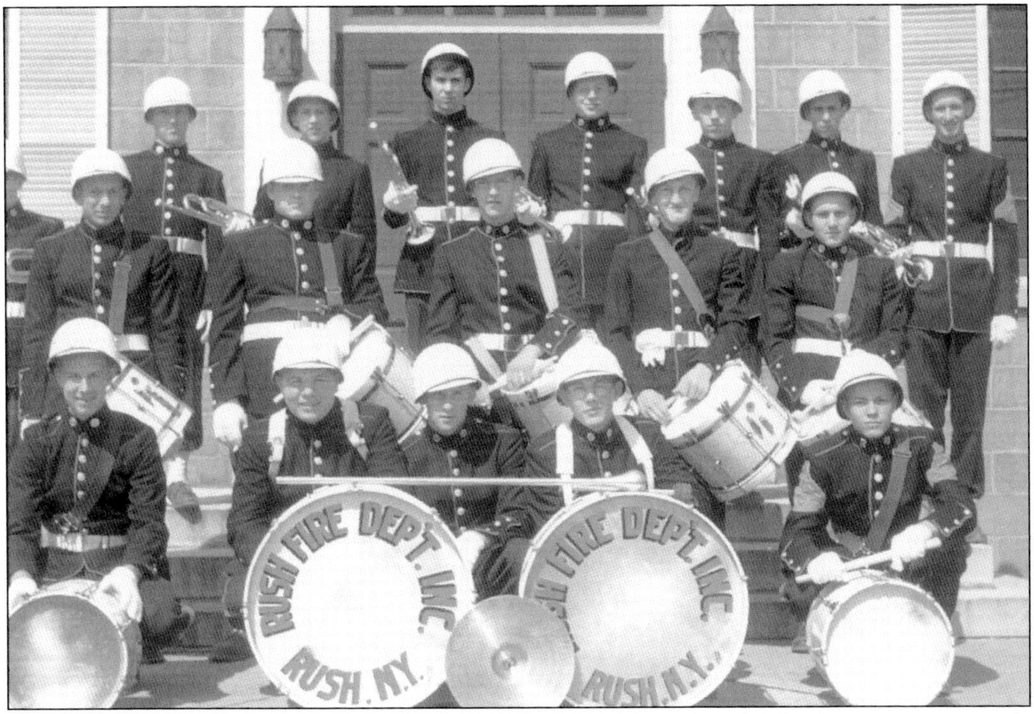

This mid-1940s photograph shows the Rush Fire Department band. Members were primarily students from the Rush High School. They are, from left to right, (first row) Don Polle, George Reese, Les Moose, Bill Monaghan, and unidentified; (second row) two unidentified, John Lozier, Dick Lozier, and Don Tobey; (third row) Norm Miller (partially shown), unidentified, Bob Bock, George Roeser, John Miller, unidentified, Harold Roeser, and Hans Stoever. (Courtesy of Norman Miller.)

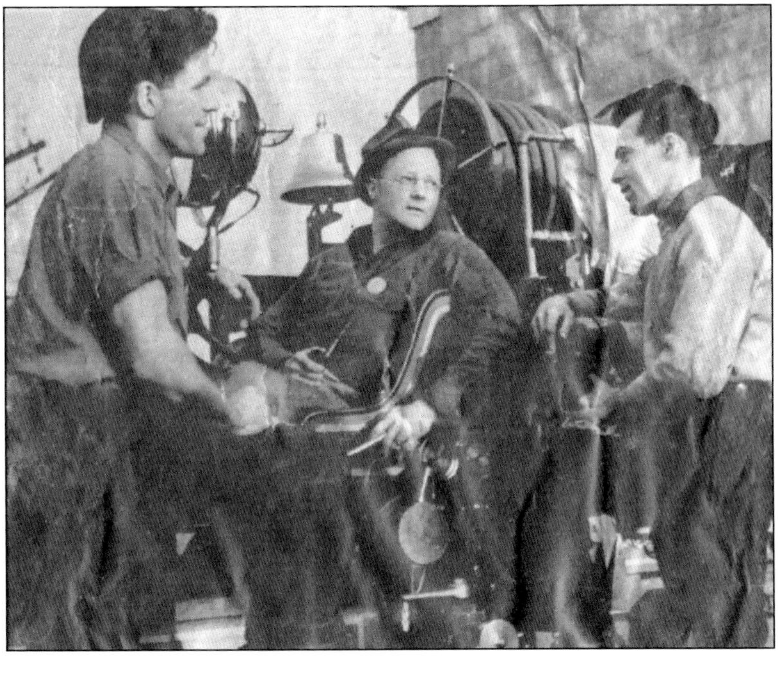

Rush volunteer firefighters Charles Goldstein (left), Ernie Parks (center), and Dick Moran are shown here with the department's hose cart in 1938. (Courtesy of *Honeoye Falls Times*.)

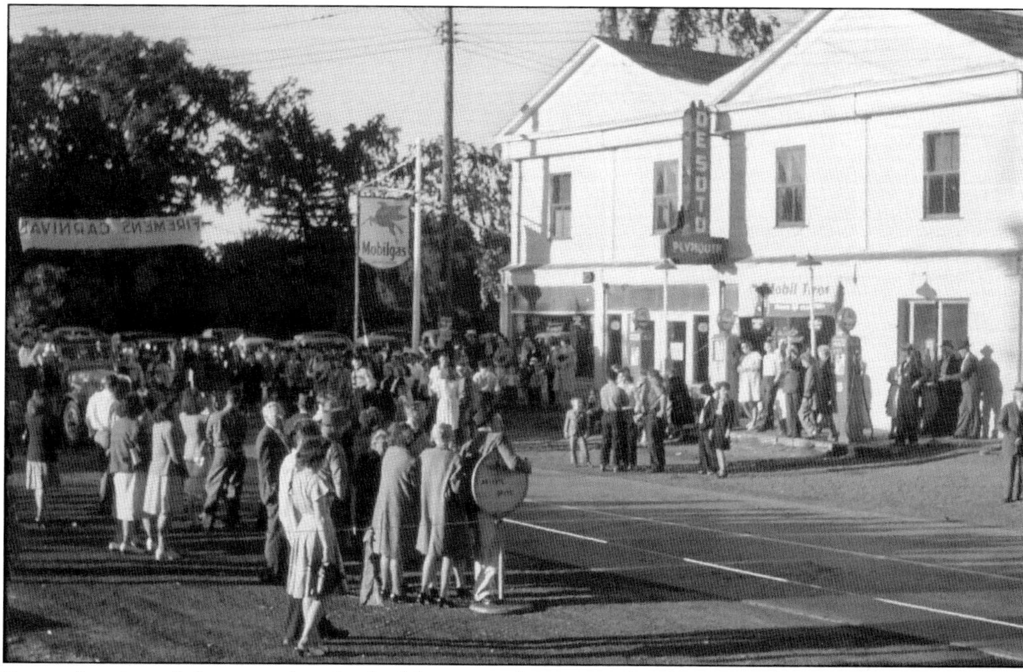

From the size of the crowd, it looks like a good turnout for the annual Rush firemen's parade and carnival. In 1937, the fire department began investigating the possibility of purchasing land for baseball games, fire exercises, carnivals, and other community events. A committee was appointed and the current firemen's field land was purchased. This photograph is from the late 1930s or early 1940s.

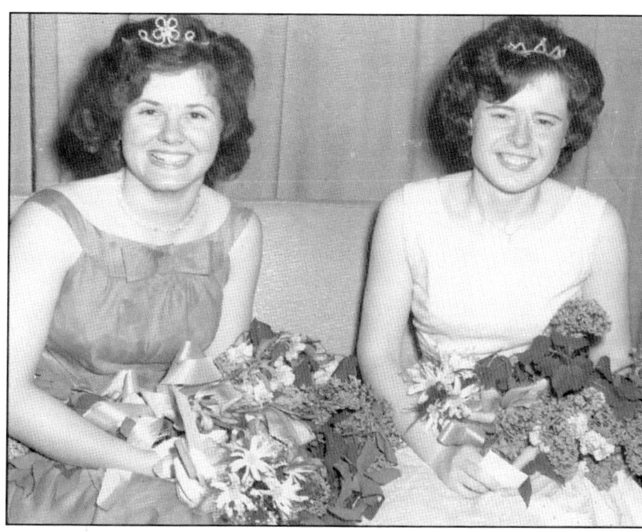

The Rush Firemen's Ladies Auxiliary formed in 1948 and has supported both the fire department and the community through a wide range of events over the years. The ladies auxiliary sponsored an annual Harvest Queen contest for Rush residents from 1949 through 1971. The contest was part of a countywide event sponsored by the Rochester newspapers, the *Democrat and Chronicle* and *Times-Union*. Nancy Reger, left, and Sharon Moran, right, were the 1964 queen and alternate.

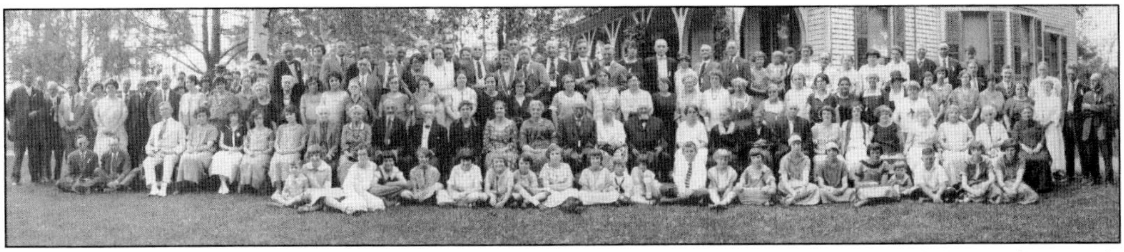

The Price, Stull, Martin, and Sherman Pioneer Association was organized to celebrate the 100th anniversary in 1901 of the settlement of the Price and Stull families in Rush. The Martin and Sherman families arrived a few years later, and the association continues to hold annual reunions celebrating these pioneer families. This photograph was taken at a reunion at the Martin family homestead in the early 1920s. (Courtesy of Robert Martin Kuhls.)

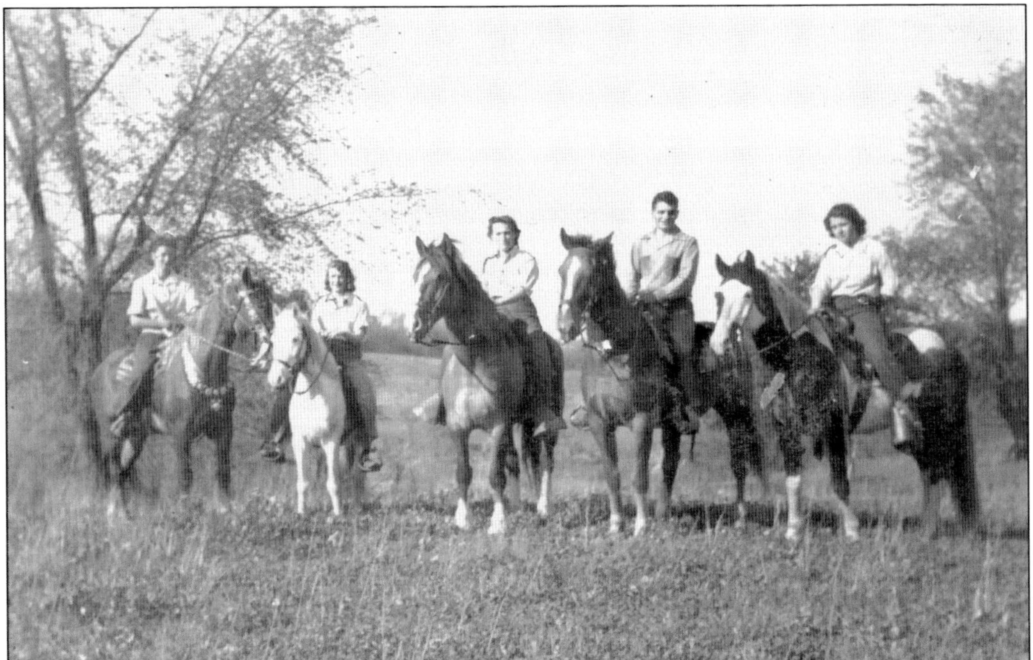

The open fields and scenic views of the area lend themselves nicely to leisurely horseback rides. This 1948 group of riders includes, from left to right, Jeanne Yawman, Dorothy Snover, Marilyn Walters, Selden Chase, and Angela Wolkin. The Rustic Riders group formed in the 1950s, riding in the town parades and participating in many trail rides over the years. The group disbanded in the early 1970s. (Courtesy of Jeanne Yawman.)

Ten

The State Agricultural and Industrial School

Established in 1846, the Western House of Refuge was the first state reformatory in the country. The facility opened in August 1849, and by the end of the year, there were 38 male inmates. In 1886, the school changed its name to the State Industrial School and also adopted a program of military instruction. By 1898, the board of managers had recommended the purchase of farmland and a move from Rochester to a rural setting. The objective was to provide agricultural training since farmwork would be the most likely employment upon release.

In 1903, the Industrial Commission selected the Edwin A. Clapp farm, along with several smaller surrounding farms, for the school's new site. More than 1,400 acres were purchased and construction of cottages and barns was soon underway. Franklin H. Briggs was superintendent during this time and was responsible for the adoption of the cottage system of living. The move to Rush was completed in 1907. The school had also undergone another name change and was now called the New York State Agricultural and Industrial School. Locally, it was referred to as "Industry."

The total acreage was divided into plots of 50-acre farms. The boys were housed in groups of 25 and lived with a supervisor and his wife. In the early years, a teacher was assigned to each cottage, and the boys spent half the day in class and half at work on their farm.

In 1908, Industry hosted its first annual exhibit where board members and the Rush community were invited to view an exhibition of farm, garden, and orchard products. Visitors were impressed with the school and its program and felt the boys were proud of their accomplishments. By 1918, the inspection by the board of managers reported that conditions were never better. The enrollment of 865 was 100 boys above the rated capacity.

Industry is no longer a working farm and is also much smaller than in years back. Today, it is a limited security facility for 13-to-16-year-old boys.

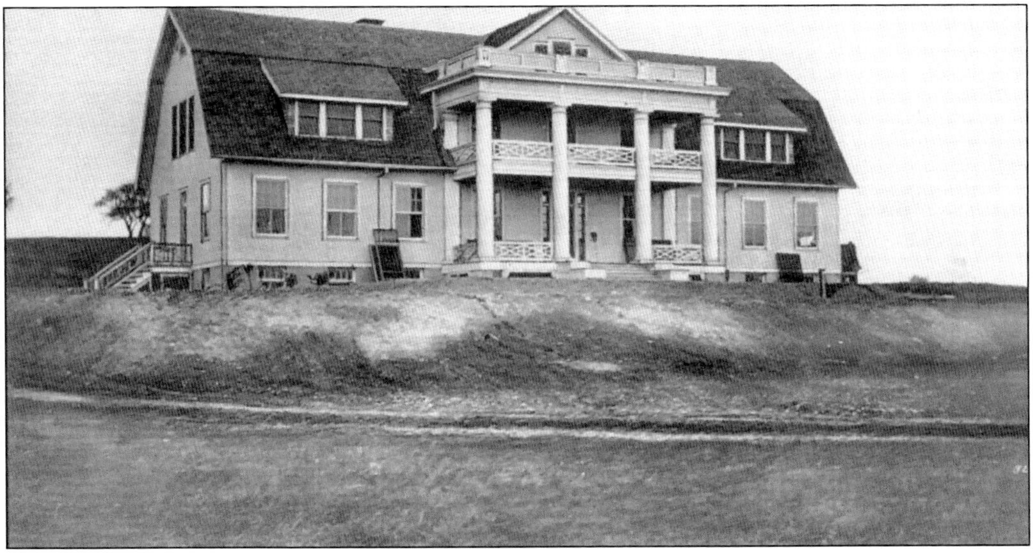

Industry was a self-contained community. In addition to having its own school and churches, it also had a hospital. The hospital was staffed with a resident doctor and nurse along with a visiting dentist and eye doctor. (Courtesy of George M. Stahl.)

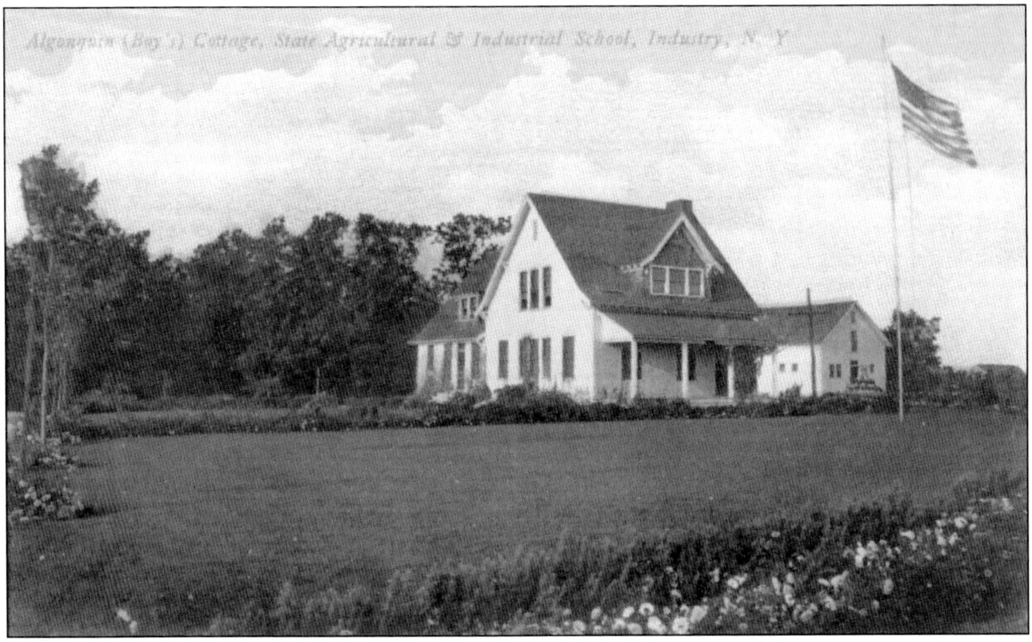

There were several cottages scattered across the grounds at Industry. Up to 25 boys lived in each cottage along with an adult supervisor and his wife, the cottage matron. Algonquin Cottage is shown here. (Courtesy of George M. Stahl.)

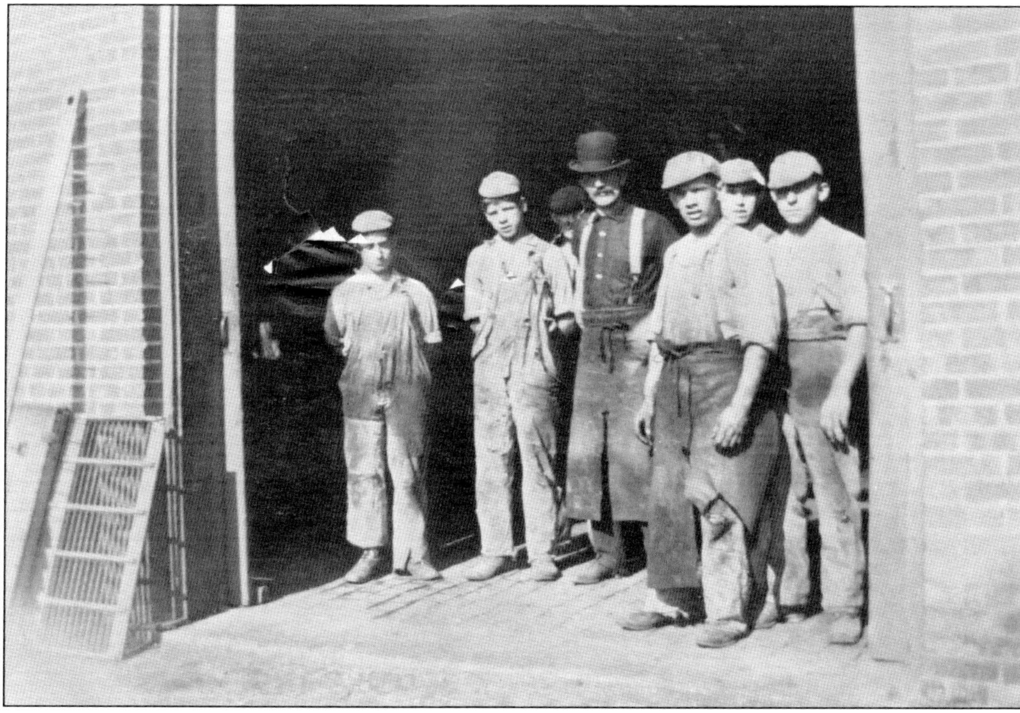

Adolph F. Kohler was the blacksmith instructor at Industry from 1907 to 1913. In this photograph he is shown with some of his students at Industry. Boys were either assigned to learn farming or an industrial trade. (Courtesy of Cathy Gretzinger.)

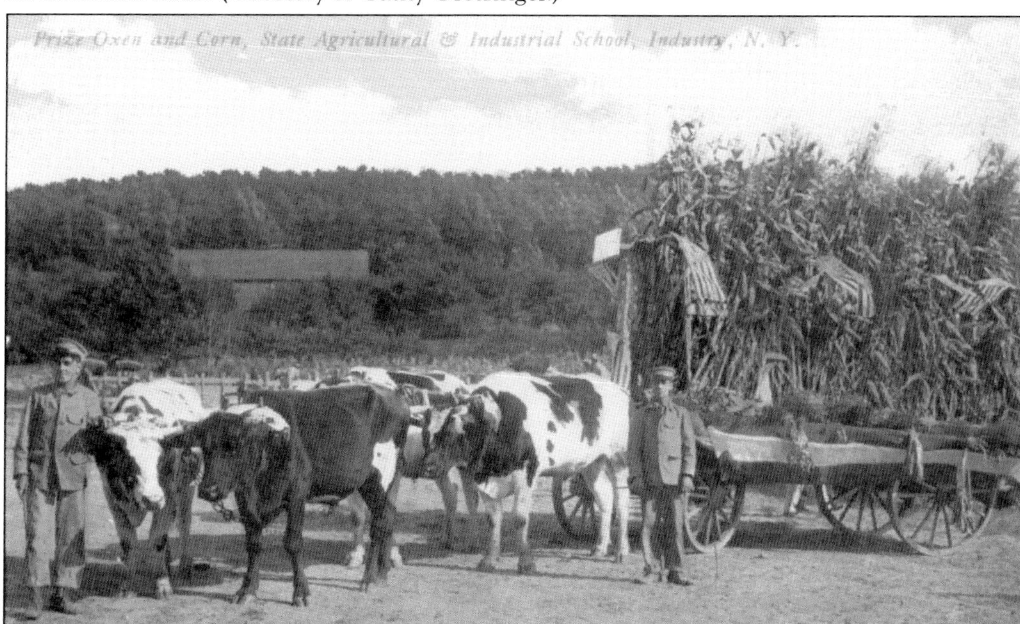

In 1912, it was noted that the last yoke of oxen in Rush were thought to be those at the State School at Industry. A pair is shown here pulling a float for the annual Flower Show. (Courtesy of George M. Stahl.)

Bibliography

In addition to materials published by past Rush historians and United States census data, the following resources were consulted:

Ainsworth, Dorothy. "Water Pumping Windmills," *Backwoods Home Magazine*. November/December, 2004, no. 90. http://www.backwoodshome.com/articles2/ainsworth90.html

Beers, Frederick W. *Atlas of Monroe County, New York*. New York: F.W. Beers & Co., 1872.

Booraem, Diotima. "Steaming into the Future," *Smithsonian Magazine*, September 1998. http://www.smithsonianmag.com/science-nature/object_sep98.html?c=y&page=1

Chapman, Barbara. "Wheatland Memories: The Story of the Wells Barn," *Rochester Democrat and Chronicle*, November 2, 2011. http://www.democratandchronicle.com/article/20111104/NEWS05/111040315/

Heidler, David S. and Jeanne T. Heidler. "The American Party," *Encyclopedia of the American Civil War: A Political, Social, and Military History*. Santa Barbara, CA: ABC-CLIO. 2000.

Henry, Marian S. "The Phelps-Gorham Purchase." *American Ancestors, New England Historic Genealogical Society*. February 25, 2000. http://www.americanancestors.org/the-phelps-gorham-purchase/

Honeoye Falls Times (1882–1986) and *Weekly Times* (Jan.–Nov. 1888).

Kringle, Harold. (n.d.) "Pea Harvest." *Chippewa Valley Museum*. http://www.chippepedia.org/Pea+Harvest

Lathrop, J.M. and Co. *Plat Book of Monroe County, New York*. Philadelphia: Lathrop and Co., 1902.

New York State. Documents of the Assembly of the State of New York. One Hundred Forty First Session. *Eleventh Annual Report of the Jewish Protectory and Aid Society*. Includes Annual Report from the New York State School at Industry. http://archive.org/stream/documentsassemb58assegoog/documentsassemb58assegoog_djvu.txt

Peck, W.H. *History of Monroe County, New York: With Illustrations Descriptive of Its Scenery*. Philadelphia: Everts, Ensign and Everts, 1877.

Peck, William F. *Landmarks of Monroe County, New York: Containing an Historical Sketch of Monroe County and the City of Rochester*. Boston: Boston History Co., 1895.

Simonson, Mark. "From Unusual Silos to Laminated Products," *The Daily Star: Newspaper for the Heartland of New York*. December 17, 2002. http://old.thedailystar.com/opinion/columns/simonson/2002/12/simonson1214.html

Thomason, Betty. 1998 "Windmills that Helped Settle the West," *American Windmills*. http://www.windmills.net/?page_id=197

Wolf, Gregory H. *Howie Krist*. Society for American Baseball Research. SABR Baseball Biography Project. http://sabr.org/bioproj/person/6b2a0e5b

INDEX